I HEARD THE SILENT RING
A Return to Self

William Whelan

Raider Publishing International

New York   London   Johannesburg

Cover design by R. Mayer Web Desgin at www.kauai-computer.com

Images of and references to Meher Baba used by permission of the Meher Baba Trust.
©Avatar Meher Baba Perpetual Public Charitable Trust.

ISBN: 978-1-61667-062-7

Published By Raider Publishing International
www.RaiderPublishing.com
New York London Johannesburg
Printed in the United States of America and the United Kingdom

Thank you to:

John-Roger
Paul Kaye
Pam West
Ron Hulnick
Robert Waterman
Kirby Benson
David Thompson
Carol Meyer
Susan Shyne
Sue Johnson
John-Clarke McDougall
Kathryn Ninos
Marjorie Eaton
Brenda Reyes
Phil Danza
Barbara Martin

Come, fill the cup, and in the fire of spring
The winter garment of Repentance Fling:
The bird of time has but a little way to fly
And lo!
The Bird is on the Wing.

RUBA'IYA'T OF OMAR KHAYYA'M

I HEARD THE SILENT RING
A Return to Self

William Whelan

Contents

Foreword

I DID NOT WANT TO WRITE THIS BOOK. IT WAS NOT MY IDEA. I was asked by a spirit years ago to write a book about my spiritual path; a very personal and private story. I remember my friend John Roger once asking me, in reference to another area, "What would you do if the Holy Spirit asked you for a favor?" Geeez. So I agreed to write it. That night around 3 A.M., my/the spirit sat me straight up in bed and the words "I Heard the Silent Ring" were branded on my brain— the title of the book. A few years later after receiving a spiritual initiation I was given the subtitle: *A Return to Self.*

Over the years in writing this book, my goal became clear. I see this world as starving spiritually. This story is about a saloon keeper from New York with little education beyond high school who never heard of anything spiritual; just an ordinary guy, who had these amazing spiritual experiences that are available to everyone. I didn't have to go to India or an ashram. I also hope this book will be a primer for hope.

Years ago, I had the same occasional recurring dream: A knock on the door. When I opened it, it was me. I would tell me to go away, as I had too much to do in the world of illusion. Other times I would tell me to go away as I wasn't ready to deal with why I came here, my spiritual growth. It was like I was awake and asleep at the same time. This dream was incessant in its recurrence. Always the same: "Go away. I'm not ready," over and over. I don't recall

when I invited myself in. It was somewhere in the late
sixties. And away we went.

Maximum Confusion

I USED TO SAY THAT I WAS A RECOVERING CATHOLIC, but when I was fifty, I realized I had recovered. I was raised in an Irish/Catholic family and went to Catholic school until I was twelve. I still have indentations in my skull from Monsignor MacAavoy's blackjack.

The teachers/nuns (I think they must have been from the "Sisters Who Show No Mercy" order) beat us on a regular basis. My confession was even compromised by a priest. In my eleventh year, I sold cards at the county fair church bingo tent. We kept the money in a carpenter's wraparound cloth mail pouch. Every few hours my four years older brother would come around and bug me for money. I always gave him a few bucks out of my pouch. After the fair I was riddled with guilt that I had stolen from God. I went to confession as soon as possible. When it came time to be paid, the priest told the other boys that I wasn't getting paid as I had stolen from the church booth.

With my father leading, for a time, my family would say the rosary after dinner. I used to play a silent game during rosary, guessing how long it would take before my sister or brother would catch my eye and we would snicker, with the ensuing reprimand. We even went on the radio once a month as: "The Whelan family prays the rosary." It was boring.

My less than illustrious altar boy career came to an abrupt end when I was caught making sure the altar wine was okay. Geez, no sense of humor. I grew up with a truly distorted view of God and his minions, and don't ever recall hearing the name Jesus Christ. Who would have thought the second half of my life would be consumed searching for God?

My family was a typical Irish Catholic family. Most of my childhood friends were Onondaga, Mohawk, and Iroquois Indians as we lived near the Onondaga Indian Reservation. I had difficulty with the white world I grew up in, but was always able to relate to the Indian world. I became disgusted with what happened to the American Indian; unconscionable, I thought, though probably inevitable.

They weren't all drunks like my Mom insisted. And she was furious when she found out I had Indian friends. Mom was "old school" and believed in severe discipline – old church, old school, old Irish. Her punishments meted out on a regular basis were swift and brutal.

The day I realized there was a God she had me cornered in the basement behind the coal furnace. She was winging large pieces of coal at me and a rat fell off the ceiling beam down the back of her dress. I waited around just long enough to watch the most amazing dance I'd ever seen trying to get that rat out of her dress. It was hilarious.

When I was ten, as long as my little mongrel dog, Blacky, was under the bed, Teddy under my arm, and my little blanky over me at night, all was bearable. Then Blacky was run over, and Mom made fun of me for crying. Shortly after, she decided I was too old for a Teddy bear and a blanky, so in front of my brothers and sister, she threw them into the fireplace. As I screamed hysterically, we all watched them die. It was truly the all-time worst thing she ever did to me. All the beatings, all the days she told me I was a mistake and shouldn't have been born, that I was worthless, were nothing compared to this. My heart was broken. I was stripped bare and barely functional. A few weeks later, I was hospitalized with rheumatic fever, resulting in damage to my heart. But, alas, after a long recovery, like all of us, I grew up.

My father was never aware of the abuse as he worked for the state of New York and was away on business Monday through Friday. I loved weekends because "Jekyll and Hyde" Mom took Saturday and Sunday off.

When violence becomes the model in a family, children spend most of their time, energy and thoughts on survival rather than growth and development. They develop a sort of violence-oriented ESP, an early warning system that provides split-second notice for self-protection. In order to stay alive in that unlivable reality of depressing, traumatic circumstances, at a very young age they learn the technique of numbing.

Andrew Vachss in his novel "Down in the Zero," describes emotional abuse as the systemic diminishment of another. It is designed to reduce a child's self-concept to the point where the victim considers himself unworthy – unworthy of respect, unworthy of friendship, unworthy of the natural birthright of all children: love and protection.

Regularly I would sneak out of the house after bedtime by climbing out my second-story window and shimmying down the rainspout. Onondaga Creek from the Indian reservation ran through the back of the property and would freeze solid in the winter. I would skate for hours, especially on full moon nights.

At thirteen my drinking problem commenced. My parents went away for the weekend and my older brother and I were allowed to stay home. I had a few buddies over and mixed a large container of orange juice with a quart of gin. I drank so much I threw up on the couch. After I recovered and was sober, I turned the cushions over, figuring no one would be the wiser. NOT! I didn't consider the odor. Mom was especially creative in the punishment meted out.

I always worked as a boy, delivering newspapers, cutting grass, shoveling snow, picking currants and selling them to the local grocery store. Plus Mom, an amazing poker player, taught me how to play poker. To this day I've met few people with her poker ability. In my early teens, I occasionally had friends over for penny poker. When Mom would return home, she would sit in, win everyone's money and then give it back.

At sixteen, I took a job as an usher at Loews State theater. The minimum wage was fifty cents an hour. I always had money. This job lasted one year until I was caught letting my friends in a side door. I then found a job at the local War Memorial as a laborer, making ice for pro hockey, laying the floor for the NBA and setting up the ring and seats for boxing. Besides pay, I got into these events free. It was really a thrill for a kid to sit on the bench with the pros.

When I was seventeen, I enlisted in the Army for three years. It was the only way I could get away from her. I was probably thirteen emotionally, and had no business in this man's world. January basic training at Fort Dix, New Jersey brought thirty degrees below zero.

A month into training I was assigned the all night job of keeping the coal furnaces burning. Instead, I fell asleep and three hundred recruits awoke to icicles. Wow! I received more than a few punches. My less-than-illustrious military career was marred by my drinking. I earned the rank of Corporal three times in three years and was busted three times.

One week prior to graduating from Basic Training at Fort Dix, New Jersey, three of us went AWOL, and headed for our friend's hometown, Pittsfield Massachusetts, where he was immediately arrested for felony charges incurred prior to his enlistment. After a week of sleeping in the park and exhausting our meager funds, we were broke. We went to the Salvation Army and they put us up at a hotel and gave us meal tickets.

After using up all this good will, we went to the Red Cross, whose rep immediately locked us in a room and called the local Army recruiting Sergeant. This Master

Sergeant was a World War II veteran and near retirement. He told us we had two options: (1) He would call the Fort Dix Military Police. They would send two officers to take us back in cuffs. We would have to pay their expenses and would probably be court marshaled. Or, (2) we could give him our word that we would go back and turn ourselves in. The choice was obvious. The phone call to my father for money was difficult for me and probably painful for him as he was a wonderful father.

Returning to Fort Dix, no one knew who we were. We were assigned to an empty barracks with mess hall privileges. My friend was sent to another base and I never saw him again. The Colonel assigned to my case decided that my punishment would be to take Basic over again. My second basic was fairly easy except for one small problem.

Firing a grenade from a rifle had been introduced. This part of our basic training was attended by four companies. I figured I wouldn't be missed among 400 solders so I snuck into the woods for a much-needed nap. That night a buddy showed me how to mount the grenade. Next day I was the first one called up to fire. I mounted the grenade onto my rifle, aimed and fired. Waking up in the hospital with a shattered cheek bone, I began to seriously consider the possibility of growing up, someday, maybe. A rifle grenade is always fired with the butt of the rifle on the ground so the earth takes the recoil.

After graduation I was assigned to a Tank Battalion at Fort Hood, Texas. Not having been raised in a prejudiced environment, (except my Mom's dislike of Indians) I wasn't prepared for 1954 Texas. Even though President Truman ordered the integration of the military in 1952, it wasn't. All headquarter companies were white, and line companies black. My fellow white solders were mostly southern, country music playing red-necks. The cool was in the line companies where I spent most of my free time with my new name, "Young Blood." The prejudice in this part of Texas was appalling, and this was a few years before the integration of Little Rock High School.

Originally I was assigned as driver of an M-48 tank Somehow, I was promoted to Corporal and assigned Tank Commander with a driver and a gunner. (Had someone lost his mind?) Approaching was the fourth Army war games at Fort Hood with four Divisions participating. We were divided into two armies and my team was sent out as reconnaissance FO's. Somehow, around that time our radio went out and I got us lost. I guess I must have slept through map reading class also. We had a couple weeks of water and rations and pulled up in a small group of trees below a hill that evening.

Whenever on winter maneuvers, tankers would sleep on top of the flat motor compartment for the warmth. Then we all got some much-needed sleep. Three days later, we heard a loud ominous humming sound. I walked to the top of the hill where I observed a huge line of enemy tanks approaching directly toward us. I high-tailed it back to my crew and thought we could out-run them. Apparently one of their FO's had spotted us earlier and we were flanked on both sides. Captured, and our tank confiscated, we were placed with other captured soldiers in detention. When the war games ended and I returned to my company, I lost my stripes for the first time.

Orders were issued for my new duty station in France, called "Pass the buck, with me the buck", where I was assigned to an Amphibious Truck company in an old French garrison in Rochefort, eventually moving to a camp between Soulac and Le Verdun in the Southwestern part of the country. I absolutely loved France and the French loved me. Possibly, the best karma in my life. I rapidly learned street French, by living with a fishing family, weekends, where no one spoke English.

Even though I had no training and knew nothing about amphibious trucks, I was assigned my own vehicle. Young French kids would hang out near my Dukw as I spoke the language a bit and always had candy for them. One afternoon working on my Dukw with a couple of French kids aboard, the Battalion Commander, a Colonel, did a surprise inspection and told me to get those kids the hell out of there. I told the kids in French that this goose wanted them to leave, which they laughingly did. A month later I was ordered to report to the Colonel's office. As he heard me speaking French in the motor pool, he assumed I spoke fluent French. His battalion interpreter had lost his job over an infraction and he told me he wanted me to be his interpreter.

Believe me this is the all-time best job in the Army. No duty, no KP, no guard duty and my own jeep. Hang out all day and run errands for the man. And of course, make fun of my friends. Most days I went into town for dry cleaning or errands and of course I had to stop at Madame Mickey's. The Madam ran the best whorehouse in Soulac and her girls were like my sisters. The only drawback: it could be scary if I visited too early when they just woke up.

Once while unloading a cargo ship of condiments, a box of twenty-four 8-oz. tins of black pepper broke open in my Dukw. I threw them into a dry part of the bilge, and the next time I was in Soulac, I gave a tin to Madam Mickey. Pepper on the black market was worth around sixteen bucks per lb. She was really excited, as condiments were impossible to obtain in post World War II. She asked me if I could get any more and would I come back to meet some friends later in the day.

I was curious as to why her friends had guns but didn't think much about that as I agreed to bring in an occasional case. I didn't find out until later they were part of the French Mafia.

The end of my fabulous job came a few months later when the entire Battalion was sent to Southern France to Biarritz, on the Spanish border. This is Basque country. We were to unload cargo ships at the three-mile-point. The problem I had was who in hell had a clue what the Basque were saying. I received the daily weather report from a

Basque speaking and writing person. Now I didn't know if they had their own language or not, but it sure wasn't any French I ever heard. So, I faked it. I guessed the weather report each day. And I guessed really well until the law of averages caught up with me. Because of my report, the Colonel sent a company of Dukws out into what was to be the worst storm to hit the coast in years. Fortunately no one was killed, but two Dukws sank. Private Whelan once more reporting for KP.

Reporting back to Dukw driver duty, I was assigned to take a Dukw with another soldier to the northern part of France. We were given a week to get there and back. (Oh dear, would they ever learn?) On the way north, I noticed a small town on the map a few miles out of the way and decided to detour to get a bite to eat. This was a decade after World War II and these people hadn't seen an American since the war. They treated us like conquering heroes. Wine, wine and more wine. Dancing and partying. We stayed three days and would probably still be there if my buddy hadn't insisted we leave. Naturally we were a few days late returning, but I was already a Private.

Upon return the Army had finally decided to integrate us and ordered every barrack to place a black man in every other bunk. Those southern red necks went ballistic. Occasionally an event called "bed-check" would occur. It was not pretty. In the middle of the night some coward bigot would sneak into the barracks with an army shovel, called an entrenching tool, and smash a black man in the head. Finally, integration in the ranks occurred and people got used to it.

I was always curious about a message on the dashboard, warning to never engage the land transfer case while moving on land. Not having Amphibious Truck training, there was a lot about the vehicle I didn't know. That sign bothered me for months. Finally I could resist it no longer and while driving to the beach I kicked the water transfer in gear. Whoa, now I knew why not to do that. Gears busted and ground. I was towed back to the motor pool. A lieutenant in the company, who didn't much care for me, ordered a court-martial. He had gone over all the motor-pool trip tickets and had me.

Maybe. Whenever taking a vehicle out of the motor pool one had to fill out a trip ticket, and upon return, write any problems with the vehicle. Nothing unusual had been noted (until that night.). I convinced my Motor Pool Sergeant friend to leave the office unlocked. Late that night, flashlight in hand, I went through the tickets and wrote with different pens on many of the tickets – "Unusual noise in transfer case." When we got to court, after reviewing the records, the judge threw the case out and reprimanded the lieutenant for his sloppiness.

This is the same lieutenant who, while in Basque country, with me drunk in my tent one night, was punched in the nose when he stuck his head in. Too drunk to have a clue what I was doing. What he did next, I still feel was really cool, albeit painful.

A few weeks later the company was sent on maneuvers. I was ordered to stay behind. Just the lieutenant and me. He was a West Point grad, and a boxer. What a beating I took! I was no match for his skills and was bloodied and bowed. He inadvertently taught me a bit about being a man.

I was obviously out of control and this incident slowed me down a bit. Everyone in the company was aware of what had happened, especially in light of my face and I'm sure many were glad.

One of my favorite dancehalls was in Le Verdon-sur-Mer, close to the Ocean, on the "Pointe de Grave," where the estuary of La Gironde, starts in Spain (in the Pyrenees Mountains), picks up La Dordogne River north of Bordeaux, and empties into the Ocean. Le Verdun is a small fishing village, where I had many local friends. One evening, I was AWOL but no one knew it, because I would walk the train tracks back to my barracks in time for morning roll call. This time MP's showed up and took me out of the bar. Before they could get me to their paddy wagon, around twenty of my local friends, (men, woman and children), made a large circle around me singing and dancing. As the Military Police were forbidden to touch a French national, they finally left.

My American Indian best friend married a French woman from the village. The reception was held in a large garage. Bottles of homemade wine were everywhere. It seemed everyone in this village made their own Vin Blanc. After the reception, the bride and groom took off for their honeymoon for the weekend, which was in a home owned by a relative. Now the fun really began. Unbeknownst to the groom or me, there is a custom in this part of France where everyone gets another bottle of wine and dances in the streets, stopping at every house looking for the married couple. It's called "Cherchez les Maries" One person leading the dance knows where they are. But every street and every house must first be traversed. A soup called Tourin made of onions, cheese, and what ever else is available is made and also carried through the streets. When we finally got to the 'honeymoon house', around thirty of us, in various stages of drunkeness, spilled into the house, got in their bed, and were dancing around, just having a grand old time. My friend thought I put everyone up to this to ruin his honeymoon and punched me. Our friends separated us and explained the custom to him. Lucky for him! (Really, me.)

In 1956, miracle of miracles, I was once again promoted to corporal, and my time to rotate home arrived. Leaving the compound, I'm sitting on the back of an Army truck with a few other short timers, heading for Orly field in Paris to fly home. As we exited the base my lieutenant walked by and I flashed him the finger. Ha! Ha! And we're off. One hour later a Military Police officer on a motorcycle turned us back to camp. I just know the lieutenant had brought us back to get me. Fortunately he was nowhere around when we arrived. What actually happened was the Hungarian Revolt began and all military planes were sequestered for their use. We finally took a slow boat to New York.

The day I was discharged after hours of some moron trying to get us to re-enlist, I was assigned KP. I attempted to explain that NCO's don't pull KP duty and I refused. So once again, number three, I was busted to private. Okay, you win, AND I'M A CIVILIAN.

It's truly a miracle I was discharged honorably.

As a new civilian, I desperately wanted an education but unfortunately I only had four credits from high school. I was so hyperactive (child abuse, thank you) and screwed up, my high school career was less than stellar. I had a GED from the Army, but this was far from a foundation. With the G.I. Bill I enrolled in a Prep School next to the Cornell University campus in Ithaca, New York. In my year and a half, I completed Elementary, Intermediate and Advanced Algebra, Plain and Solid Geometry, Trigonometry, English and all the other classes required for a high school diploma. The school was open till 10 p.m. every night, and I utilized this extra assistance regularly. I was focused on having an education.

Early evenings, I would make twenty sandwiches and sell them at Cornell Fraternity houses. I also washed dishes part-time at two local restaurants. Some of my classmates, rich kids shipped up from New York City were a constant distraction. Another veteran and I decided to straighten them out, something their 'never home' parents should have done. We caught three of them in an alley, told them we were not happy with their disruptive ways in class and slapped them around a bit. We also told them if it continued we would really hurt them. It was amazing how cooperative they became. The Dean of the school called me into his office a week later and asked me if I took part in "assaulting" them. I responded, "Why? Are they still being disruptive?" Oh and you're welcome.

My older brother, a Korean Navy veteran was attending

San Diego State on a football scholarship and suggested I apply, and stay with him and his wife. I was accepted and in 1959 I enrolled. The counselors, (actually graduate students assigned to fill slots) convinced me to take courses that would prove to be way over my head, like Chemistry and Physics. I also enrolled in a French class, and a few weeks into the course, I informed the professor that no one in France spoke that way. Haughtily, he informed me that this was High Parisian. I was pretty much lost as the street stuff I knew was not applicable. As I was not used to 600-700 students in two balconies, with no individual assistance, I was lost. These courses were also definitely interfering with my drinking.

The coup de gras arrived the day after I stayed up all night studying "Principles of Economics." I spoke to the professor and shared some of my frustrations with the course. He responded by stating that if I opened the course book once in a while I might learn something. That was it! I slammed the book into his stomach, called him an asshole, and walked off campus, never to return.

The Beginning or the End?

AFTER COLLEGE, I WENT TO WORK FOR A PUBLISHING company in San Diego, Calif. selling encyclopedias door to door. I was really good at it, even earning a National Salesman of the Year Award. Eventually I was promoted to sales manager in Tucson, Arizona, and was living in the old Pioneer Hotel, downtown. One of my Mexican salesmen, Raul, was my best friend and was as wild as I was. Many weekends we would go down to Nogales, Mexico, drinking and partying.

One weekend we took my girlfriend with us in my rented Cadillac. We started out at the bullfights with a couple of large botas of wine, then on to dinner and more wine. My date wanted to go to the red light district as she had never seen one before. We go to a brothel with tables and a long bar. Raul is quite taken by a sixteen-year-old prostitute. An hour later he informs me we're taking the girl back to Tucson. No way! Way! NO WAY! WAY! The house owned all the girls and we were not allowed to leave. Raul heads for the door with the girl and two bouncers stop him. I jump up and he and I are now fighting them back-to-back. Then he disappears and I'm taking way too many fists. A few minutes later, Raul returns with a .38 pistol he had hidden in the glove compartment of the Caddy. He fires one round into the ceiling and lines everyone up against the bar and we take off with the girl. Right out of the Ole Wild West.

15

We had parked a few blocks away on a side street hoping the car wouldn't be stripped. We put the girl in the trunk and head for the border. At the border the guard walks the length of the car and stops at the trunk. We're both feigning sobriety and Raul wants to shoot him. NO WAY! Finally the guard comes back and says, "Nice car" and waves us through.

Entering Tucson, I come to a screeching stop and ask, "Where's Judy?" Oh shit, we left her in that bar. No way to go back now. Oh, well. We sneak Raul's new life companion up the back way and go to bed. He makes her sleep against the wall with me on the outside. He didn't want me near her. Next morning, headaches splitting with post drunk hangover, Raul and I head down for coffee. First thing he says to me is "Why in hell did you let me bring her across the border? What am I going to do with her?" After feeding her and giving her some money, he puts her on a bus back to the border, as we had books to sell. Judy caught a ride with some Air Force guys and wouldn't go out with me any more. Geez, no sense of humor.

Soon after, my drinking got to the point that I was unable to continue my job. I decided to return to Calif. I climbed up the fire escape and snuck away without paying my bill. Over the months this bothered me, as my Dad was such a wonderful influence on me, with an attitude of one of Shakespeare's quotes, "To thine own self be true." I could hear him teaching me about honesty as a way of life. I had to go back to Tucson and take care of that bill, which I did on my way back to New York. My 18-year-old kid brother had recently quit a landscaping job, and the owner wouldn't give him his last paycheck. I suggested we go to his ex-employer's house, and I'd get the money for him. When we arrived, the owner stated that his business was slow and he couldn't pay my brother. I told him to get the money. He tried to close the door but I had my foot in it, forced the door open and chased him around the house, finally cornering him in the basement, where he reluctantly paid him.

My brother was probably the only Irishman who belonged to a Polish-American club where one could purchase a shot and a beer for twenty-five cents. We spent a lot of time there, and one day after spending a buck and a half, decided to start our own landscaping company. Hence the birth of "Whelan Brothers Landscaping."

Dad thought it a good idea and lent us $1000.00 and we bought a 1954 Dodge pickup and some tools. We decided to canvas wealthy neighborhoods. One woman wanted a rock garden in her back yard. We told her we needed to measure the area and would be back with an estimate. On the way to the truck, I asked my brother, "What the hell is a rock garden? "

He replied, "Never heard of it." Neither one of us had any idea what a rock garden was. At the library we got a pretty good idea and submitted a bid. Our first job.

Then we picked up some regular maintenance jobs and hired some part-time help. We really did well. We purchased an electric hedge clipper and while working our best maintenance account, decided my brother would start trimming the very beautiful ten-foot high, one hundred-foot long hedge, while I worked the other side of the estate with two helpers. An hour later I walked around to where my brother was trimming and was absolutely incredulous. Somehow he cut a long chunk out of the hedge so it looked like a severely swayed-backed horse. (Dude, what the fuck are you doing?) We both backed way up so he could see it. He totally screwed up that hedge. We had to lower the entire hedge four feet to make it level.

"Grandmother" had our check, which she would give us after inspecting our work. She was reading in the backyard and had real thick glasses on. Seeing as I was our fearless leader, this was the plan: We would approach her and tell her we were finished and could we get paid? Then I would stumble, bump into her really hard and knock her glasses off, my brother would step on them, and we'd help her up, get our check and get the hell out of there. It worked perfectly and she wasn't injured except for her glasses. That evening the owner called me. Uh oh! She said our work was brilliant, and she had been thinking of lowering that hedge for months. Always quick on my feet, I told her that many people didn't view their property through landscaper eyes and it was critical for the health of the hedge to lower it. Pure BS.

Under the dashboard of our pickup was an air vent that when opened, not only allowed air in, but the eight-inch rectangular opening allowed one to see the road in front of the truck. Some days we would take the seat out, and drive around sitting on the floor. We would stop at red lights and stop signs and it would appear the truck was driving itself as we couldn't be seen. It really freaked people out and we thought it hilarious. It appeared I still hadn't completely grown up.

The demise of our business was facilitated by my drinking. A series of large checks arrived, and I went on a week-long bender, and my brother decided he had had enough. I had been tending bar part-time and now went to work full time.

One of my full-time jobs was tending bar at Marty's Hideaway on Rock Cut Road. This road was full of automobile junkyards outside of town. Marty's was a haven for college kids from Syracuse University, junkyard guys, Seneca, Mohawk, Huron and Onondaga Indians and a motorcycle gang I ran with for a while. No two groups got along and as booze flowed, every night was "rock and roll." Rarely a night went by without a major fight.

One evening I showed up for work and there was a very drunk, mean guy at the bar. The bar maid was afraid to cut him off and left him for me. So, I threw him out and a half hour later he returned with a double-barreled, sawed off shotgun. He placed the gun on the bar and laid his head down. His wife called, and said I pissed him off, and he was going to kill me. I didn't like that. I shook his shoulder and when he lifted his head, I hit him on the side of the jaw as hard as I could, hid the shotgun and dragged him outside, where he slept off his drink. This was an amazing year in this crazy saloon and I loved it.

Four years later, after working very upscale clubs I decided to open my own club. I found a location in a shopping center, borrowed ten grand from the bank, ten grand from a friend and built the "Honey Bucket," a little jazz-club restaurant, outside of Syracuse, New York. While working nights tending bar in a club, my days were filled with building my saloon with a contractor.

One night a kid I had known from Marty's came to the bar and asked me if I had some marijuana. I told him I didn't smoke dope. I found out later he was a junky, working undercover for a narc and had a recorder in his shirt pocket. He returned three or four times always asking if I could get him some dope. As many college kids staffed the club I asked one of the waiters if he could get me a joint. He brought one to the bar and I gave it to the kid.

A week later, while working in my saloon, a detective from narcotics walks in and shows me my liquor license that hadn't been issued to me yet. He obtained it from the Liquor Control Board. He told me he knew I gave the joint to the kid and if I didn't become his snitch I wouldn't be able to open. I told him I needed to think about it.

Next day, in a neighborhood saloon I hung out in, frequented by some cops, I told a police sergeant friend the story. He told me to tell the narc to kiss his ass. Whoa! He said he really had nothing on me and was bluffing. When the narc returned I told him I couldn't help him and to either arrest me or get the fuck out of my saloon. A week later I received my license. A month after I opened, the narc arrived with a hooker. He ran up quite a large bill and told the waitress I would pay for it including the tip. I went to his table and informed him he was paying the bill or I would call his lieutenant. He paid. I never saw him again, thank you.

I had a standing rule in my club that any time a waitress got stiffed, they were to come get me. I would meet the party in the parking lot and ask if anything was wrong; was the waitress rude to them, or was the food not to their liking? Usually drunk, they would always tell me every thing was fine. I would look very puzzled and mention that they forgot to tip the waitress. They'd always come up with a generous tip.

Approximately a year after opening, I got married, and had the reception in my club.

Once a year I would enter the "Demolition Derby" at the state fair. In order to qualify for the main event you had to provide your own car and place at least third in your heat. (The promoter provided the main event cars.) The last year I competed, I entered a 1949 two door black Cadillac. It was in "cherry" shape. Whenever I entered a car, I had the number "69" painted on the doors, with the words "Breakfast Off" in a half moon above and the word "Champions" below. There was an entire section filled with people from my saloon who were usually loud, raucous and in various stages of drunkenness.

Just prior to the race, the drivers with their cars would meet with the promoter at the fourth corner of the track. This time when it was over. I jumped in my car and raced toward the grandstand. Right in front of the crowd, I did a "Brody," jumped out and took a bow. My saloon fans went wild. As soon as the race began, because of my grandstanding and the beauty of the car, all the other guys tried to immediately knock me out. I was able to keep it running just long enough to qualify for the main event. It finally quit running after the engine compartment and undercarriage caught fire. I couldn't get the doors open and knew the gas tank, which was a converted beer keg I had anchored on the floor of the real seat, would soon blow, so I climbed out the passenger window, ran to the fence separating the track from the grandstand and rapidly climbed to the top of the fence. One of my saloon guys was waiting at the top with a can of beer, which I drank to raucous cheers.

In the main event the car the promoter provided had no seat belts and we had to sign a release that if we got hurt or killed, he wasn't responsible. But I was ready. I brought a piece of chain with seat belts attached, a small sledgehammer and a large metal chisel/punch. I punched two holes on either side of the frame as close to the seat as I could and secured myself in. I didn't win, but came real close. I placed second.

*   *   *

THE NEWSPAPER HAD DUBBED TWO ROBBERS, A WHITE GUY and a black guy, "The Salt and Pepper Bandits." They were robbing saloons late at night. One night, at 2:45 A.M., just before closing, two guys walk in, one black, one white and sit facing the waitress end of the bar. I ask if they would like a drink. No, just waiting for someone. So obvious!

I kept an English Fox-Sterlingworth side by, double-barreled twelve-gauge shotgun under the waitress station and pointed it at them, telling them to get out, which they started to do. I said, "Leave your guns." They started to tell me they didn't have guns, so I cocked both hammers. It probably looked like a canon and the cocking sound is real loud.

Suddenly they remembered they in fact did have a couple of guns and laid the pistols on the table. I walked them to the door and told them if I saw them here again I'd blow their fucking heads off.

I was drinking enough VO and beer to have serious liver problems. I also smoked three packs of unfiltered camels a day for twenty years— when it all started to unravel.

When I was in my mid thirties, every morning upon arising, I started coughing up large black chunks of some nasty looking, foul smelling, and gooey stuff. Real chunky, really disgusting. I also had a constant cough. The problem was addiction to nicotine, like a junky to a fit. After a medical examination, the doctor told me I had a pre-cancerous lung and showed me the x-ray with the large offending spot. He further explained it could turn into full cancer at any moment.

A few weeks after the exam, still undecided as to what to do, I had occasion to see a friend in the hospital. A visitor was there who had suffered with cancer of the jaw from smoking and the doctors had surgically removed his lower jaw from below each ear and had sewn an aluminum artificial jaw onto his face. He looked right out of the "Star Wars" bar scene. He couldn't talk because his tongue had also been amputated and he wrote on a note pad. He made these disgusting gasping, gurgling, slurp sounds. He was so addicted to nicotine; he'd get a cigarette burning and then try to inhale the smoke from the burning end, as he had no lips to suck the smoke in with. I felt like a person on an airplane that's about to crash and it's too late to take another flight. And I thought maybe I could change my flight.

Which I did! That day I smoked my last cigarette. I wasn't afraid to die, but Star Wars wasn't an option, nor was being hooked up to a machine for the rest of my life or having to drag around an oxygen tank. So I quit smoking. Cold turkey!

Then my wife ran off with a car dealer and I was devastated. I felt like I was bleeding emotionally. My drinking accelerated to the point where I was drunk most of the time. My business was suffering and I didn't care. One night at home, one of the barmaids knocked on my door. I was two-thirds into a bottle of VO, sarcastic, rude, and angry.

Feeling quite the victim, I wasn't in the mood for company. Once inside, she asked me if I had ever done any mescaline. I had no idea what the hell she was talking about. She told me it would help me feel better. I washed the capsules down with VO and within thirty minutes experienced my first psychedelic trip. That night I cried most of the night, wallowing in the emotion of my wife leaving.

The next morning I was free. The pain and emotions were gone. I felt liberated and grateful. I was a different person. What an amazing experience! As I was to find out later, mescaline is derived from the hallucinogenic cactus, peyote, which will be covered in a later chapter.

Meher Baba

I DECIDED TO TAKE A LITTLE R&R IN COCOA BEACH, Florida. But I wanted to sell my cabin cruiser first. I advertised it and didn't get any takers, so I decided to torch it and collect the insurance. I took the boat up the St. Lawrence River and started a small fire up under the bow right on the electrical box. After putting it out, I went to a large marina to have them check out my boat, as I smelled something burning. They told me it was an electrical fire and I needed to re-wire the boat, as it was dangerous. I made an appointment to have them do the work the following week. I wanted it all on record.

I waited until the fireboat was way upriver, poured five gallons of gas in the bilge and dropped a match. I'm lucky to be alive as the explosion blew that boat to hell and me up into the air and into the water. The remains were roaring fire, drifting toward a dock adjoining a private island and an expensive home. The dock caught fire just as some boaters picked me up out of the water. My rescuers and I were able to put the dock fire out. Whew! The insurance company wrote me a check, no questions asked.

Unfortunately, after I cashed the check and spent a good chunk of it in Florida, it bounced. The insurance company questioned my ex-wife's signature, which I had forged. It was my boat, in my name, with my insurance, etc. But because I hadn't removed my ex's name from the insurance, the check was made out to both of us. She agreed to sign the check for half the money.

Prior to leaving New York, I had my bartender friend

purchase a large quantity of mescaline for me. Upon arriving in Florida, I rented a small one-bedroom house right on the beach. The first week in Florida, I went out on the beach late at night with my tape recorder and took bits of this marvelous tan powder and recorded my reactions.

One night a few weeks later, after making myself a cup of coffee, I decided to pour a little of the mescaline powder into the cup. Accidentally, I dumped the entire bag, approximately seven grams, in. There was no way to separate it and take it out, so I stirred and drank it. This was probably enough mescaline to get half the city of Cocoa Beach off. At eleven PM, thirty minutes after I lay down on the beach with my recorder, I died. And when I was re-born, I would never be the same again. In a split-second, somehow, I arrived in a heaven-like place. I could see my body lying on the sand. The wind had pulled the tape out of my recorder and it was billowing down the beach like a long wounded kite tail anchored to the machine. This place where I was pure spirit, was a snow white, billowy, cloud-like place that resembled what I've observed peering out of airplane windows, looking down at the clouds.

There was a man sitting in front of me, all dressed in white. He had a very prominent nose and a large mustache. He looked exactly like Jerry Colona the Hollywood cartoon voice master from the forties. No words were exchanged. I knew I was in the presence of a god-man. I knew I was pure spirit. I had no human reference point for this experience, but it was more real to me, more familiar than my life on earth, before or since. There was no right or wrong, good or bad. There just… was. I knew in the silence that every moment was eternity and perfection manifested into each new moment. With this silent teaching, I understood that this is the way it is on earth also. I was aware of wishing that this "now" would last forever and realized that forever was just a pathful of nows, and all I could do was to walk each one fully in its turn. I was aware that life on earth was but a reflection of reality— like when glancing into a mirror, one knows that what they see is just a reflection of themselves. My mind was gone, yet I knew everything. Somehow this god-man imprinted a spiritual encyclopedia on my heart and I've been turning the pages ever since.

This encounter also commenced my ability to see into spirit. The peace, joy and calm I experienced was extraordinary. It was like I came home. I knew that I knew. I know I am - that I am. All without a sound. I was home. I could have stayed there forever. I now know I did. I get a kick out of hearing people say the last frontier is outer space. I know the last frontier is inside. Jesus proclaimed the kingdom of heaven is within and God lives within that kingdom, I now know that to be true. To this day, my time with this angelic being was the most all-time profound occurrence I have ever experienced.

It changed me and my life forever. My feeble attempt to describe this sacred encounter with my limited mind is, at best, ludicrous. When I arrived back into my body, quite alive and well, it was daylight. And I was truly born again. I had been gone over six hours. I wasn't immediately sure whether I was alive or not. I was seeing the world and the ocean/surf through different eyes. Finally, I was able to get up. I was truly humbled by this miraculous experience. To this day, I have never lost the depth of peace I was given that night. I now knew there was more going on than the material world. This experience took the fear of death from me, as I now knew there was no death, just the dropping of one body for another. I knew there was a God. I knew I was a spiritual being.

How could I ever be the same again? I was obsessed with sharing this encounter with anyone who would listen. As I was quite hungry I went to a restaurant and attempted to share my experience with a waitress and some customers. I went over to some new friends' house and "bothered" them. They probably thought I had become a Jehovah Witness. Finally, in frustration, I heard inside: "If I wanted anyone else to have your experience, I would give it to them." I have rarely spoken of this event for thirty years.

I spent time alone at a large bird sanctuary north of Cape Canaveral, walking the beach day after day, reflecting on this experience, reliving the peace and grace that had been extended to me. I felt like I had been to the "Cosmic School" forever and now I knew I had all I would ever need; I still feel that way.

A week later I met an old man on the beach who was living in his pickup truck. He had a camper shell on the bed and invited me in to smoke some hash. Inside were over fifty pictures of the man I had been with in Heaven. I was incredulous and speechless, as I looked lovingly at each picture. He told me this was the avatar, Meher Baba, his teacher from India who had passed away a few months earlier. I told my new friend, "Believe me, he's alive and well." This was amazing. The old man shared how this man called himself the "Awakener." Man, he sure woke my booze-sodden ass up.

I borrowed all of his Baba books and discourses and devoured them. I started exploring Baba's teachings and they made sense to me. I felt I understood them. I wasn't doing any formal studies, just reading on my own. What made sense to me was the love he taught, the heart, the possibility that we are all love if we choose to be. I especially related to that; it's something I had been searching for all my life. All the anger and violence in the world, especially my own, never made sense to me. And here was a man, no longer alive, from thousands of miles away in India, who was saying things that were in my heart all along. I was really clear on not becoming a Baba follower or following Hinduism. I was committed to exploring the possibility of love on an unequivocal basis. I still haven't reached it yet. I've learned that this level of study goes on till our last breath. Like the Nike ad: "There's no finish line."

Meher Baba was born Merwan Sheriar Irani in Poona, India, in 1894. His parents were Persian and devout seekers of God. When he was 19, while in college, he met the aged Muslim saint, Hazrat Babajan, considered one of the five perfect masters of the time. He visited with her on many occasions. One day she kissed him on his forehead, revealing to him his state of God-realization. At first he was dazed but gradually the focus of his consciousness returned sufficiently to lead him to Sai Baba. After receiving Baba's teachings, he eventually found the Hindu, Upasni Maharaj of Sakori. For seven years Maharaj integrated Merwan's God-consciousness of the mundane world, preparing him for his role as the Avatar of the Age.

Years later Baba explained that the Avatar comes every 700 to 1400 years, depending on the cycles of time. He also identified the following spiritual figures as incarnations of the Avatar: Zarathustra, Rama, Krishna, Buddha, Jesus and Mohammed. This avataric mission started in 1921 with the gathering of his first disciples, who gave him the name "Meher Baba" or "Compassionate Father."

An old military camp called Ahmednagar became known as Meherabad. Here he started a free hospital and dispensary, shelters for the poor and a free school where no caste lines were imposed. His life time instructions, offered to all, included moral discipline, and love for God, spiritual understanding and selfless service. He taught to love God and become free in this life. He would explain that this love could be expressed in various ways, ultimately resulting in union with God. He also taught that the practical way for the common man to express this love, while attending to every-day life's duties is to speak lovingly, think lovingly and act lovingly toward all mankind, irrespective of caste, creed and position, taking God to be present in everyone. He didn't ask his followers to leave their respective religions, saying all religions are revelations of God, but he asked them to follow the innermost core of their religion.

Commencing in July 1925, Baba took a vow of silence

where he never spoke again. He communicated with an alphabet board and a unique short hand system of represented gestures. He traveled extensively in India, Europe and the United States. He lived a simple life, did not marry, ate little and slept even less, and spent long periods in seclusion, often fasting totally for months on end. However, he laid down no rules in these matters for others, telling them that outer renunciation had little value. What counted on the path to God was honesty and the inner and real renunciation of all forms of selfishness and back-biting. He owned no property; never handled money except to give to the poor and sick; and was plainly indifferent to ceremony and ritual, emphasizing that the only real prayer was pure praise without asking or complaint.

A persistent theme throughout his five decades of ministrations has been his seeking out the God-intoxicated (mentally ill in the US) and his homage to lepers and those lamed by disease. With infinite care and love he washed the feet of lepers, many times bowing his forehead to the often twisted stumps on which they hobbled, and sent them on their way with renewed hope and peace. He once wrote: "They are like beautiful birds caught in an ugly cage. Of all the tasks I perform, this touches me most deeply."

He continually emphasized 'that he had come not to teach, but to awaken.'He stated that truth had been given by the great messengers of the past, and that the present task of humanity is to realize the teaching embodied in each of the great ways. His mission was to awaken man to that realization through the age-old message of love. He taught acceptance by inviting people to look at themselves, to accept their egotistic self not as good or bad, clever or stupid, successful or unsuccessful, but as illusions of their true selves, and cease to identify themselves with the illusion. He never sought to form a new religion or sect. I really liked that as God only knows this planet doesn't need another religion. He attracted and welcomed many faiths and every social class, with a message emphasizing love for

God and one's fellow man. He always encouraged people
to grow through their own faiths towards the goal of
elimination of the selfish ego and the potential of realizing
God within themselves. In his book "The God-Man" he
states: "I have not come to teach but to awaken. Understand
therefore, that I lay down no precepts. Throughout eternity
principles and precepts have been laid down, but mankind
has ignored them. Man's inability to live God's words
makes the Avatar's teaching a mockery. Instead of
practicing the compassion he taught, man has waged
crusades in his name. Instead of living the humility, purity
and truth of his words, man has given way to hatred, greed
and violence. Because man has been deaf to the principles
and precepts laid down by God in the past, in this present
avataric form I observe Silence. You have asked for and
been given enough words - it is now time to live them. To
get nearer and nearer to God you have to get further and
further away from 'I', 'Me', and 'Mine.' You have nothing
to renounce but your self."

And at a public meeting in Nagpur, India in 1944 he
stated: "The organized religions of the world often fail to
express the real vision of those who have been the
fountainhead of inspiration for their very coming into
existence. Dogmas and beliefs, rituals and ceremonies can
never be the essence of the true spiritual life. They are
generally not only superficial and ineffective, but also
positively harmful and misleading. Often, they not only
feed the ego of the priestly class, but also serve as an
instrument for the exploitation of the credulous. When
religion becomes merely a matter of external rituals and
ceremonies, it becomes a cage for the soul. Nor does it help
very far to change one religion for another; it is like going
from one cage to another. If religion does not help man to
emancipate the soul from spiritual bondage and realize
God, it has no useful purpose to serve. Then it is time that
religion should go to make room for God. I am, therefore,
not interested in founding a new religion. The world is

already divided by numberless sects, based upon dogmas and beliefs. I have not come to give another cage to man but to impart to the world the illimitable truth. The world needs awakening and not mere verbal instruction; it needs the freedom and the amplitude of Divine Life, and not the superficiality of mechanized and pompous forms; it needs love, and not the display of power."

All of these teachings were so similar to some of the quotes from one of my favorite books, Paul Twitchell's "The Tiger's Fang" where the lord of the Etheric realm, Sohang states,: "Every religion, cult and philosophy formed principles and attributes which they gave their god. Each disagreed, usually violently, in principle with one another. Mighty wars have been waged with one religion seeking to destroy the other. Christians attempted to kill off the Muslims but failed. Yet more Christians were murdered and slaughtered by one another in the Thirty Year's War of the earth's Middle Ages than through the whole Crusades against the Muslims.

Man is more concerned with God taking care of his machinery, which consists of a brain, heart, bowels, and kidneys. As he comes closer to death, his prayers are stronger, louder, and more pathetic to his God to save him and allow these plumbing works to continue their piddle-patter for the sake of nothing. What man has given to the world is nothing, except for his spite for revenge against a society that rejects him. This and nothing more.

Spiritual logic? Man has none, but then sometimes his feet come close to the fires of hell and he quickly develops logic. So man, in his stupidity as the superior being he thinks he is, devoid of the slightest imagination, establishes a God which is a fallacy. What man cannot understand is that pure love and self-sacrifice are the requirements of character and goodness to others is the only contingent. It is always difficult to find happiness in one's self and impossible to find it anywhere else. Love is like charity; it begins at home. The world is naïve and simple and as old and evil as hell; there is a spirit of world-old evil that broods over all, with all the subtle sophistication of man's own invention-Satan. Greed, deliberate greed, is crafty, motivated, and masked under the guise of world groups for the betterment of mankind; yet man murders his saints and hangs his philosophers. It is a disgusting spectacle, the thousands of industrious and accomplished liars engaged in the mutual and systematic pursuit of their professions, salting their editorials, sermons and words with the sweetness and lightness of religious and philosophical platitudes.

It is the habit of the world to persecute the saints and prophets, but when they are gone, the people weep and repent. Jesus was crucified by his people and Nanak underwent hardships in the Punjab. Then in Baba's discourse on "Renunciation" he states that when a "pilgrim" (I don't think he meant the John Wayne kind) or "disciple" feels drawn to renunciation, it means the spirit of renunciation was already latent in him. And if the latent spirit is simply a spiritual indigestion from a temporary surfeit of pain, combined with a mild desire for something more pleasant, the overt renunciation will be only of a fleeting and feeble kind, a mere temporary escape from unpleasantness.

At its best however, this latent spirit is a secret pact of aggression between 'an incurable disgust for the world and an ardent and burning thirst for God.' When it comes to the surface it shows itself as an invincible determination to marshal the entire being to the attainment of victory over the lower self, and to reject everything that is irrelevant to this great and terrible struggle.

We might call renunciation the fruit of the flower of spiritual longing, fertilized by the pollen of disgust for the futility of endless births and deaths. And because this spirit of renunciation is latent, it needs some exciting cause to bring it to the surface."

Meeting Baba in the manner I did, was my "exciting

cause to bring it to the surface." And here, now, thirty years later my dormant spirit of renunciation is awake, 'my incurable disgust for the world' intact and my ardent and burning thirst for God continues unabated as I persevere on my journey home.

In my studying Baba's teachings, I came across information about the Meher Spiritual Center. One weekend I drove to the center to check it out. What I found was 500 beautiful, pristine, natural acres, several miles north of the Resort City of Myrtle Beach, South Carolina. Dense forest, with several fresh water lakes, covers most of the property. Throughout the property are a library, communal cooking and dining facilities, meeting halls, walking trails, a meditation cabin and residential cabins for visitors.

Founded in the early fifties, it was visited three times by Baba. The center is a designated wildlife sanctuary, protecting more then 100 species of birds including golden and bald eagles. River otters, alligators, black bear, bobcats and mink are among the 44 species of mammals sighted at the center. White tail deer still move quietly through the forest. More than two hundred plant species have been collected and documented, including endangered species of state, regional and national concern. As I walked around the property I was aware of the quality of peace present.

Unfortunately my visit was cut short. On the first and only day of my visit I was thrown off the property. In wandering around, I discovered "The Throne Room;" a small room where Baba would sit on a beautiful throne and hold darshan. As I sat in the room for a few minutes I wondered what it would be like to sit on his throne, which really looked like a king's royal seat. As the urge was overwhelming I climbed up and sat down. It felt really good. I was only taking poetic license. While I was sitting on this beautiful throne, the Director, Elizabeth Patterson walked in. She went ballistic and really freaked out. She screamed at me to "get off the throne" and also to "get off the property." Man. You'd think I killed someone. So much for love and brotherhood. Jeez, no sense of humor.

A few years later, while driving around Upper Ojai, about eighty miles north of Los Angeles, I came across a "Meher Mount" sign on top of Sulfur Mountain. I parked and walked up the driveway. As I walked past a couple of burned out homes I came to a small trailer, where I found the owner of the property, Agnes Barron. She was near ninety and stooped over by age. She invited me into her little trailer for tea. The inside walls were covered with pictures of her beloved Meher Baba. I shared with her my experience with Baba in Florida and asked her to tell me about him. She told me that during World War II she had been a correspondent in Europe where she met Baba and became a follower. At one point, Baba asked her to find property in California for a center.

In 1946, she purchased 170 acres of dense woodland at the very top of Sulphur Mountain in Ojai, California. It's a place of great natural beauty. At 2600 feet above the Ocean, it has a 360-degree view, where one can see for hundreds of miles, including the nearby peak of Topa Topa, the Los Padres National Forest, the Ojai Valley and the Pacific Ocean. She told me about the fire that roared through the property and destroyed all the buildings, hence her living in a small trailer. Prior to her nap she suggested I walk the property and eventually end up at what she called "The Baba Tree." During his first visit to Meher Mount, in 1956, Baba would sit alone on the bed of dry leaves under the tent of leafy branches beneath this beautiful, huge, old, red oak tree.

The tree sat at the very edge of the mountain facing the Pacific Ocean. The view had the feel of sitting on top of the world. This was Baba's favorite place on the mountain. As I sat under this huge old oak tree, I felt the presence of spirit. I spent many hours trimming the Baba Tree. It had been severely burned in the fire and over the next few months, I cut and stacked most of the dead wood.

As my meetings with Ms. Baron increased and I assisted her with her shopping and errands, she started to believe that Baba had sent me to her and she wanted to leave Meher Mount to me in her will. She felt that if she left it to Baba people, they would only allow his followers to use the property and she had a dream that any group could use it, churches, children's groups, etc. I told her I wasn't interested in spending the rest of my life managing her property. It was more than I wanted to take on. She was furious and hit me with her cane. I told her if she ever struck me with that cane again, I'd break it. Finally over the next few weeks she came to see that leaving me her land was inappropriate.

Years later, just prior to her death, I visited her one more time. She was in a wheel chair and incapable of taking care of herself. Some of her Baba friends were taking care of her. She left the property in a trust and today it's a universal center.

On January 31, 1969 Avatar Meher Baba left his body behind for good.

It was time to return to New York and dispose of my business. I went over my books and determined I still owed approximately $20,000.00 on the saloon. My head bartender wanted to buy the business. I told him to come up with $5000.00, sign a note for the remaining debt and I was out of there. Truly a gift. And I gave everything away including my 1954 two seat Jaguar. It had a brass plaque on the passenger side dashboard commemorating it winning the 1953 French Le Mons Grand Prix. What a sweet car! But everything had to go including the beachfront property in the Bahamas.

Before commencing my journey I visited my mom. She had been paralyzed and speechless for many years from a series of strokes. She could move only one arm. Even though I had suffered unspeakable abuse at her hand as a child, I loved her very much. As I leaned down to kiss her and tell her I loved her the last time I saw her, she grabbed my beard, gently tugged it twice and winked. It was the clearest communication we ever had.

Back in Florida, my one-bedroom beach house where I could step out my front door onto the white sand beach was perfect for my new life. I bought a twelve-foot Hawaiian surfboard and spent many hours in the sun. I changed my diet, cutting out most of the fat, and jogged each day on the beach. At first, I lay on the sand wheezing like a beached whale after one block, but eventually I worked up to a couple of miles. A year later, my weight was down from 245 pounds to 180 pounds. I was free from stress and societal conditioning. I was dark tan and my normally dark brown hair was bleached from all the sun and salt water. I spent many hours on the beach just laying around, looking up at the stars and listening to the surf. I was having the time of my life. I had put some money away, so I was truly carefree. I always wanted to sail, so I bought a twenty-foot Bahamian sailboat. It was a beauty, with twin keel fins, poured with five hundred pounds of concrete for ballast, yet drawing only six inches of water. It was sloop-rigged with a mainsail and spinnaker. It had a small galley/head area, a tiller and a couple of bunks below. Never having sailed before, it must have been humorous for anyone watching me teach myself. For weeks, I was all over that bay, usually grounding myself in shallow water. But finally I was ready for deep water Atlantic. Sailing opened up a new world for me. I also bought a small fishing boat with an outboard motor to tow my sailboat out through Navy Channel to breakwater.

I contacted a local blue crab processing company and bought thirty crab traps. Then I talked to local crabbers to make sure I didn't infringe on their territories. Every morning at daylight, I set out my traps in the Indian River. I spent the rest of the day sailing, surfing or diving. Then at dusk, I checked my traps.

I tied empty gallon bleach bottles to my traps as buoys. During this time I went to scuba diving school and became certified. I wanted to dive for lobster 30 miles out in the Gulf Stream. My final purchase was an 18-foot powerboat, so that I could get there quickly. I had a small set of shrimp nets made so I could drag for shrimp on the way back. I ate lots of seafood. It sounds like I was taking on a lot, but I really wasn't. I was taking care of myself for the first time in my life, and I needed to stay busy. I taught myself to use my outboard boat as a surfboard. I could catch a wave just right and power the motor and surf in, then full throttle out through the break. I was having a lot of fun. I was fully involved in the sub-culture. I loved my new family and was impressed with how free and liberated they were. Irresponsible was probably a more appropriate adjective, but I didn't see that initially.

I really thought I had found "my people." People who were kind and loving. Lord, how naïve and idealistic I was. The only difference in these people and the so-called straight crowd was clothes, drugs and attitudes. They were truly the same. Negative, angry, lying, stealing, etc., under the guise of liberation. For a while I hung out with a fundamentalist Christian group; probably the most hypocritical bunch I ever met. I already had the Meher Baba experience inside of me. When I would attempt to share this experience with them, I was told that Baba was going to hell because he wasn't into Jesus. Well, he was into Jesus, but just not their way. Their attitude always went klunk inside of me. I've never been much of a follower and pretty much had to check things out for myself.

I'm always amazed at the mind numbed robots this country produces seeking anyone to lead them. I was in trouble with this crowd from the beginning. Dialoguing with them was frowned upon as I was supposed to buy everything they said because they had memorized the Bible and quoted it constantly.

When I would ask them why they reached up to the skies in thanks, when their book "The Bible" said through their leader Jesus, that the "kingdom of Heaven was within and God lives within that kingdom," I was told I just didn't understand. Adios amigos.

I headed for California with some friends to visit my brother. I knew there were many shipwrecks off the Mendocino coast and we were talking about building a scuba salvage business. First a stop in Silverton, Colorado to visit friends. I met an older woman who made Elk hide clothing. She was leaving for the Taos Pueblo in Northern New Mexico and suggested I look her up if ever in New Mexico.

Heading west we stopped at Yosemite National Park. After visiting Old Faithful, we entered the park's beautiful hotel. The lobby appeared three stories tall and was woven with hand-hewn logs. Every floor around the hotel had public bathrooms with old tubs for guests, which we definitely weren't. We found an empty one and decided that my two friends would take a bath while I went out for beer. Unbeknownst to me we were being stalked by the hotel cop. As I was walking toward the bathroom, the hotel dick came up behind me with a holstered gun, and walked me to the bath. I'm sure I was a sight with my dirty hippy clothes, long hair and beard. Arriving outside the bathroom we could hear my friends laughing and playing in the tub. They had the door locked and when I banged on the door and informed them there was a guy out here with a gun, they thought that was hilarious and thought I was putting them on. They were obviously stoned and having a good time. They also thought it quite funny that I was locked outside and they were in the warm stoned tub. They got real loud about how hot the bath water was and how much they were enjoying themselves and how they were smoking dope. I thought it really funny and couldn't stop laughing, which really pissed the cop off. Finally, I pleaded with them to open the door and the cop was hard banging on the door with his gun. Right out of the Wild West. At least he didn't shoot the lock. This went on for another ten minutes before they realized I/we weren't kidding. Then, naked, they unlocked the door and we all got thrown out of the hotel.

No sense of humor; and I'm the only one who didn't get a bath. Upon resuming our trek west we spent some time in the Grand Canyon in Arizona. We found a series of ancient Indian caves above Hermit's Gulch on the South Rim and lived in one for a while. One late night, in the pitch dark, sitting by my campfire, a voice came up from below: "Excuuuuse me." Without thinking, I yelled back: "Whhhhy?... Diiid... yooou... faaart?"

It was two stoned guys who had lost the trail, one with a broken ankle, and they were attempting to come out using our campfire as a beacon. Getting out on the trail in the daylight was a chore and these two guys were coming straight up. Hell, it was only about a 2,000-foot fall. We helped them up and to a hospital.

Probably the most interesting night of my life was over the fourth of July at Oak Creek Canyon. We had gotten there real early and got a good camp. The place was quite crowded. Around 6pm, at sunset, the Oakland Hell's Angels roared in. There weren't any campsites open and we welcomed them into ours. There must have been fifty or sixty bikes. Campers around us left in a hurry. We shared our dope stash with them and sat around the campfire watching the most incredible "movie" I have ever seen. Those guys and their women were totally whacked out, drunk, stoned, fighting with each other and roaring around on their bikes. This was the wildest, craziest group of people I had ever encountered. That night was one of the all-time great movies I have ever experienced. I just sat back and watched. Their women were really bad and some were beautiful. One would have to have a death wish to hit on one of those chicks. They raced around on their bikes, fought with each other, fucked on the ground and were generally just pretty nuts. I loved it. They had half-a-dozen campfires going and the Arizona State Police had roped off the area so no one else could get in and maybe get hurt. They just left them alone. They reminded me of what the barbarian hordes must have been like. Fortunately the Angels liked us, or we probably would have gotten hurt.

Arriving in San Diego, my friends wanted to go into Mexico and I wanted to spend time with my brother, so we parted company. I spent a month with my older brother and his family, then purchased a 1953 Chevrolet long bed panel truck. It was originally a bread truck that had been stored in a barn for twelve years and was in mint condition. My brother had a mechanic friend who let me paint it in his garage. I painted it the light beige color of mescaline, placed India Red Madras print curtains on the walls, and in between the driver's compartment and the rear and a yellow shag rug on the floor and was ready to go.

Upon my return to Florida, I discovered the vehicle I had brought from New York, a 63' Chevy El Camino, was a wreck. In my absence I had allowed one of my new friends to house sit. She found the keys to my car and let her boyfriend drive it. Late one night, while drunk, he hit a cow and ruined the front end; probably ruined the cow too.

I took a welding torch and cut the car in half attempting to make a trailer out of the rear end, but instead set the whole damn thing on fire. Next stop the junkyard.

For the first time, my life wasn't dominated by alcohol, although the problem wasn't completely solved. I was thoroughly enjoying my self.

One day word spread through the sub-culture that magic mushrooms containing the psychedelic Psilocybin were discovered north of Cocoa Beach. What a sight that was, hundreds of hippies, some naked, roaming the cattle pastures picking mushrooms.

I had learned a new trade and started a business called "Billy's Bongs." I learned from a freak who was probably the best bong maker in Florida. They were constructed out of Oriental Bamboo, which only grew in a few places in the United States. It's the best bamboo for bongs. Each branch is used as legs so the bong stands up. Cajun country in Louisiana was the closest place where this cane grew and I made a couple of trips there for bamboo.

In 1969 the moon launch was scheduled at Cape Canaveral. A friend had a small rental house in Titusville directly across from the launch. We could see the shuttle sitting on the gurney. We decided to have a launch party. Using the sub-culture moccasin wireless we got word up and down the coast, up into Georgia and the Carolina's that Leon Russell the great pianist/rocker and his band was playing at our house for the launch. Then we set up tables on the lawn selling everything from bongs to crafts. A couple hundred freaks showed up, and camped out all over the property. What a great party! Leon never showed. Oh well.

When the launch commenced I had a couple of hits of mushrooms in me. What a spectacular sight!

Once, while nude sun bathing with friends on the roof of my little home, the police arrived and arrested us. My house was hidden by thick forest. A very tall condominium three blocks away was the only sign of nearby life. Apparently someone in the condo spotted us with binoculars and called the police. All four of us were taken to the police station. We refused to dress. Next day, the headlines of the local paper read: NUDE MAN DISCOVERS BAN ON TAN. I knew that normally one in this position would plead guilty and pay a fine. We refused and demanded a jury trial. They dropped the charges. My days in Florida were numbered, as the police would arrive at my house every morning from 2 to 5 a.m. shining lights in my window and generally harassing me. Then a strange thing happened. I started getting seasick every day. It was truly a devastating condition. I had no idea what was going on, as I had been on and around the water all my life. I could no longer sail or go boating. Finally, a friend asked if he could try my outboard as a surfboard. He capsized and apparently salt water and internal combustion machines don't match. So, with police harassment, no more sailing or boating, and disillusionment, it was time to move on.

Lama Foundation

Until one is committed, there is hesitancy, the chance to draw back, always ineffectiveness. Concerning all acts of initiative (and creation) there is one elementary truth, the ignorance of which kills countless ideas and splendid plans: that the moment one definitely commits oneself, then Providence moves too.

JOHANN WOLFGANG VON GOETHE

HEADING WEST ONCE AGAIN, I DECIDED TO DRIVE the northern route taking me through New Mexico. Stopping in Taos, New Mexico, I never found the Elk lady, but while browsing a bookstore I came across Baba Ram Dass' book "Be Here Now", a read I had thoroughly enjoyed a few years earlier. The book was published in San Cristobal, New Mexico at a "Lama Foundation." I asked the clerk where it was. Nineteen miles north toward Colorado. I decided to check it out. At the Lama turnoff I drove up a rough, rutted, dirt road as far as I could, then parked my truck and started walking. It was a warm, late fall afternoon. As I had recently left Florida, I was dressed in shorts and sandals and was enjoying my hike at 8,500 feet. Three miles up the road as the Lama Foundation turnoff wasn't marked, I walked right on past. Another three miles found me near the little town of San Cristobal.

The afternoon had turned very cold and a snowstorm surrounded me. I came across a woodcutter and he directed me back to the Foundation turnoff. As I entered the Lama turnoff I had now hiked approximately nine miles, three in a very cold blizzard. I was freezing. As I came up over a rise, a large building came into view. The Lama Foundation dome is a very large geodesic type circular adobe building. When I first saw the Dome, I had this powerful feeling that I was "home." I had no idea what this place was, but I knew I needed to be here.

Behind the dome was a small two-story building, housing the kitchen. I saw smoke coming out of the chimney and was in desperate need of warmth. My hair, eyebrows and beard were caked with snow and ice.

After I knocked on the door a person opened it and told me to go away. I pushed in past him and went directly to the stove. He told me no one was allowed at the foundation and I was to leave. I would have told him to kiss my ass, but I was so cold, I was unable to speak. I stood mute, warming myself over the stove. I must have looked like the proverbial abominable snowman. He was quite upset with my staying. After a few minutes another man, the coordinator, entered and observing my obvious stress state, went to the refrigerator, brought out soup and heated it on the stove. After a bowl of broth, I explained who I was and asked if I could stay. As it was now dark and below zero, this second person told me I could sleep on the floor in the library near the stove. He brought me to the bookroom, gave me a blanket, banked the wood-stove and told me to be gone after breakfast. I slept on the concrete floor.

The following morning I was once again instructed to leave. I knew I needed to be here, and suggested they put me to work as I was staying. The co-coordinator of the Foundation was a follower of Meher Baba and took me under his wing. I was allowed to sleep in the library and each day assigned various tasks.

At the first Lama Counsel meeting I attended, held

weekly, I was once again asked to leave, and they voted me out. The six people living at Lama appeared to be well off and hiding from the world. They were non-violent and I knew they would never attempt to physically remove me. So I stayed on, participating in whatever was going on.

For a while I lived in the yellow school bus Ram Dass had left behind. It had a small cook stove and was toasty warm. Finally, a few months into my stay, I was voted in as a member. I thought that really funny. The 150-acre property Lama Foundation was created as an eclectic spiritual ashram where members could live a reclusive spiritual life. In the early days of Lama, leaders from the Taos Pueblo spoke to the founders and told them basically: "You are on our land and we would like to teach you about this place."

They spent a few hours teaching them, walking the land, and sharing about certain plants and certain sacred areas that needed to be preserved. They took prayer smokes over many sacred places. Then they wanted to know if they understood and said they'd be back to keep telling them. One of their main points was, "We have our ways which are not yours. You people or Americans have lost your way and you've got to find your way. We're here to help you." Some of the leaders were Little Joe Gomez and his brother John and Tellus Good Morning covered in a later chapter and Frankie Zamorra the focus of Frank Waters' "The Man Who Killed the Deer." Frankie built a house on Lama Mountain the old way by cutting all the trees by hand and after trimming them placing them into the shape of a one-room long house. He then left it to cure and dry and then chinked it with mud. I knew him when he was very old. He sure liked the ladies. One evening I visited a lady in Taos as Frankie bolted out the bedroom window.

These Pueblo leaders were often there the first three summers, teaching the early residents basic skills: how to make bricks, which trees to cut for wood. "They showed us how to kill an animal correctly, in a sacred manner, and the rhythm of working and the rhythm of rest, and the rhythm of life. And lots of family things— generations living together in ways that many of us had not really experienced because of America being the way it is— and loyalty and friendship and companionship and silence."

MISSION STATEMENT

The Purpose of The Lama Foundation is to be a sustainable spiritual community and educational center dedicated to the awakening of consciousness and spiritual practice with respect for all traditions, service, and stewardship of the land.

The Lama Foundation was founded in 1967 as a Meeting of the Ways for followers of all spiritual traditions who have sought to be more fully human.

One of the many landmarks of Lama's history was Ram Dass' collaboration with Lama Residents in 1970 to produce his famous book, Be Here Now. The income from the sale of this book not only provided for the daily needs of the community but also enabled them to donate sums of money to outside projects deemed appropriate. Life at the Lama Foundation observes two distinct seasons and modes of operation. In the winter, a small group of 10-15 residents live as an intimate community practicing conscious living and co-creation together. In the summer months, Lama opens its doors to the public, expands to include a much larger ensemble of summer staff, and hosts a diverse calendar of spiritual and educational programs. This last aspect of Lama was not implemented until approximately a year after my arrival. Throughout the year, Lama also operates two cottage industries -- one offering hermitages to the public for solo contemplation and Flag Mountain Cottage Industries, which produces hand printed prayer flags. Lama is relatively unique among spiritual communities in that it is a living organism that remains unbound to any particular creed, tradition, or teacher. At Lama, all spiritual paths and traditions are celebrated as equally beautiful expressions of the Divine; at any given time, many different paths are practiced, both individually and collectively. Lama is also unique in that its resident body is constantly shifting, and consequently the particular practices, character, and engagements of the community are likewise always evolving. Lama is partly an on-going experiment in co-creation in which the residents continually evolve the course of how Lama can best serve the Awakening of Consciousness. Lama residents try to conduct all daily and long-term business through a consensus process, an endeavor that can be richly rewarding at times, deeply challenging at others. Lama residents are ostensively dedicated to a constant exploration in how individuals can learn to live most harmoniously together and with the earth.

Living quarters were for the most part one-room wooden structures with lofts scattered about the property, and one two-story house. Wood stoves were the only means of heat and there was no plumbing or toilets. There was one large outhouse. Peristalsis at 30-below zero was difficult, and most of us used honey-buckets.

Each week, a watch was assigned. This person was responsible for the daily routine, visitors, office tasks and the general well being of the Foundation. We all took turns. At five thirty a.m. and five p.m. the watch would ring the large gongs in front of the kitchen calling everyone to the prayer room for meditation. These gongs could be heard all over the mountain. The prayer room was an underground room at one end of the dome. It had a very small door that one had to crawl through to enter. Inside was a circular room set underground in three levels, plastered white. A puja was in the center at the bottom level and a small fireplace in the rear was the only source of heat. Once inside, sitting in various forms of meditation, the watch would ring a small bell and we would sit for an hour. I loved this room and spent many hours there. Members had a variety of spiritual practices including Zen and Tibetan Buddhism, Sufism and Hinduism. Then there was me, who had never heard of any of it. Master spiritual teachers were invited from all over the world to come and provide their practices from one to three-week increments. Every member was invited to participate in these events, and for me it was a crash course in spirituality. Behind the prayer room was the library/office. And near the front of the dome were showers and a yoga room. The center of the dome was a two-story hollow structure large enough for a couple of hundred people to Sufi dance. Breakfast was served a half-hour after meditation and in the winter was normally hot porridge and tea. All meals were organic and vegetarian. When membership was low we would just hang out and eat in the kitchen and when there were more people, we would all eat upstairs in a more formal setting.

From the beginning of my stay, everyone at the Foundation had difficulty with my sarcasm and anger. As I had lived with it most of my life, I was unaware of this negative aspect of my personality. In retrospect it was definitely a problem. These two defense mechanisms were my forte through life and had become second nature to me. I guess it's okay that we don't always see how we truly are, how embarrassing. But I was learning and was reminded of it by members on a regular basis. When I arrived at Lama there was a 1,500-pound Holstein cow named Emma, and a flock of chickens. Members were talking about getting rid of her, as no one wanted to milk her twice a day. The organic gardens were also in disarray. I suggested I take over the garden, chickens and responsibility for Emma. As I had absolutely no experience with gardening or animal husbandry, nor had I ever been within a freeway of a cow, little did I know what I was in for. Everyone thought it a good idea as they liked the organic milk. That night I headed for the barn, milking pail in hand, excited about my new adventure. Emma waited patiently near the gate to the milking stand. I measured out the proper amount of feed and let her out. She stood quietly eating in the stanchion. Bear in mind this is a 1,500-pound beast standing in an area with barely enough room for her, let alone me. I put the stool sideways next to her, washed off her teats and proceeded to milk her. Never having milked anything before, nothing came out. As I would painfully find out, she gave approximately nine gallons of milk a day. She was a milk-producing fool. After almost an hour she became a bit impatient, moving back and forth and leaning into me, crushing me into the wall. Occasionally her belly and I became one. Three hours into this fiasco, she was around three-fourths empty, beyond patience, and my hands had become frozen into grotesque caricatures of their original selves. I wasn't sure they would ever open again. I released her from my apprenticeship. The next morning the dance resumed. My hands were beyond pain and were mostly useless.

At one point I attempted to milk her with my wrists that were only partially ruined. Anything to get the milk out. I kept at it, day and night. Finally the day arrived when I could milk her pain free. She was a wonderful teacher for me. A pattern developed between us. During milking time, whenever I was angry or off-center, she would gently lean into me, pressing me into the wall. The degree of the lean was predicated on the severity of my imbalance. She constantly reminded me to stay positive. I grew to love her. She really did "cow" well. I realized she needed to graze as she had been constantly locked in the barn pen. I started leaving the gate open and every day she would wander around the property contentedly grazing. I knew she would find her way back to the barn, every evening, which she always did. Every day other Lama members would chase her all over the property trying to get her back to the barn. I knew it couldn't be good for her to have that huge bag flopping from side to side as she ran. I finally convinced them to just leave her alone. Next I started working the gardens. This also was my first exposure to farm life, but being the dedicated didactic I am, like everything in my life, I figured it out for myself. There was a large, full, compost bin and I mixed in chicken manure and the enormous defecation leavings of Emma. Carrots and lettuce were the first the earth gave. Situated at 8,500 feet, the growing season was short. I was really enjoying this new adventure. The two dozen chickens had quit laying prior to my arrival. Not knowing anything about chickens but having first-hand proof of the power of Spirit, I created a small puja. I put a picture of Meher Baba, some incense and a large glass candle in it. I built a chicken-wire pen around it to keep the chickens from incinerating themselves. Within a few days, egg production resumed. HA!

Lil Joe

There's no way, there's only "Way."

GRANDPA JOE GOMEZ

THIS WAS A GOOD DAY TO DIE. GRANDFATHER WOULD leave today. He left the same way he lived his long life: gently, into Spirit. I'm not sure how old he was. 95, maybe 100? Was that him on the wing? Did I hear him in the wind?

I was at his hogan on the Taos Pueblo reservation all day. Even though he was a spiritual leader and elder Shaman of the Taos Pueblo, and head of the Sacred Clown clan he had been forced to live outside the Pueblo years earlier because he had married a white woman.

There were more or less fifty people, mostly Indians, around the property. Campfires were burning, people were drinking coffee, and some were praying the Indian way with tobacco. Lil Joe was beloved all over the southwest and the recognized spiritual leader of the Peyote Way. He reminded me of Carlos Castenedos' Don Juan.

That afternoon, his wife, Adrianne, came outside and started screaming at us, "Let him go. You're keeping him here. Let him go. Get out of here." She was pissed! People stopped praying, some left. Then he died.

I wasn't sad, just grateful for the teacher and friend

51

Grandfather had been to me; he who taught me the Peyote way and where God is. I met him at Lama Foundation on one of his many visits. He was the local resident guru, a Peyote Master, a teacher of spirit. He was amazing in his innocence and loving. His eyes were light blue and he stood barely five-foot tall. Over the years I spent many hours at his hogan sitting at his feet, listening to the wisdom of the ages, or at Peyote meetings when he was Road Man. At home, Joe would sit on his bed, which was against one wall, and a few feet above chair level, throne-like. He was probably the must unpretentious person I had ever met.

As the unofficial head of the Native American Church, the Peyote Way, The Way` Joe (named "Standing Buffalo Watching" at birth) spent a lifetime presenting and teaching the Way. Over the years, on more than one occasion, the peyote meetings, up in the mountains, would be interrupted by the Pueblo sheriff and they'd have to complete the meeting in jail. Once, Little Joe, all 120 pounds of him, crawled up the cell fireplace chimney, escaped and was arrested by a confused sheriff at another meeting a few hours later. Sometime in the late 1800s, after the harvest, Joe, his brother John, friend, Tellus Good Morning and his father "Red Willow" buck-boarded to Oklahoma to meet with the great Comanche Chief, Quanah Parker, and brought the Half Moon Peyote Way to the Taos Pueblo.

In their early teens, Joe and John, along with their orphaned friend, Tellus Good Morning, took a vow of secrecy with this outlawed Way, conducting meetings all over the southwest for over seventy years.

Though Tellus was very young, Quanah Parker gave him his Chief Peyote Button and to John an eagle tail, beautifully beaded and wrapped in snow white hand-tanned leather. What he gave to Joe was the best gift--the "Way."

Quanah Parker was born in 1845 to Peta Nokoni, Chief of the Nocone Comanche Band in Texas and Cynthia Parker, a white captive. From 1867, when he became Chief of Comanches at age 22, until his defeat at Adobe Walls in 1874 he led numerous raids against white settlements.

Before discovering Peyote, Parker had dedicated his life to destroying every white man he ran into, counting more coup than all of the other chiefs combined. After a while Parker realized he was fighting a losing battle. He believed he could play the white game and win, not only for himself, but for his people. Everyone would have preferred the old ways, but at least they were in a better situation than most of the tribes. He had seen Geronimo and his Apaches when they came through Fort Sill.

They were a beaten people. They had nothing. No land. No horses. No lodges. All they had left was despair. The same was true for most of the other Plains Tribes. They were not able to change, so they suffered terribly. He called together his Council and they adopted the Peyote ritual and the killing and wars ended.

The Peyote Way, required complete abstinence from alcohol and brought a sense of solidarity and brotherhood among the tribes within their subjugation by the white man. In 1875 Quanah settled in Fort Sill, Oklahoma, and counseled his people to adapt to White ways without surrendering Comanche customs and heritage. He was appointed Judge of the Court of Indian Affairs, was a successful businessman and rode in Teddy Roosevelt's inauguration parade.

Quanah Parker died in 1911 with seven wives, twenty-five children, a forty-room mansion, was part-owner of a railroad (The Quanah, Acme, and Pacific), judge, a millionaire, and friend and adviser to a President. He also established the Native American Church, the only church legally allowed to use Peyote as a sacrament. After Quanah died, the Comanche tribe voted to designate him, "The Last Chief of the Comanches." On his tombstone it is written:

Resting Here until Day Breaks
And Shadows Fall and Darkness Disappears
Is Quanah Parker Last Chief of the Comanches
Born 1852 — Died Feb. 23, 1911

While still at Lama Foundation, we purchased a couple of Mexican mules from an old trader. One was a Palomino mare that was faster then the breeze and the other a dark brown crazy that I gave the Indian name: "Stands Trying to Kick Head In", as he was obviously committed to kicking my brains in. After a few weeks, I was finally able to get a saddle on the "Mino" and off we went at breakneck speed. A mile down the road she dug her hoofs in and stopped dead in her tracks. The belly-cinch broke and I became Superman, without the super, and flew over her head. When I was able to function again and catch her, we walked back to the barn. She won Round One. A few more weeks passed with my attempting to gentle her. Then I jerry-rigged a second belly cinch out of thick, wide latigo leather and had at it once again. As I always used a Sioux saddle, the cinch was tied to the saddle blanket.

I took her out every day attempting to calm her. I knew that in Mexico, a mule is rarely gentle broke. The damage was already done and I never could gentle her. The only way I could trust to ride her was to keep the stirrups a bit ahead of the saddle in preparation for her stopping short, so I could dig in the stirrups. Unfortunately, she lulled me into trusting her and a month later, double belly-cinched. I once again gave her, her head. Lord, she could run like the wind. Once again she stopped dead in her tracks, both belly cinches broke and I, once more, in fleeting retrospect, flew over her head. This time, I was knocked unconscious. When I came to, my shoulder was broken and she was grazing a few feet away. Her silent communication was clear. "Stay off me and we'll get alone fine." I told the doctor I didn't want a cast and asked if the shoulder would set properly without one. He assured me it would and shared in parting that I would never be able to stand the pain. I wanted to work with the pain. Sometimes it was difficult rolling over in my sleep. But I healed sans cast. There was no Round Three. I never rode her again. I'm a lot of things, stupid not among them.

Stands Trying to Kick Head In, lost a shoe and there was no way I could replace it without putting myself in cemetery way. Lil Joe suggested I bring the mule to his hogan. It took me three hours to load him in a borrowed horse trailer.

Unloading him, we tied him close to a stout post. Joe sat under a tree, silent, just staring at the mule. He rolled a smoke and stared some more. I always knew when to be quiet around him. I knew he was figuring it out. Finally after a half hour he got up whispering and gentle with the crazy and looped a small lariat to the shoeless foot and tied it forward, tight to the halter. Now he stood on three feet. Very still and calm. He was so devoted to not falling over, balancing on three legs, that he just stood quiet. Then Joe nailed on another shoe. Nice and easy. Whole thing took about ten minutes. Then I asked Joe if he would help me load him back into the trailer. I figured after what I had just observed he would know an easy trick to load him. Turning to face me, he smiled and said, "Your job." Okay, okay.

"Half Moon Way"

PEYOTE (*LOPOPHORA WILLIAMSII LEMAIRE*) IS A SMALL *spineless, carrot-shaped member of the cactus family, growing wild in the Rio Grande Valley and into Mexico. Nine psychotropic alkaloids are contained in Peyote. Contrary to the religious zealots and the uniformed public, the Peyote Ceremony is one of the most beautiful worship services I've ever attended. In its totality, the Peyote Ceremony, commencing at sundown, with singing and praying all night, and ending at sun up, is a well- designed and beautiful vehicle of worship, which produces in the person attending, a feeling of security, warmth and communion with God. It's the total design of the ritual, with its attendant prayers, singing and dignified ritual acts, that has made the Peyote religion the most popular and widespread American Indian religion in existence today. For many Native Americans, practicing the Peyote Way brings an ability to reach out of their physical lives and communicate with the spirits, to become complete. The contemporary Peyote ceremony has a veneer of Christianity. Syncretistic aspects are seen in the fact that the Native American deity is equated with the Christian God, Peyote with Jesus, and messenger spirits, in the form of birds, eagles, hawks, et al, with the Christian dove. Ethical concepts embraced by Peyotists include both Indian ideals and certain fundamentalist Christian rules such as temperance, brotherly love and care of family. One of the most interesting claims is that Peyote was sent to the Indians and afterward Jesus was sent to the Whites, with the same purpose. However, the Whites killed Jesus in their ignorance, and thus have only the cross left; whereas the Indians never killed Peyote, with the result they still have him." Of great significance for some Native Americans is the fact that their spirit-force is represented by a*

56

plant: Peyote is the Indians' Christ. White people needed a man to show them the way, but Indians have always been friends with the plants and have understood them. So Peyote came, and not to Whites.

Peyote people firmly believe they are in direct communication with Jesus, or God through Peyote. "The white man goes into church and talks about Jesus, the Indian goes into a teepee and talks to Jesus." Albert Hensley, the great Winnebago Peyote leader and missionary stated, "Our favorite term (for Peyote) is 'Medicine', and to us it is a portion of the body of Christ, even as the communion bread is believed to be a portion of Christ's body by other Christian denominations...It came from God. It is a part of God's body. God's Holy Spirit is enveloped in it. It was given exclusively to Indians and God never intended that White men should understand it, hence the folly of any such attempt."

For many Native Americans, the Peyote ceremony has considerable influence, offering "prayer for his soul, food for his stomach, health for his body, prestige, and self expression. It allows for the venting of certain aggressive feelings and, to a certain degree, soothes the ever-present sense of cultural loss."

Peyote also allows the participant to enter the world of the unknown in a visual encounter of mind-expanding dimensions. Peyote ingestion allows the user to go beyond the material world and into the spirit world, to reach out of the physical world, to communicate with spirits and become complete. This ceremony is part of a serious, valid, and meaningful religion— a demanding, moralistic faith that requires much emotional and physical involvement. The ceremony itself is a means, or a tool, by which believers can find and attune to God through the sacramental use of Peyote.

PEYOTE BY EDWARD F. ANDERSON, PUBLISHED BY
UNIVERSITY OF ARIZONA PRESS

This way that Joe, John and Tellus Good Morning taught was the Kiowa-Comanche ceremony. This is the form most Peyotists subscribe to from Mexico to Canada. The preferred structure is a Plains Indian teepee, erected on a three-pole foundation with sixteen additional poles spiraled around the basic tripod, although occasionally a meeting would be held in someone's home.

The teepee cover is always white and undecorated. The entrance always faces east and great care and respect is maintained during ground preparation and teepee erection. In the afternoon, the Roadman or Road Chief, standing alone, directly in the center of the teepee, facing west, prostrates himself on the earth, with face downward, and head to the west. A complete act of humility. He then stretches his arms to the sides, reaching as far as he can. Dragging his fingertips on the ground, he brings his arms up over his head. This forms a rough half-circle, and is the outline for the altar. The altar is called "half moon" or "way," hence the name "Half Moon Way." Then sand and earth are used to construct the altar. On top of the crescent, a thin line is trailed in the sand. From teepee to teepee, this represents the "road of life," or the "Jesus" road, the avenue of communication between participants and God. In the center of the altar will be placed the Father Peyote or Grandfather, a usually large and well-formed peyote button or top of the peyote cactus. This button represents Christ. To the east of the altar or moon, close toward the entrance is the ceremonial fire. Fire sticks are placed in a "V" shape, criss-crossed on top of each other, with closed end of the "V" to the altar or west.

At the beginning of the ceremony the Roadman enters first, clockwise, and sits in the place of honor directly opposite the door, on the west side. Everyone always moves clockwise in the teepee. Now the other officers enter, Chief Drummer, sitting to the right of the Roadman, Cedar man to his left and the Fire Chief takes up his position inside the door. These four divide the responsibility of conducting the ceremony at the direction of the Roadman. The rest of the participants now enter and move all the way around until they come to the first empty space, unless otherwise instructed by the Roadman. The drum, used with everyone who sings, is made by tying a circular buckskin head over the top of a small (6" to 8") three- legged iron or copper kettle. A clothesline is usually used today and a twisted vine or handmade woven rope in olden times.

Seven stones are spaced under the head, around the sides of the drum, and the rope is secured around the sides of the drum, and around the skin at each stone to hold it in place and tighten it. Sometimes a deer antler is used in tying the drum. When properly tied the rope used produces a unique "morning star" design on the bottom of the drum. The drum is now filled to about one quarter with water.

Water is occasionally added to it during the ceremony by pouring it through the skin with the drummer sucking it in. Tuning is achieved by blowing air into it through the hide.

The sequence of the meeting is as follows:

When everyone is seated on the ground, Cedar Man takes cedar needles and sprinkles them on the fire. As the smoke rises, the Roadman holds the Father Peyote button in the smoke for a while, then places it on the road. He then states the purpose of the meeting, which could be someone's health, a funeral, a birthday, a holiday or honoring a friend. The Drum Chief rolls a long prayer cigarette out of corn husk and loose tobacco and hands it to the Roadman. Corn husk and tobacco is now passed to everyone. A specially carved "smoke" stick, smoldering in the fire is passed around clockwise from the Fire Chief. Everyone now smokes and prays aloud. When finished, the butts are placed on the ground and collected by the Fire Chief and placed behind the altar, near the ends of the crescent.

In the morning they are burned in the sacred fire by the Fire Chief. Sprigs of sage are passed around and everyone rubs some on themselves to acquire some of its 'cleansing power." Plains Indians consider sage a holy plant and a powerful counter to bad medicine. Peyote buttons are passed around and everyone eats some. Once, Grandfather Joe told me human beings have a snake in their stomach making the peyote taste bitter and harsh. And over the years, when enough problems are worked through, the snake shrinks and the medicine starts to taste better. I think he was referring to arrogance and ego.

Ritual articles are removed from Roadman's box, and are 'cedared' individually in the smoke. A small, decorated altar cloth is spread on the ground in front of him, just behind the altar. Then, from east to west, he places an eagle bone whistle, golden eagle tail feathers, staff, sage sprig, gourd rattle and his personal feathers. Behind the cloth, separate from the other articles, he places a bag of tobacco and corn husks. Now Fire Chief is called forward and handed a single feather, usually an eagle's. This constitutes Fire Chief's symbol of authority and his credential for leaving and re-entering the Teepee during the ceremony without first asking permission. No one else leaves without the consent of the Roadman and only after midnight.

With the staff in his left hand, sprig of sage and a single eagle feather with the gourd rattle in his right hand, the Roadman begins to sing the opening song, repeated three times while shaking the gourd in a four-four beat. Then he sings three other songs of his choice, each sung four times. The Drummer loudly taps the eight note "Peyote beat" on the water drum. One shake of the rattle is made to every two-drum beats. Now the meeting is completely underway. When these songs are complete, Roadman passes the staff, sage, eagle feather and gourd rattle to the Cedar man on his left and plays the drum for him while he sings four songs of his choice. The staff is always held in front of the singer pointing to Grand Father Peyote on the altar creating an imaginary line between the singer and God. This line must never be broken by someone walking through it or the singer's connection to God could be severed. The singing and drumming proceeds in this manner all night, always proceeding in a clockwise direction. The person who sings is expected to drum for the person to his left. Occasionally someone else like a relative or close personal friend will be asked to drum. Anyone not wishing to sing passes the ritual articles to the left. Women never sing before midnight. The belief is because they bear us, they have knowledge or wisdom and have no need to make sound, which is contrary to the White world, where some women never shut up.

At midnight, the Roadman orders the staff, et al, returned to him. And the drum and drumstick are returned to him. The Fire Chief cleans the fire, pushing the hot coals into a crescent shape between the fire and the altar and the Cedar Man sprinkles cedar on the fire. Then Roadman calls for water, and with the staff, sage sprig, feathers and gourd rattle accompanied by the drum, sings the Midnight Water Song, a beautiful but difficult song sung four times. At the end he blows the eagle bone whistle in a pattern of one long note followed by several short ones. Then he sings four personal songs, each sung four times, and each time blows the eagle bone whistle at the end. When the first of the four songs are sung Fire Chief leaves the teepee and returns with a pail of clean water. Prior to entering, he circles the teepee once outside, clockwise, then enters, placing the bucket in front of the fire. Cedar Chief sprinkles cedar on the fire and Fire Chief "cedars" himself and the water by drawing the smoke toward himself and the water with his hands in a slow fanning motion. Then the Drummer brings corn husk and tobacco to the Fireman who rolls a cornhusk smoke, lights it with the fire stick and prays. When finished he walks clockwise to Roadman and hands him the tobacco husk. Making sure it is still lit, he hands it to Drummer. After a few puffs he returns it to Roadman who passes it to the Cedar Chief, who puffs on it and hands it back. Now Roadman prays at length. Plains Indians believe the tobacco smoke takes their prayers to Wok On Tonka, the Great Spirit. Fire Chief now brings the water bucket and sets it in front of Roadman. Taking the single eagle feather and the Eagle bone whistle he places the tip of the feather in the water and draws a cross on the surface, then dips the feather in the water and shakes it towards each of the four directions, north, east, south and west over his shoulder in that order, then on either side of himself and finally himself, on head and shoulders.

Lastly he takes the Eagle whistle and draws the same design in the water. The Christian influence is always evident. Now he blows one long high note and several short ones. This is done four times. He concludes by lowering the whistle below the surface of the water. This blesses the water and it is ready to drink. Once more he prays at length, than drinks from a cup out of his tool kit. He passes the cup and bucket to his left to Cedar Chief, who drinks, and passes it on till everyone has drunk. Then the Fire Chief retrieves the bucket and takes it outside. As soon as the water bucket has been removed, Cedar Chief burns more cedar needles so the staff, drum and other paraphernalia are cedared off. After midnight individual members may use their personal feathers or rattles, but they must be cedared first. Again peyote is passed around with peyote tea, as Roadman takes his Eagle whistle outside for the "Whistling to the Four Winds" ceremony, while the staff, feathers and drum are returned to the point where they stopped before midnight and singing rounds are started again. Once Roadman returns, members, with permission, may leave the meeting to stretch or relieve themselves. Occasionally someone needs to vomit. People are encouraged to vomit on the ground in front of them, loudly, as the belief is this is a form to release negative spirits from within. Then the Fire Chief, with a shovel, removes it from the teepee. Elders can be heard murmuring, "Ah hoo" during this time or after a song is sung, exceptionally well. During the night, Fire boy adds new fuel, at his discretion, to the fire, and arranges the sticks so it doesn't smoke. Dry cottonwood is the wood of choice as it burns hot, is smokeless and makes strong, lasting coals. If the wind shifts strongly, he may go outside and adjust the smoke flaps to create a proper draft.

Toward morning, the Fire Boy arranges the coals in the

form of the "Water bird" or "Ash bird," representing the water turkey which, Peyotists believe, along with tobacco smoke, carries their prayers to God. This is the bird that while sitting still on water, takes off, going directly up into the air.

Upon arrival of first dawn light the Road Man tells the Fire Boy to awaken "Morning Water Woman." It is her duty to bring in the morning water at which time she represents "all woman kind" and the "blessings" woman brings to man.

When Roadman is advised that water woman waits outside, he immediately signals by blowing the ritualistic long and short notes on his eagle bone whistle four times, even if someone is singing. As soon as the person has finished singing, he calls the staff and drum back to the altar, takes in his left hand a full set of eagle tail feathers (twelve) which are fixed in buckskin sockets attached to a beaded and fringed handle, also the single eagle feather, the sage sprig and staff with the gourd rattle in his right hand.

The Kiowa way calls for a black and white young golden eagle tail and the Comanche way a speckled mature golden eagle tail. Some of the Northern Peyote boys use Owl feathers. The Kiowa and Comanche Peyote boys, et al, get agitated when someone brings owl feathers into the Teepee. Sometimes arguments would ensue. This was the only time I ever heard Indians arguing at meetings. (Owl feathers have a burr on the end of their feathers that dissipates the wind allowing them to fly silently, and they only hunt at night and attack their prey from behind.) Accompanied by the Drum Chief, he sings the beautiful morning song, four times. During the singing of this song, Morning Water Woman comes in carrying a pail of cool water, setting the pail between the door and the fire. She sits behind it facing west. After singing the morning song, the third of the official songs, the Roadman sings three personal songs, each four times, then places the staff, gourd and other articles on the altar cloth. Cedar Chief puts cedar needles in the fire and Water Woman "smokes" or "smudges" herself and the water. Now Drum Chief rolls a corn husk/tobacco smoke that Fire Chief retrieves and brings to Water Woman, first lighting it with the fire stick.

She smokes and prays at length and when finished the Drum Chief retrieves the partly consumed smoke and brings it to Road Man who puffs it, prays and hands it to the Cedar Chief who puffs it and hands it back. Fire Chief now spills a small amount on the fire to "feed" it and gives the cup and bucket to Morning Water Woman, who drinks. The bucket is passed from person to person, clockwise, until all have drunk.

When the bucket reaches the Fire Chief and he has drunk, Water woman circles the teepee clockwise, picks up the bucket and goes out. Roadman now announces he is about to sing the quitting songs. Again four songs. In this case, the official quitting song is song last. While he is singing, Morning Water Woman brings in the four sacred foods of the ceremonial breakfast. This breakfast consists of water, corn, fruit and meat. The exact forms these dishes take varies. They could be home grown and cooked or canned. Fruit consists of whatever's available and the meat can run from venison to hamburger.

When Roadman completes the four quitting songs, the meeting is officially over. The Drum Chief unties the drum and pours the water out along the inside of the "Way".

The ritual paraphernalia are passed around for everyone to handle, including the staff, gourd, sage and feathers and also the drum kettle, rope and drum stick. Someone is asked to pray over the food, an elder, man or woman. Roadman now retrieves Father Peyote from its place on the altar and when all the ritual items are put away the atmosphere changes from formal restraint to friendly familiarity. The food is passed around, again clockwise, with each person taking a small amount of each dish, either eating it on the spot or putting it aside for later. Complete informality reigns, as the food is passed. Visitors are asked to speak, jokes are told and the elders teach by talking to each other across the teepee. Wiser younger members listen intently as the oral tradition is passed down. When the Fire Chief has finished eating (he being the last in order,) Roadman indicates that all are free to leave. Most rise, stretch cramped limbs, and the Fire Chief leads the line out of the teepee.

Participants usually hang around for the social gathering, and around noon a completely secular dinner, in larger quantities than the ceremonial breakfast, are served by the sponsor. Someone is asked to pray over the food. I always loved listening to Indians praying in their native tongue. When someone would pray for an exceptionally long time, I always got a kick out of someone remarking they must be Navajo, as Navajos pray for so long. Some participants rest or doze in the teepee till the noon meal is served. This was always my practice. And some of the younger members would tie a new drum and practice songs that they "caught" during the evening. Those who have come long distances are given quantities of food for their trip home and everyone always gives money to them for gas and expenses. By mid-afternoon most have departed for home and the teepee is taken down.

A friend brought me to my first meeting. The person bringing you to your first meeting is supposed to be responsible for you. I wasn't aware of this nor obviously, was my friend. It was a very cold fall night. We were next to the last two allowed in. I sat one seat from the door on the south side with my friend to my left. After midnight the person sitting to my right was singing and praying. One of his friends was squeezed between the singer and me to drum. There was a cold breeze blowing on me from the door flap that wasn't completely closed. I tried to get to it by reaching behind the drummer and singer, but couldn't. I obviously wasn't paying attention to anything but my discomfort. To close the fly, I got up and walked directly between the singer and road, breaking the line between him and God. The next thing I knew, the Fire Chief, hit me like a linebacker and slammed me down on the ground. Everything stopped. The only other time I saw a meeting stop was when someone dropped an eagle feather and the Road Chief had to cedar it off. Everything went silent except for whispering. Everyone was incredulous. No one could believe what had just happened. Apparently this never happens. I was now totally present and aware of what a major screw up I had just created, although it wasn't until much later I learned what I had just done.

It was the only time I ever saw Grand Father with tears in his eyes and I would never forget it. I got to my feet and humbly stood there. I apologized to Grand Father and asked if I should leave. He said 'no', then walked over to me clockwise, had the Cedar Chief drop cedar needles into the fire, and smudged me with cedar smoke with his eagle feather and did the same with the singer and drummer.

People, only white people, started quietly hurling insults at me. With a glance, Grand Father silenced them and told me to sit, shook his eagle feather once at my friend and said, "Pay tention!" For the next six hours I was abject attention. It was the beginning of my considering the possibility that I might have some work to do in the area of arrogance, work that continues to this day. I shall never forget that meeting. To this day, thirty years later, there are people, only white people, who cannot forgive my mistake

After this meeting I knew I needed to go this way and started hanging out with L'll Joe whenever possible, and participating in meetings on a regular basis; sometimes two meetings in a row.

Years later, after marrying, I was invited to a healing meeting with Grandpa Joe as Road Chief and his brother John, also attending. John was sitting on the south pole.

As my wife entered ahead of me and a few feet into the teepee, instead of going around to the first available seat, which in this case was all the way around on the north side, Grandpa John told her to sit next to him which put me to her right. At midnight Grandfather John went out of the teepee. As he left, he handed her his eagle tail to hold for him, the one Quanah Parker gave him sixty years earlier. She sat up straight as the power and energy of that beautiful tail, entered her. Without a word, she knew. Man, I loved this Way.

One day, while at Lil Joe's hogan, we were hanging out near his garden, having a smoke. I had been thinking of going to India in my quest for God. It seemed to me, from what I had seen, God was in India. He sure didn't seem to be in decadent America.

Joe turned to me and asked, "You want God?"

I replied, "Of course."

He pointed to a Red Tail Hawk soaring above us and said "God," then pointed to a Pinon tree and said "God." Then he pointed at me, in the direction of my heart, and said "God." Whoa, I don't know what he did, but a gentle surge went through me similar to what I experienced when I met Meher Baba. I knew that I "knew." I understood I didn't have to go across the street to find God, let alone India. All I had to do was sit down and shut up. This informative encounter was the beginning of serious meditation, reflection and introspection as I was reminded once again that the last frontier, so to speak, was inside.

Another of my Peyote teachers, born in the 19th century, Usually Good Morning, became one of my mentors. I spent many hours with him in his Pueblo home, learning old ways, and sat in many meetings with him. When Tellus was Roadman, at the end of every meeting, a funny thing always happened. It was custom in the morning before everyone left the teepee for the Roadman to go around and shake everyone's hand and say, "Good Morning." Grandfather Tellus would shake the first hand saying "Good Morning," and the person would respond, "Good Morning, Good Morning," or "Good Morning— Good Morning Good Morning, Good Morning— Good Morning Good Morning," and so on. Finally, everyone in the teepee was laughing.

Some of my Indian Peyote friends were silversmiths. I was intrigued with how they could take a bag of silver scraps and turn it into beautiful Concho belts, bracelets and rings. One day, I asked if they would make a ring for me. They replied that they would teach me to make it myself. Thus began a long apprenticeship where I eventually became a master silversmith.

These artists were silversmiths, not jewelers. They taught me how to melt scrap silver into ingots, anneal them and pound them to the proper gauge. They taught me how to make metal stamps out of old buckboard spring steel. I was completely into this new occupation and began making a few bucks from my creations.

One day I asked one of my mentors to teach me how to make cabochons out of raw turquoise. He threw me a one-pound bag of raw nuggets and told me to go to a mutual friend's house that had a complete lapidary shop. I spent hours grinding and polishing my cabs, teaching myself the process. I returned to the shop proud of my twenty-one cabs. My silver teacher asked where the rest of them were. His sister said, "Down the drain." and they all laughed. In fact, I had ground them down way too far and was about fifty cabs short. But now I knew how to make my own cabs.

Back at Lama, I erected a teepee to live in. I loved living this way. As Lama was situated over 8,500 feet in the Sangre de Christo mountains, winter nights occasionally approached twenty-below zero. The fireplace in the teepee center created plenty of heat, until you went to sleep, and then the fire also went to sleep. Many nights I would bring goats in for their body heat. Sometimes it was a 'four goat night'.

I regularly hung out at some of the local communes, Magic Tortoise (where I lived for awhile) and New Buffalo.

Many summers New Buffalo Commune in Arroyo

Hondo, had a solstice party, sometimes lasting a couple of weeks.

People would come from miles around, from Texas, Arizona, Colorado and all over New Mexico. Rock and roll drumming and dancing went on day and night. Teepees were put up all over the property. One year we made electric cool aid by placing a couple hundred hits of LSD in five gallons of Kool-Aid. That was an amazing day.

A few days later, after spending a night with one of the Buffalo ladies, I found my '54 Chevy van with four flat tires. As these were fairly new tires, I knew something was amiss. I asked around if anyone knew anything about them. Someone told me to talk to Army Joe who was interested in the lady I had spent the night with.

He had in fact let the air out of all my tires. Army Joe was a bit of an animal and I didn't think I could take him in a fight so I had to hustle him. I convinced him I would seriously hurt him if he didn't pump up the tires. I got my hand pump out and he pumped all four up.

While living at Lama, I became friends with Spanish Eddie Gaudet. He was a Creole from Southern Louisiana. When I met Eddie he had been living at Morningstar Commune, where he had built a secret tunnel in and out. He was quite paranoid and thought the government was after him. Little did he know they would be. He had caches of weapons and food all over the mountains. I met him late one morning while working around the Lama barn. He came out of the trees on a stallion he had caught and broke, with two bandoliers across his chest, a scabbarded rifle, long beard, camouflage clothes and a nasty, untrusting attitude.

I invited him down and offered him water, suggesting he tether his horse loose near the stacked alfalfa bales. We shared a smoke and I invited him to the kitchen for lunch. My Lama colleagues' enthusiasm was less than overwhelming. Many times, I would find Eddie's horse tied to the alfalfa, with him gone scouting new cache locations.

On his second lunch visit, I convinced him to leave his bandoleers with his horse, as they freaked out the other members. Once, a Sufi member told me to tell him not to come back. I replied, "You tell him!" Eddie and I became friends, with his knowing he always had food and water at the Foundation.

Another time I convinced him to let me ride his stallion. He claimed I wouldn't be able to. I persisted and one-half mile later, down the mountain, when we approached a small pond, I guess because the stallion knew I had 'over head' experience, he threw me into the pond.

On one occasion, during a motorcade in New Orleans, someone threw a gas-soaked flag at President Nixon, apparently hoping to light it. As Eddie had recently visited his parents, someone notified the police that Eddie was the culprit. Eddie had already returned to New Mexico prior to this incident.

Soon thereafter, State law enforcement personnel from Sheriff, National Guard, FBI, and Secret Service agencies, some with helicopters, converged on Taos County. What a "movie" this was! Mass paranoia! Dozens of law enforcement officers were searching the mesa looking for Eddie. This was his turf and he had hiding places everywhere. This was what he had been preparing for. As he was an expert rifleman, he fired real close to an ear a few times. A couple of times he was spotted and they'd open fire on him. With his tunnel into Morningstar, he spent most nights with his wife in his own bed. This saga went on for weeks. They never caught him. Once, very seriously, he told me they should have been home taking care of their families and he was just trying to scare them home. He always escaped.

ABC, NBC, CBS and the BBC had arrived along with Eddie's mother and brother from New Orleans and it was finally realized that on the day in question, Eddie was applying for food stamps in Taos. He was finally convinced to turn himself in to the Secret Service and they took him to

Albuquerque where he pled guilty to a negligent discharge of a firearm with a suspended sentence. And everybody went home.

For years I had researched early American Indian lore and wanted to make an authentic Indian necklace. Hollywood movies always showed breastplates and necklaces as shiny white plastic, but they were actually made, in part, from the small hollow shin bone of the coyote. I asked one of the local trappers what he did with the carcasses of the animals he caught. He told me that after skinning them, all the trappers dumped them at the same place southwest of town and gave me directions. I drove there and found a large pile of carcasses, probably three hundred or so, in various stages of decay. Some were fresh from that morning. The putrid odor was sickening. I was appalled at this obvious disregard for life. My heart was heavy for the unconsciousness of the world I lived in.

I dropped to my knees, weeping tears of grief for this wanton killing. Then, realizing the foolishness of my sympathy, I composed myself, and as Grandfather had taught me, rolled a smoke and prayed the Indian way, to the four corners for all these animals. Then I cut off thirty front legs, hung them to dry on the back porch, and a few months later, made the necklace. (The breastplate on the Quanah Parker photo is made from coyote shinbones.)

I was given the opportunity to work a turquoise mine in Orogrande, in Southern New Mexico, in exchange for raw stone. While there I become acquainted with a local trader and on cold winter days, he shared coffee with me in front of his warm wood stove. One morning, he showed me a complete bald eagle he had picked up off the road on a trip to Albuquerque. Apparently, this magnificent bird had gone down for road kill and was struck on one wing, as that was the only part of the bird that was damaged.

My friend had called some Arizona friends and found out the bird was worth a lot of money in Indian country. The feathers were worth at least twenty dollars each and the tail was worth even-trade for a new pickup truck.

He also found out it was against Federal law to have it, and if caught, he could do some serious time. I wanted to give Grandfather Tellus the eagle for the kiva ceremony or for meetings. The trader and I agreed on a trade for some jewelry I had made. Soon I was heading back to Taos to spend Christmas with friends and give Grandfather the eagle. I wrapped it up like an Xmas present in case I was stopped for a traffic violation. Elder Pueblo people usually have two homes. The Pueblo itself, which is a multi-storied adobe structure, made of mud and wood and used in winter, and a summer home somewhere on the reservation, which is normally wood. After I arrived at Grandfather's summer home on the reservation, we had coffee, and then I handed him his Christmas present. When he and his wife, Pauline, saw what it was, they became quite excited and started speaking in Tewa, the language of the Pueblo.

This sacred bird was the center of Pueblo life, and they could hardly believe they had received such a magnificent gift. But then a strange thing happened. Whenever I ran into Grandfather, he avoided me. Sometimes, when he saw me approaching he crossed the street. Something was obviously amiss. I called on a Cheyenne friend and told him what was happening. He thought for a moment and said the Tewas were very superstitious, and like most of the Plains Indians, believe the eagle is a symbol of bravery and wisdom. He further explained they believe the eagle is in direct contact with God and suggested they might feel that someone who had the power to obtain one, then just give it away, must have strong medicine. He thought Grandfather was afraid that I would ask him for his truck or one of his daughters or something very valuable, and of course he would have to give it to me. Welcome to the 20th Century.

I drove back to Grandfather's house. When Pauline answered the door and saw me, she tried to close it, but I had my foot in it and forced my way in. I told them to sit down and listen carefully. I don't speak Tewa and their

English was poor, but I told them I was grateful for all they had taught me, that I gave them the eagle as partial payment and to show my gratitude for all they had done for me, that I felt I still owed them and I wasn't looking for anything in return. Once again, they started speaking in Tewa until they both understood. Then they laughed and shook my hand. We had coffee and our friendship resumed.

Back at Lama I was having trouble with the closed attitude of the core group of foundation members. With the success of Ram Dass' book "Be Here Now," people from all over the world would gather outside the locked front gate, some living in vans, some pitching tents in the surrounding forest. I became acquainted with some of them. They were all spiritual seekers and Dass' book had touched them deeply. Finally I couldn't stand it any longer, and smashed my van through the front gate, and invited them all up for lunch. As I was unpopular with members, this was just business as usual.

Now these people had to be dealt with. Some were put to work and all were allowed to participate in the various spiritual practices. Some of them had journeyman skills and were able to assist with the many ongoing projects. And I always needed help in the garden. Out of this incident came the summer work program where, in exchange for camp sites and meals, people could live and work at Lama and take part in whatever spiritual programs were being offered plus participating in the twice a day meditation and classes.

Originally, this area was a place where the elk outnumber people and bighorn sheep grazed. Snow-capped pink granite skylines, views of forever and the siren call of the wilderness still permeate this beautiful area. Deer still summer grazed above us as Taos Pueblo Indians hunted nearby every summer, occasionally stopping for coffee. One morning, after milking, I came across cat tracks in the snow, four inches in diameter. Had to be a mountain lion, an animal not seen in these parts for decades. I decided to track him and headed up the mountain.

The tracks turned south toward the village of San Cristobal. Approaching above this rural community, I heard a rifle shot. A group of locals had gathered around a very old female mountain lion, shot dead. She was huge, gaunt and scrawny, had neither teeth nor claws and was probably starving, as this magnificent beast would never have ventured this close to civilization. She had mauled a child and the father shot her.

Late that fall, I started boarding horses for neighbors. I will never forget one beautiful mare belonging to some friends in Arroyo Seco, ten miles south. I boarded her for a couple of months. She was gentle broke, but oh so headstrong. My equine karma continued. Besides caring for her, I rode her every other day, much to her chagrin. She also preferred to be left alone, but at least she tolerated me. When her time with me was up I decided to ride her home.

On the chosen day we started out at first light.

The night before it had dropped below zero and we headed out. As the property bordered national forest, the timberline was just above us at 9,000 feet. We headed up and over Flag Mountain. This was a perfect excuse to explore the rugged Southern tip of the Rockies. Snow was deep in places and the air crisp and clean. As the crow flies, Seco was only ten miles away. With no maps or roads and only my good sense of direction, I allowed my self around ten hours to arrive before sunset. Well, the best laid plans, etc…. The mare was definitely not into this trip and fought me all the way. Although grass was rare at timberline, I walked her quite a bit and let her graze when appropriate. Knee deep snow occasionally slowed us further.

We parted company close to three in the afternoon. We approached some wild crab apple trees, I got off, she bolted and took the reins from me and my party was over and hers just begun. She grazed on grounded crab apples. Every time I approached her she would walk outside my reach. I went from really pissed to frustration to tears. It was snowing again and the temperature was dropping rapidly. I knew I could gather enough wood to keep warm through the night. I was concerned about her being exposed to the elements all night. Even wild horses know better than timberline in the winter.

I decided to gather up all the apples and place then in a small pile near where I was sitting, and completely ignore her. Now she was in a dilemma. I was ignoring her, and I had all the apples. Very coolly and slowly, she moved toward me. I felt I'd only get one chance at the reins. The most difficult part was sitting very still in freezing weather. It was now past five and snowing really hard. Her need for apples overcame her fear of losing her freedom and she stuck her nose in the pile of apples. I waited, waited and than lunged at the reins, catching them in both hands. I knew she would bolt, if for no other reason than out of being startled. We both rose up in the air, me involuntarily, but I had her. I took a spare rope from my saddle bag, tied it around my waist and secured it to the pommel. We were now one.

I could always find my way with the stars at night, but it was snowing so hard they were not visible. I knew better than to wander directionless, so we waited another hour moving past 7 P.M. Finally the snow stopped and the stars came out. I located the Big Dipper and the North Star and off we went. It was slow going in the dark. Finally, around midnight, we came over the edge of the mountain and I could see the lights of the tiny village of Arroyo Seco. As I rode into town I saw the Seco bar was still open, not a good place for a gringo at any hour. My freezing need for brandy overcame my apprehension of a fight. Tying my sort of trusty steed outside, I entered. Two Chicanos at the bar eyed me suspiciously and the other four at tables were equally wary. As I approached the bar my snow laden cowboy hat covered my long hair. I could barely speak. I finger pointed around the room in a circle and said "Drinks," hoping I had some money. Than I said, "Brandy," and held out two fingers. He poured two shots and set up the house. Everyone said, "Gracias," and one of them bought me another shot. I found a twenty, paid my tab and left. Arriving at the mare's home, the owners were really concerned with my late arrival and put me up for the night. I never saw her again.

That Thanksgiving, just this once, the counsel wanted to have a turkey for dinner, breaking a long vegetarian fast. I also would like some turkey, but in light of consensual thinking, I thought it hypocritical. My suggestion was I would obtain a live bird and we would all kill, dress and enjoy it. Vegetarianism ruled.

Sundays, visitors were allowed to visit, have lunch and participate in events. One Sunday as one of the members and I were cleaning up in the kitchen after lunch, we were laughing and kidding around. At one point I said to him, "Up yours." We both laughed, finished our task and he left. One of the female visitors, observing the exchange, came over to me and piously stated, "That wasn't very spiritual!"

I thought a moment and replied, "Up yours, too."

My last meeting was held at Grampa Joe's hogan on the reservation. This was a healing meeting for one of Joe's grandsons. The boy, having grown up on the Pueblo, now lived in L.A. No wonder he was sick. As this was an all-Indian meeting I knew I wouldn't be invited in, but attended to assist with the outside fires, morning meal and what ever else I could do. After the last person entered, one of Grandfather's boys, who was Fireman, stuck his head out and motioned for me to come in. I thought he was gesturing to someone behind me and looked around to no one there. He gestured to me to come in again. As I entered I saw one seat vacant on the north pole, to the right of the Road Man and just before my friend Joe Sun Hawk Sandoval, an aged Apache man married to a Pueblo woman. He was the grandson of Goyahkla ("He who yawns") or Geronimo, the great Apache warrior.

I had known Sun Hawk for a number of years and always enjoyed his company and his wonderful sense of humor. As I settled in and the meeting commenced I observed over fifty Indian people attending, all dressed in their finest Levis and cowboy shirts out of respect to the Way. This was my first and only all Indian meeting and it was as different from mixed white meetings as day and night. There was no talking all night, just singing and hand gestures. No squabbling, arguing or dissension. Sun Hawk had a large bag of green peyote buttons he recently cut in Northern Mexico peyote gardens. Some of the soft succulent buttons were three inches across. He and I ate that entire bag. They tasted like sugar candy as the snake receded. As the meeting passed midnight, where people were allowed to go out and relieve themselves, I was anxious for Sun Hawk to leave. Every meeting I attended where he participated, whenever he would go outside, it would rain on the teepee and out approximately six inches, even during years of extreme drought. Everyone knew he had "powers", or as the Hindus call "siddis". It wasn't discussed, but all knew. It was just a fact of life. Many times I would follow him out and stand in the always rain. This night was no exception as a few minutes after he left, sure enough the rains came for a few minutes.

I caught Grampa Joe's eye and gestured with a finger toward the door flap. He swept his hand up, pointing toward the door and I went out to stand in the rain. I wanted to ask Sun Hawk about his power but knew it would be a stupid question.

Rabbi Zalman Schacter-Shalomi

Vos noenter tsu der shul, alts vayter fun Got.
[*The nearer to the synagogue, the farther from God.*]

"REB ZALMAN IS ONE OF THE MOST CONTROVERSIAL RABBIS on the American Jewish scene," writes Roger Kamenetz in *The Jew in the Lotus* (Harper: San Francisco), his journal of the historic 1990 meeting between the Dalai Lama and eight Jewish leaders. "He was our loosest, freest spirit-heir to the joy and zest of the Hasidic masters. He has been a canny and perceptive theoretician of Jewish renewal and a source of contact with the vast wealth of wisdom that might otherwise be inaccessible. To his detractors, he is irresponsible; condemned for his excesses, personal and doctrinal. He has danced with Sufi masters, meditated with Buddhists, experimented with psychedelics and is a pioneer in interfaith dialogue." I found him a man who loved life and lived it to the fullest. He has transmitted his personal wisdom to his 10 children and 21 grandchildren, the 50 students he has ordained and the countless others who have learned from him."

Rabbi Zalman Schachter-Shalomi was founder of The Jewish Renewal Movement, former head of Judaic studies at the University of Manitoba, professor emeritus at Temple University, author of *From Age-ing to Sage-ing*, and holding the World Wisdom Chair at the Naropa Institute, an accredited, nonsectarian private institution of higher education that offers contemplative education combining Eastern and Western educational traditions, in Boulder, Colo. Walking the two worlds of ancient Judaism and the contemporary world of the "New Age," Rabbi Zeb is an internationally recognized teacher of the heart who draws from many disciplines and cultures. He grew up in the cosmopolitan Vienna of Beethoven and Freud, and attended a Zionist gymnasium and a Hungarian yeshiva. After fleeing war-torn Europe, he arrived in New York in 1941, entered the Lubavitch yeshiva and was ordained in 1947.

He has a degree in psychology from Boston University and a doctorate of Hebrew literature from Hebrew Union College. Reb Zalman has woven these seemingly disparate strands into a brand of counter-cultural Judaism. He was active in the inception of the havura movement and in 1962 founded the P'nai or (Faces of Light) Religious Fellowship. Now called ALEPH: the Alliance for Jewish Renewal, it seeks to update Jewish theology and enhance Jewish spirituality. Its literature describes its "full inclusion of women, respect for other spiritual paths and a commitment to healing the world's personal and sociopolitical and ecological levels."

When the Camp David peace accord was signed, Reb Zalman adopted the name Shalomi, meaning "My peace". "The intent was to drop Schachter when peace became reality," he says. He's still waiting.

His sensitive translations of prayers have been included in Reform, Conservative and Orthodox prayer books and songbooks. He valued the role of feminism early on, ordaining a woman even before the Reform Movement did. "Women are the white letters of the Torah," he says borrowing Rabbi Levi Yitzhak of Berdichev's metaphor.

"As long as we looked at the black letters— the men— we also saw the white spaces, but we didn't take account of them. Judaism wants to survive, we have to bring in the feminine mind," and again, "Every person has a certain amount of holy spirit. My job has been to love people to God."

Rabbi Zalman Schacter arrived at Lama Foundation as a scholar guest. We immediately became friends and spent many hours in my "A" frame talking and smoking dope. During his short stay he ministered to all. I shared my peyote church experiences with him and he asked if he could participate. I contacted Grandfather and received his permission for the Rabbi to attend a meeting planned for the upcoming weekend, where Little Joe was Road Chief. People came from all over, white and Indian alike.

All night Rabbi wore a furry animal skin yarmulke, the only one in the teepee with his head covered. It looked like bear skin.

After the morning feast and as people were chatting around the teepee a Cheyenne man, Martin Fingernail's white wife, during a lull in conversation, said out loud, to no one in particular: "You'd think that when people come this way they'd have enough respect not to wear a hat." Only a white person would be this disrespectful. Zalman was one of the most respectful people I had ever met and there were no rules that I knew about about head covering. Silence spoke, in the teepee, as all eyes were on Rabbi. Zalman, sitting to my left, was obviously upset. He was quiet for a bit, than he spoke. "This yarmulke was given to me by my father who was also a rabbi, given to him by his Rabbi Father and handed down generation after generation. It is only worn for very special occasions, to show the utmost respect."

After a silent pause, Grandfather spoke, "It's your head!" He was always direct and succinct.

After the meeting Zalman brought a young man to me and said that I needed to baptize him. "Smuck, are you nuts? I don't know how to baptise."

He replied "I'm a Jew, I can't baptize him." The "boy", actually 21 years old, was now in tears as he had a vision during the meeting and needed to be baptized with his new name, Christian. We take him to a sink where I fill a cup with water, and work to access my memory bank. Then I remember. Slowly pouring the water over his head, I say, "I baptize thee in the name of the Father, the Son and the Holy Spirit. You are now, "Christian." I just decided to throw the last part in. He was now weeping and soaking wet.

The wonderful work Reb Zalman's done on aging and his philosophy on aging is encapsulated in the following: "Most of us feel a certain kind of depression as we age because on the inside we don't feel older yet we look older when we see ourselves in the mirror. Most people haven't paid attention to the elder years because there's no model for the elder years in our society. It's a youth culture. Look at all the ads. Even the ads in the AARP magazine "Modern Maturity" features people who look like teenagers with white hair going on cruises. We don't have models of people who have become elders; we have people who feel ashamed that they are old. So I wrote *From Age-ing to Sage-ing*. The earth today truly needs sages, people who have wisdom. We have an information glut but not enough wisdom about how to use the information. We have high technology but we don't have the wisdom to apply it to enhance life. We have become the servant of technology, which is another way in which we abuse our emotional life. I see childhood as the winter, the lessons in youth as spring, the main opus of a person's life as the summer. But beginning with age 63 and up, we are in the fall and fall is harvest time. If people only see that leaves are falling, they don't realize that falling leaves means that the apples have ripened and life has harvested."

Zen Buddism
Kyozan Joshu Sasaki, Roshi

What is the sound of one hand clapping?
Bring me the sound of rain.
Bring me the essence of flower.

KOANS

THREE DAYS INTO MY FIRST AND ONLY SESSION, I KNEW I was going to die. We had been sitting zazen for nineteen hours a day for almost three days. My legs were beyond pain. I was totally into sanran. I couldn't believe I had agreed to this. It was time for my sanzen. The sanzen procedure is formal and includes ringing the kansho bell, bowing etc. Sanzen is given twice a day. It's not optional - you have to go. I could barely walk. My legs were not functioning normally, they were in so much pain. When I arrived at the small two-storey building where Roshi was, I immediately went up to his room. I gasshoed and prostrated before the master in sampai and sat cross legged on the ground. He looked like the Buddha, perhaps five feet tall, and weighed around 250 pounds. He was sitting in full lotus with a small highly polished, carved stick. The end was round and glass-like from centuries of hand polish use.

He always says the same one word: "Koan?" to everyone. And you repeat your koan and whether you have the answer. Any other conversation is absolutely forbidden.

Having always had difficulty with rules, when he said 'Koan', I said to him, "Can I ask you a question?"

What happened next was extraordinary. I have never before or since seen or heard anything like it. Faster than the blink of an eye, with a blood curdling scream, he brought his staff down onto my right shoulder, stopping just before the touch. I've studied some martial arts but had never seen anyone move this fast before, especially someone this large.

I was certain that if he hadn't stopped he would have cleaved my shoulder. I didn't blink or move. Actually there wasn't time. He slowly returned his staff to his lap and with squinted eyes and a slight tilt to his head, very slowly asked, "No a-fraid?" with accent on the latter syllable.

I replied with a bit of trepidation, "No disrespect, Rosh, but no!"

A very slow he-he-he laugh came out of him and he stuck out his hand and said, "Sasaki Roshi."

I shook his hand and said, "Billy Whelan, How ya doing, Rosh?" I guess I thought we were going to be old buddies.

Then he immediately and very sternly said, "Koan!"

I didn't have a clue and he harshly said, "More zazen!" So I dragged my aching butt back to the zendo to sit some more.

Joshu Sasaki was born into a farming family in April 1907, in Miyagi Prefecture in Japan. As Zen is the largest school of Buddhism in Japan, he became a novice Zen student at the age of 14 at the preeminent Rinzai temple in northern Japan. He was ordained an osho at the age of twenty-one, receiving the name Kyozan. At the age of forty, he received authority as a Roshi.

In 1953, Roshi became abbot of Shoju-an in Liyama, Nagano Prefecture where he served for ten years. In 1962 he was sent to the United States. He arrived in Los Angeles with his wife, who was very much in the background, for she married him to be a wife and caretaker, not to become a student of Zen. He eventually authorized the purchase of an abandoned Boy Scout camp on Mount Baldy which became Mount Baldy Zen Center. This center, in existence today, is used as a monastery and residential training center.

Many of Roshi's students and ordained priests have established centers around the world, besides the fourteen in the U.S. including Jemez Springs and Albuquerque, New Mexico, Redondo Beach, CA; Mt. Cobb, CA; Ithaca, NY; Princeton, NJ. Miami, FL; to Vienna, Austria, Puerto Rico and Vancouver, BC.

The original purpose for practicing Zen was to reach Satori, to achieve health of body and mind and to attain the spiritually highest way of life as a human being. Satori is not an understanding obtained through intellectual analysis, but rather it is an "intuitive awareness" obtained through direct experience. Zen masters teach one fundamental lesson: that one should leave behind any clinging or striving toward extinguishable things and instead live every moment in a free, natural and fulfilling manner. The formation of this kind of personality is the purpose of Zen practice, and its attainment can be gained through all daily activities including Zazen.

"From the Buddhist point of view, God is not a living thing you can look upon," said Roshi, who speaks in Japanese and uses an interpreter. "God is not something you can take as an object. Buddhism says there is no God; there is no absolute personified being other than the manifestation of the complete self. The person who takes God as an object is the mistaken self. Zen practice brings people to their true selves. That is a dangerous concept in a country where most people believe in God." The goal of Zen is zero, or the state of emptiness.

One of the most important aspects of Zen study is the use of the Koan. Every koan presents us with a problem that cannot be solved by thought or reasoning.

The common sense of ordinary people will reject it as absurd. Learned people, such as philosophers and scientists, will feel repugnance at the lack of reason in the koan. Such people are often perplexed when confronted by the strange and even abnormal expressions found in the language of the koan. They cannot be understood by logic and cannot be transmitted in words; cannot be explained in writing; cannot be measured by reason. They can only be understood beyond the mind. Koan is a Japanese word that comes from the Chinese, kung-an, that means public dictate. It is a reference to examples that are meant to guide life, or, in the case of Zen, these dictates are meant to be catalysts for awakening one's true/deep/pure nature.

Attempting to figure out a koan with the limited mind is impossible, and yet, it is only when we exhaust our minds that a deeper level of inquiry becomes possible. Eventually, sometimes, after years of practice, the koan will do its work, the mind will open in gentle deep understanding, and any number of simple direct responses will seem obvious. Koans act like swords to stab at your ego and draw forth your Buddha Nature (your fully natural nature that is not dependent on your self-definition). I always felt koans could only be understood through the spirit mind. It took me decades to understand that the answers are in the silence. Koans are like seeds of awakening. Sometimes there is a prolonged and difficult growing period, sometimes the growing period is short and direct. I saw the koan process as a metaphor for our spiritual growth. To fully resolve a koan one must allow it to grow to full maturity; a koan must reveal itself, in its time frame, not the minds. Like all spiritual growth.

When we decided to invite Roshi for a session, I didn't intend to sit. I wasn't a Zen student and none of it made sense to me. The council decided that everyone not involved in the session would leave the Foundation for the week. I agreed to come into the foundation through the back road near the barn to take care of the animals and then leave. A few days before Roshi arrived I asked one of the Sufi students why he was sitting in the session as he wasn't a Zen student. He replied he would probably walk across hot coals to be with a spiritual master.

I thought back to my life since meeting Meher Baba and my ensuing spiritual quest and how much I loved spiritual smorgasbord. I realized that I was probably missing an opportunity if I didn't sit the session. I informed the Lama coordinator, who was also to be Jikijitsu, that I would sit the session and also take care of the animals twice a day. The day before the session we had a practice day. We sat for nineteen hours. I thought I would die. How in hell was I going to get through the next five days? I couldn't believe how undisciplined I was. I had a gallon of white wine in my truck and put it under my bed. Every night prior to my four hours sleep, I would take a long pull, spacing the gallon to last the entire session.

The five-day session, with meals, kinhin and Sanzen breaks commenced. When entering the dojo, everyone is required to bow in the direction of the altar which reminded me of my Catholic upbringing where, when entering the church the tips of fingers are dipped in holy water and the sign of the cross is made.

A circular wooden deck was built around the wall of the dome (dojo) and acted as the structure we sat on, facing the center of the room.

The three essentials of session: no talking, whispering, or looking around at others is strictly enforced by the Jikijitsu (jikki). The jikki keeps time, corrects, admonishes and inspires. It is the leading position in the zendo. The jikijitsu also carries the keisaku. Everyone sits with the hokkaijoin mudra.

The point is to transcend the background chatter of our busy minds. My mind was frenzied as I had never taken the opportunity to just sit for great lengths of time and be still. Having been hyperactive since childhood, sitting quietly took every ounce of my will power. It was torture. Slowing my mind down, with all my unresolved issues, was impossible. My quest for no mind, took me over twenty five years, through a variety of meditation techniques to achieve and I am grateful for this session experience as it truly opened my love for meditation.

The schedule and seating arrangement for the dojos are constant. Keeping strictly to your allocated place is important. Black floor length gowns called monk's robes are worn by everyone attending. Watches, perfumes and lotions are prohibited. Promptness is expected and after the bells have rung, entrance is barred. When one steps into the dojo, you bow in the direction of the altar. This is your show of respect to the Buddha. When you arrive at your seat you bow towards your seat. This is your bow to the Dharma. During the day, when the bell rings twice, every fifty minutes, it is time for kinhin. Every hour I looked forward to kinhin. Occasionally I couldn't walk, and would stand and wait until the line came around to me and then I would join. When Jikki claps the clapper everyone stops at their place with backs to the zafu and everybody gasshos together, then all turn in the direction of the altar, gassho again and take their seat. The principle is "everyone moves together." Every morning the bell rings at 4 am. Everyone gets up quickly and goes to the dojo.

The kyosaku is an effective way to relieve tiredness and tension in the shoulders or on either side of the lower back. The smacking sound of the kyosaku, brings us back to our practice. The kyosaku and brief 'massage' (I got a kick out of it called a "massage" as it is truly more of a solid whack) is offered during the session but only at your request. The way one requests the "whack" is to move while jikijitsu is approaching. Then jikki stops in front of you (Occasionally jikki will indiscriminately pick you out for kyosaku).

Either way, when jikki stops in front of you, you place both hands on right knee and extend neck by bowing head slightly to the right, and the kyosaku is brought down soundly between the neck and shoulder. The order is reversed and a whack is given on the other side. Then you gassho and resume sitting. I found my legs, especially my knees, in such pain that I was requesting kyosaku regularly just to have a different pain to focus on. The jikijitsu for this session was the Lama coordinator, my Meher Baba friend. Once, when I requested kyosaku, he accidentally struck my ear and blood ran down my neck. It felt like I lost my ear. What the hell, this was all pain anyway. After the session, I mentioned it to him. I recall something about, "Shit happens. Did you want me to stop and apologize?" At one point, when the jikki asked a woman to walk the kyosaku, she stopped in front of a man and he silently smashed her in the face with his fist, knocking her flat on her back. She got up, blood and all, and resumed the walk. I mentally noted to stay away from him.

That evening, while milking, a friend of mine joined me in my chores. I shared the incident with him. He listened to the whole story and then replied, "We're supposed to be silent." I pointed out that he waited to hear the entire story before reminding me.

Next day the jikki told me to walk the kyosaku. I replied "Are you nuts?"

He screamed, "Silence." Jeez!

So after some instruction, next session, I walk the stick. I felt very conscientious walking kyosaku. It requires slowly walking around the zendo, close to the meditators. One is supposed to sense when someone needs the stick or when they request it by moving. I took this responsibility very seriously. I only hit a couple of people, the fist thrower not one of them. Finally the end arrived and I thought everyone would yell and shout in joy. Not a sound as we all trekked out. It was an extraordinary experience and opened so many doors into the areas I needed to work on. Other than the obvious physical discomfort I experienced, this "formless" way, had way too much form for my taste.

Recently, Joshu Sasaki Roshi was given a new title: "Kyozan," meaning "Mountain with apricot trees." This is his new name, and is a higher and more significant title than "Roshi," implying the need to give greater respect to the bearer. The title was given by the Japanese school to which the Roshi is attached, because he is now the oldest living Roshi in the school, a significant attainment in the Japanese culture in 2003. He is 96.

Hari Dass Baba

Ask yourself if what you are about to say would be an improvement on silence.

I ARRIVED AT THE HOME OF MA RENU, BABAJI'S SPONSOR, at Sea Ranch in Northern, California a few hours north of San Francisco and was ushered into Baba's bedroom. He was sitting in full lotus, with around six foot of black hair laid out in round ringlets around him, all seventy pounds, at the pillow end of the bed. I stood near the end of the bed, gasshoed, and said namaste. He placed one hand in gassho and made a sucking sound by sucking his tongue against his teeth and roof of his mouth. It was the only sound he ever made other than the scratching of chalk on his little chalkboard. He patted the bed in front of him. I sat cross-legged at the other end of the bed. He shook his head no, made the sucking sound and patted the bed again. I moved up half way and resumed sitting cross-legged. Once more he shook no, made the sucking sound and patted the bed again. Without thinking I said, "You want me to sit on your fucking lap?" He threw his head back and laughed uproariously, composed himself, making the sucking sound one more time and re-patted the bed. Now I was sitting a few inches away from him. He looked into my eyes and wrote my astrological chart on his little chalkboard.

The best way to offer something useful is to be an example of that in yourself. To emanate the qualities of love and light is the surest way to affect someone positively. A lamp doesn't have to say anything, but by its light, others can see the way and won't stumble in the darkness. Most of us enjoy being around someone like that, someone who has evolved enough that they bring these qualities into their being. It feels great to be with them, like basking in sunlight.

After one darshan Ma Renu asked me if I wanted to participate in a Hanuman ceremony. Sure. She and I entered a small room with a puja on one side and a small container of water and another container with a fire burning on the other. She gave me a child's noise maker and we awaited Babaji. He entered dressed in his usual white dhoti.

Then, while we continued making lots of noise-maker noise, after silent prayer, he reached into the fire, scooped up a handful of ash and gracefully threw it across the room where it landed in the urn. Then he reached into the water urn, cupped a handful of water and gracefully threw it into the air toward the burning puja urn. The water gathered in the air and like a magnet attracting metal and dove into the fire urn, putting the fire out. I was impressed. He then appeared to be in silent prayer, and it was over. Later I asked Ma Renu what that was about, and how he did that. She didn't know but said he did it every day.

As I was leaving, she walked me to the door, handed me a fifty-dollar bill and said, "Baba wants you to have this."

I hadn't shared my dilemma with Hari Das, that I didn't have enough gas money to get back home, but this was certainly a God-send. I started to refuse and she sternly told me, "Don't. Please, take it." Okay.

His teacher had given him this advice when he was but a small boy studying the way to enlightenment in the jungles of India: "Don't ever ask anyone to come; don't ever push anyone away; and don't talk." Though silent, to sit in his presence is extraordinary. He has no expectations. He just is. And you feel that Love. It's unconditional and non-attached. We spent around an hour and a half together, me asking questions and he writing. I loved being in his presence. It was like being with a child.

Baba Hari Dass, born near Almora, in northern India in 1923, is a silent monk, a mauna, or silent saddhu who has not spoken since 1952 and communicates through inner communication or by writing on a small chalkboard. Babaji is first and foremost a monk and a master yogi, having practiced the disciplines of yoga since childhood.

He was initiated in the Vairagi Vaishnava order in 1942. He was classically trained in the authentic traditions of yoga that have been passed along from guru to disciple over thousands of years. At the age of eight Hari Dass went to a brahmacharya school for spiritual instruction, During this time, he had several experiences with Indian saints, though he doesn't discuss his personal instruction or association with other spiritual teachers.

Hari Dass was discovered by several American aspirants traveling in India who persuaded him to come to the United States to teach. He arrived in America in 1971 and began teaching the classical "eight-limbed" path of Patanjali known as Ashtanga Yoga as developed and preserved by the ancient sages of India.

In 1974 a group of students founded the Hanuman Fellowship to foster the teachings inspired by Babaji. Two sister fellowships, Dharma Sara Satsang Society/Salt Spring Centre near Vancouver, and Ashtanga Yoga Fellowship in Toronto, also take their inspiration and teachings from Babaji. They, too, are involved with yoga teaching, retreats, service, and publishing. This system is comprehensive as it includes methods which take into account every level of life, from right thinking and concentration for the mind, to postures and purifications for the body.

In 1978 the Mount Madonna Center for the Creative Arts and Sciences was established as a spiritual community and seminar and retreat facility to "nurture the creative arts and health sciences within the context of spiritual growth."

Mount Madonna Center comprises 355 acres in the redwoods overlooking Monterey Bay. There are over 100 residents at the facility, which includes a children's boarding school, a bookshop and library, as well as the retreat and seminar facility.

There are also centers in British Columbia, Ontario, Canada, and in Mexico City, Mexico. In addition, Babaji is an accomplished author, teacher, builder, philosopher, sculptor, and proponent of Ayurveda (the ancient Indian system of health and healing). He is also conversant in several languages. He teaches weekly classes in the Yoga Sutras, the Bhagavad-Gita, and yoga practices, and teaches other related subjects at various yoga retreats.

He also works on building projects, writes on many yoga topics and spiritual stories, creates theatrical props and masks for the Ramayana, and always has a special welcome for children.

In 1984 Babaji created the Sri Ram Orphanage located in the village of Hardwar in northern India, with the hope of providing at least some of India's homeless children a better life. At first there were only two children. Within a year thirteen more arrived. After the earthquake of 1991 nineteen more were admitted. Sri Ram Orphanage has now adopted approximately 50 children. It also supports the surrounding villages with medical assistance and a school.

He is present every Sunday for Satsang gatherings open to all without charge, at the Pacific Cultural Center in Santa Cruz which provides an opportunity for spiritual singing, meditation, and questions for Babaji. In his presence it is evident that he has found a way to be at peace despite the pain and confusion of the world. His teachings, his actions, and, more importantly, his example communicate the realization that this peace is available to each of us, if only we make the effort to be peaceful.

Silence fell upon the dome at Lama Foundation as white-clad Baba Hari Dass appeared. He stooped to remove his shoes, and then moved rapidly to the small elevated stage where two large pillows arranged an unpretentious throne. He was dressed in traditional Indian clothing. A long-sleeved, full-length white gown all but concealed his white dhoti.

A large crowd of people, of all ages, was seated on the floor. Most were dressed in all white with mala beads round their necks. As he sat, he motioned to me, and patted the seat next to him. HUH? ME? He patted the pillow again. I approached from the side and sat next to him. I was dressed in my usual jeans and work shirt. I was aware of all the people sitting in front of us who disliked me, were jealous and wondered how Baba could ask someone so "not spiritual" to sit on the dais with him.

An assistant asked, "Are you ready for Satsang, Baba Ji?" Baba nodded and made his clucking sound. A question was soon asked from among those assembled. Baba Ji wrote on his slate. He works with an interpreter and consulted with him, and after a nod from the teacher, or a shake of his head, which would be followed with another communication on the small slate, his interpreter finally shared the teacher's answer. So the evening went; question upon question; responses garnered through the experience of the interpreter and written words upon the chalkboard.

> *Without reducing negative qualities,*
> *progress in spiritual life is as impossible*
> *as carrying water in a sieve.*
> *There is an unspoken language.*
> *It comes from the silence and can't be heard by our ears,*
> *only by the heart.*

What I loved about Baba was that at no time did I experience any lack of communication because of his silence, and his answers were often expressed so the questioner had to make his or her own decision. I've never learned anything when someone else attempted to make my decisions for me, as that approach robs me of the opportunity for experience and I've come to learn there's no understanding without experience. It appeared it was not Baba Ji who answered the many questions. He was merely the vehicle through which the wisdom of the ages was being transmitted.

His stillness had the voice of authority without pretense, depth of knowledge without vanity, and wisdom drawn from within, as silence spoke.

> *God to me is inner peace.*
> *When the mind is freed from the outer turmoil's of the world,*
> *it becomes peaceful.*
> *In that peaceful state of mind, God's love can be experienced.*
> *Ultimately, this love has no explanation,*
> *but rather is a pure state of mind*

During darshan I became aware that every time I became angry or judgmental, Baba would quietly glance at me and then leave the stage and go to the other side of the room. Powerful, silent teaching: "Practice staying neutral in loving."

What is threefold karma?
It is:
(1) Samchit (collected), the unfinished mass of actions of past births, both good and bad, yet to be worked out and which appear in this birth in the form of desires— in other words, samskaras
(2) Prarabdha (detained), the result of karma already worked out in a previous life which appears in the present life in the form of fate
(3) Agami (present), the karma we are continually making in our present actions and will be making in our future actions.

The following morning found Baba Ji and me sitting on

a bench in the Lama forest. It was very early morning. We were both silent, which was rare for me. A woman walked by, gasshoed to Baba and said, "Good Morning, Guru." He made his sucking sound and gosshoed in return. I was stunned. I knew she wasn't talking to me. Spirituality was new to me as it was only a few years earlier that I was running a saloon in New York.

I had never met a guru and didn't really know what one was. But I understood a Guru was like God and somehow I hadn't equated Babaji with that word. He was just the coolest person I had ever met and was my friend.

I turned to him incredulously and said, "Are you a fucking Guru?"

He looked at me very seriously and thoughtfully stroked his beard, looked away, than back at me and wrote, "Not yours!"

We both laughed so hard we fell over backward.

> *The body is the temple of the soul*
> *And the soul is the temple of God.*

During Babaji's stay we practiced aspects of Ashanga Yoga including asanas (Surya Namaskara), Sutra Neti, Mulabandha, Vastra Dhauti, Meditation and Nadishodhana, every morning. I enjoyed Sutra Neti each morning as it reminded me of the sensation of snorting cocaine, but Vastra Dhauti was difficult as it took me a bit of time to get past my gag response. You could always tell who had coffee as the cloth would come up with spots of caffeine.

> *Searching for God outside is like looking for*
> *your son who is sitting on your shoulder.*

After one session of meditation, I was walking with Babaji and he wrote on his chalk board, "Always meditate alone."

It would take me years to understand what he was

talking about. Some people cannot slow down or stop mental activity during meditation and to those who can, this interferes with meditation. I've checked this out dozens of times over the years and always in crowded meditation situations the mental activity always impedes my process.

> *Each second of our lives is like a seed of grain,*
> *And time is a hungry bird eating every seed very quickly.*
> *When the grain is finished the bird will fly away.*
> *So worship God, surrender to Him, and attain peace.*

This was also the day Baba told me, "You must even give up God." Since my encounter with Meher Baba, my insatiable quest for God ran unabated. This possibility was enormous to me and it brought tears to my eyes. It took me decades to realize he was talking about attachments.

Years later, while operating a home for abused children we were given a donkey. A sweet gentle animal that was part of the group soul of the ass Jesus rode. I loved this wonderful animal. One day one of my staff tied her on a short rope in front of the children's home to graze. It was a hot New Mexico summer day, with temperatures over 100 degrees. I wasn't aware she had been tied up, as I took care of the animals. Mid afternoon, working in the office, I sensed something was wrong, went outside and ran to the front of the house.

I found her lying on her side with her legs tangled in the tie rope. Her eyes were bugging out of her head and foam was all over her mouth. Apparently she had been lying on her side for hours in that scorching heat with no water. When I got to her she took one last breath and died. I have never grieved so much in my life. This death was so senseless. I was an emotional wreck for months. I couldn't seem to get over her death. One day I was contacted by a friend who said they had a message for me from Hari Dass Baba: "Focus on your love for her and not the pain of your loss."

What wonderful advice! It absolutely worked and became very useful in my future counseling practice.

Returning to Lama, my tenure as a member was almost over. My Meher Baba following coordinator friend convinced me I needed to do a month in silence. He was quite persuasive and I agreed. The "High Hermitage" built just prior to my arrival was 500 feet above the Foundation at approximately 9,000 feet. It's above the Maqbara ,where Sufi Sam— Samuel Lewis— is buried. Every full moon around midnight, we would go up to the Maqbara for Sufi dancing.

This one room, round, wooden structure with windows all around was used strictly as a sanctuary for individuals to meditate in silence for a week to a month. There was no electricity and there were no kerosene lamps. The view is spectacular showing all the way to the Rio Grande along the Southern Rockies. Up I went with rice, water and silence in tow, and it was heavy. My only companions were the high altitude birds and one spiritual mouse. I would leave the birds grain each morning and did my best to ignore the mouse. Little did I know that she would be my spirit's catalyst.

The birds became inadvertent teachers. One bright, sunny morning, the birds were busily feeding on the grain I had left. That afternoon it snowed. The birds busily fed. It was no difference to them sun or snow... same, same. Contemplating this, I was amazed at how appropriate this attitude would be in my life. Neutral, non-reacting, non judgmental. I recalled one of my favorite authors, Kahlil Gibran's statement: "Treat failure and success as the imposters they both are." I hadn't known what he was talking about but now had a reference point. I was starting to get into this retreat stuff. Three weeks into my hermitage, as I lay sleeping on the floor, the mouse ran into my bag. I was unaware I could wiggle, jump around, break dance, contort and wake up quite as quickly and effectively as when I danced around that poor little mouse. Harmless little thing probably thought I lost my mind. The bag and I parted company as I lit the table lamp and wide awake, sat at the table, my notebook nearby. Hours later, at daylight, head on forearms, I woke up. In front of me were twelve neatly printed pages. I normally don't print, but this was in my hand. I figured I was put into a trance and spirit dictated the 12 pages. I slowly read the text. It was the future of Lama Foundation. Exquisite detail including personal information for couples. The perfection of these suggestions was mind boggling to me.

After my hermitage time was up, I returned to the Foundation and my teepee. My coordinator friend had moved away and a new one elected. I was having difficulty speaking as my vocal cords had been dormant for a month.

That alone was a miracle and probably refreshing to the other members. I approached the new coordinator explaining what had happened. I asked him to call a meeting for all in-house members, trustees, board members and any former members that wanted to attend, as I had a message from spirit. In the eyes of most members I was someone of low spiritual stature, and for me to bring a message from spirit must have appeared ludicrous. On the appointed day, over fifty people showed up for my darshan. HA! Just prior to my presentation, I shaved. When I entered the Dome, everyone became quiet. I wasn't sure whether I would be stoned or not. (The rock kind, not rock & roll) The first thing I said to them is that no one in that room had ever seen my clean shaven face and I asked only that they treated me like any stranger and would just please listen.

I explained how the twelve pages came to be and then slowly read it. It was all about the future of the foundation. Sweet Emma, the cow, had been bred and would come fresh in a few months. Her calf (the transmission called it a bull, which it eventually was) was to be given to Grampa Joe in the Taos pueblo or it would die. Eventually members decided not to give it to Joe and it died. There was some personal information that only couples knew about.

Suggestions for increasing income, construction and how to be more open to the public. I doubt many people in the room believed a word of it. Many thought I was attempting, in a convoluted way, to take over the foundation. I couldn't care less what they believed. I wasn't selling anything and certainly not interested in taking over. I felt I had done my part.

A few months later, in January, I moved from my teepee to the little A-frame at the bottom of the garden. That day I finished shingling the roof with dry cedar shakes. A friend from a neighbor commune helped finish the roof. After milking, as it was way below zero, I banked the little wood stove and opened both top and bottom vents for rapid heat. My friend had scored some killer weed and we got stoned.

The stove got red hot and I didn't notice it. The pipe running up through the roof turned cherry red and slowly crawled toward the ceiling. By the time we noticed, the roof was on fire. As the structure was all dry wood it rapidly spread into a raging inferno. We vacated the premises while Lama members arrived and set up a bucket brigade from the kitchen. The NYFD couldn't put that fire out. The entire building was gone in less than thirty minutes. I lost everything.

Two days later, Lama members called a special meeting to discuss... me. Some thought I was devil possessed. Some were afraid to be around me. They voted I leave the Foundation immediately or... Well, they didn't have an "or". As I had arranged Darshan with Baba Hari Dass in a few weeks, I was leaving anyway. I had pretty much exhausted my funds during my Lama tenure so I told the council for $500.00 I would leave that day. They immediately wrote a check. Shoulda said a thousand.

When I arrived at Sea Ranch for my Hari Dass visit, he laughed at my "transmission" story. He wrote on his chalkboard: "They shot the messenger."

Back in New Mexico, after my silversmith

apprenticeship, I was living in a horse barn in Questa. I was making a fair living with my silver and delivering goat's milk a couple days a week. Many of my milk customers were low income and would occasionally trade, for hay, weed, whatever. Most of them couldn't afford a veterinarian and hence their animals suffered. I knew the vet from Santa Fe who traveled once a week to various feed stores and locations in Northern New Mexico. People would line up with their animals for his help. I asked if I could travel with him and learn simple, basic vet healing. He agreed and I learned the basics. He liked the idea that low-income people's animals would be treated and wouldn't interfere with his practice as he wouldn't see these animals anyway.

After my apprenticeship, he agreed to sell me medicine at cost. Anything I needed but narcotics.

I went to the Lama counsel and explained the program and they donated a few hundred bucks and a commune friend who came into some money also donated. Every milk delivery day, I would also take care of animals.

David Monongye
Keeper of the Hopi Prophecy

Koyaanisqatsi
Life Out of Balance
The Return Path

I ONLY KNEW GRANDFATHER DAVID MONONGYE A FEW years, late in his life. Until his passing in 1988, he was the Mongwi and spiritual leader of the village of Hotevilla, the most traditional of all eight Hopi villages, Hopi elder, and recognized Hopi Prophet, clan keeper of the Hopi Prophecy, weaver and artist. Even when he lost his eyesight, Grandfather insisted on continuing to respond to the numerous requests for the Prophecy. He believed that this was the most crucial time for the message to be heard and requests were coming more frequently. As keeper of the Hopi Prophecy and one of the last traditional Hopi elders, he devoted his life to sharing the prophecy with anyone who would listen. Hopi law stated the prophecy must be stated in full, at best, a three-hour process. My role with this teacher was to set up venues like auditoriums and theaters for him to share the prophecy. As his English was poor and he spoke mostly in a monotone, it became difficult for me to listen over and over. Standing barely five feet, he was relentless in sharing the Hopi vision for peace to whoever would listen. He was horrified to realize that the bombs dropped on Hiroshima and Nagasaki contained uranium mined on Hopi land. He spoke out against the nuclear arms race in the late 1940s and early 1950s and repeatedly appeared at the United Nations, warning the world about the dangers of nuclear weapon. Faithfully, a man of peace.

The Hopi prophecy truly spoke to my heart as I also believed the world could not survive in the greed filled way it was pursuing. This man was my "peace" teacher. The Hopi are a Pueblo people occupying a number of mesa-top pueblos on reservation land in northeast Arizona.

Hopi is a shortened form of the full version of the indigenous name of this nation/culture/people. The full Hopi name, Hopituh Shi-nu-mu, has a number of valid translations. The most frequently seen of these is "the Peaceful People," or "the Peaceful Ones," also "All People Peaceful," and "Little People of Peace."

They are a Native American nation that in 1990 numbered close to 12,000, who primarily live on the 1.5 million acre Hopi Reservation in northeastern Arizona. Their reservation is surrounded by the Navajo reservation. A few Hopi live on the Colorado River Indian Reservation, on the Colorado River in western Arizona.

Traditional Hopi are organized into matrilineal clans. When a man marries, the children from the relationship are members of his wife's clan. The Hopi are sedentary farmers, mainly dependent on corn, beans, and squash; they also raise wheat, cotton, and tobacco, and herd sheep. Each village is divided into clans and is governed by a chief, who is also the spiritual leader. Political and religious duties revolve around the clans. The Badger clan, for instance, still conducts the kachina (fertility) ceremony, and the Antelope and Snake clans perform the well-known snake dance at Walpi and other pueblos. A Hopi tribal council and constitution were established in 1936, but internal dissension has limited tribal unity. The Hopi, more than most Native American peoples, retain and continue to practice their traditional ceremonial culture. However, like other tribes, they've been severely influenced by the surrounding American culture. The Hopi have also been impacted by very active missionary work by a number of religions and also by consumerism and like most Indian Tribes, alcoholism. Nevertheless there is a traditionalist core that adheres to traditional ways.

The Hopi have a strong spiritual connection with Tibet. The Dalai Lama often visited the Hopi Reservation and when he first arrived there, the Hopi elders said to him, "Welcome home". The Hopi see themselves related to every race and especially to the Tibetans. A Hopi prophecy says that the Hopi and the red-suited men (Tibetans) from across the Ocean will be reunited as brothers.

A Tibetan prophecy says that when the iron bird flies and the horses run on wheels, then the Tibetan people will be spread out of their land and the Wisdom of Buddha will reach the red-faced men from across the ocean.

Part of the prophecy states: A tribe of red hat and red-cloaked people would come in great numbers from the East, traveling through the air. They would colonize the Western American lands and then scatter and disappear. The Tibetans came calling on the Hopi Elders when the first three precursory signs in their own 1,200-year-old prophecy concerning the transplantation of their religion to America was fulfilled.

On one of these trips thru Arizona the monks, dressed in their red native clothes, stopped at a motel/restaurant for a night. At dinner they were treated very rudely by the staff. When the bill was paid, a fifty-dollar tip was left. Upon return from the Hopi Reservation they stayed at the same motel. When they entered the restaurant they were treated like royalty. After dinner a note with a penny tip was left stating: This is for our last dinner here, that tip was for tonight."

This Tibetan prophecy coming from Padmasambhava, says, "When the iron bird flies (airplanes) and the horse runs on wheels (cars), the Tibetan people will be scattered like ants across the face of the Earth, and the Dharma will come to the land of the red men." Since the 1970s, the Dalai Lama and a number of marooned robed priests fulfilled Hopi prophecy by regularly paying a visit to the Hopi elders. If you went straight through the Hopi Reservation to the other side of the world, you would come out in Tibet. The Tibetan word for sun is the Hopi word for moon, and the Hopi word for sun is the Tibetan word for moon. Many Hopis also believe a later visitation in the 1980s of red cloaked and capped followers of Bhagwan Rajneesh, also completed this aspect of the prophecy.

On the seventieth anniversary of the Hotevilla village, Grandfather David, made the following statement to a gathering of Hopi and Bahanna friends.

First of all, as you come here to my village of Hotevilla, I wish to welcome each one of you. At this time we are celebrating a time in our history, which is both filled with joy and with sadness. I am very glad that you have come to share these feelings with us. We are now faced with great problems, not only here but throughout the land. Ancient cultures are being annihilated; the people's lands are being taken from them, leaving them no place to call their own. Why is this happening? It is happening because many people have given up their teachings and the Way of Life which the Great Spirit has given to all people. It is because of the sickness called greed, which infects every land that simple people are losing what they have kept for thousands of years. Here at home, it is the so-called Hopi Tribal Council that is stealing our land and life. We Hopis are a Sovereign Nation. We have never signed a treaty with the U.S. Government, or with any government.

Yet the so-called Tribal Council has let the U.S. run over them and push them around. Now they, the so-called Tribal Council, push around their own people as if they have some kind of authority. But they do not have authority over Hopis. Hopis have their own authority and their own leaders who watch over all the people like a mother and father. But the so-called Tribal Council will not admit that this is so. Yet if it was not so, how else would we be able to still be alive today? We have managed for thousands of years to survive, without wars, without laws, and without outside authority telling us how to live our own lives. Now we are at the very end of our trail. Many people no longer recognize the True Path of the Great Spirit. They have, in fact, no respect for the Great Spirit or for our precious Mother Earth, who gives us all life. We are instructed in our ancient Prophecy that this would occur.

We were told that someone would try to go up to the moon, that they would bring something back from the moon, and that after that Nature would show signs of losing its balance. Now we see that coming about. All over the world there are now many signs that Nature is close to losing its balance. Floods, droughts, earthquakes, and great storms are occurring and causing much suffering. We do not want this to occur in our country and we pray to the Great Spirit to save us from such things. But there are now signs that this very same thing might happen very soon on our own land. Now we must look upon each other as brothers and sisters. There is no more time for divisions between people. Today I call upon all of us, from right here at home where we are guilty of gossiping and causing divisions even among our own families, and reaching out into the entire world where thievery, war and lying goes on every day, to recognize that these divisions will not be our salvation. Only by joining together with love in our hearts for one another and for the Great Spirit, shall we be saved from the terrible Purification Day, which is just ahead. Those of you who have come here today are honest people. I know you, each one of you, and I know that you have good hearts. But good hearts are not enough to solve these great problems. In the past, some of you have tried to help us Hopis, and we will always be thankful for your effort. But now we need your help in the worst way. We want the people of this country to know the truth of our situation. This land which you people call the Land of Freedom has just celebrated its 200th anniversary. Yet in 200 years the original Americans have not seen a free day. We are now suffering the final insult. Our people are now losing the one thing which gives life and meaning to life: our land, which is being taken away from us. I ask you this: Where is this freedom which you all fight for and sacrifice your children for? Is it only the Indian people who have lost it, or are all Americans losing the very thing that you originally came here to find? Listen to us. We have no freedom of religion because others come to our homes and tell us that our religion is no good; that we should take theirs instead.

We don't share the freedom of the press because the only thing that gets into the papers is what the government wants people to believe, not what is really happening. We have no freedom of speech, because we are persecuted by our own people for speaking our beliefs. So you have come here to help. I hope and pray that your help will come. If you have a way to spread the truth through the newspapers, radio, books, or through meetings with powerful people, tell the truth! Tell them what you have seen here; what you have heard us say, what you have seen here with your own eyes. In this way, if we do fall, let it be said that we at least tried, right up to the end, to hold fast to the Path of Peace as we were originally instructed to do by the Great Spirit. And should you really succeed, we will all face up to our mistakes of the past and return to the True Path, living in harmony as brothers and sisters, sharing our Mother, the Earth, with all other living things. In this way we could bring about a New World. A world which would be led by the Great Spirit and our Mother could provide plenty and happiness for us all. God bless you, each one. May the Great Spirit guide you safely home and give you something important to do in this great work which lies ahead of us all.

HOPI PROPHECY

THE HOPI PROPHECIES WERE GIVEN TO THEM BEFORE the coming of Jesus. It is mainly by word of mouth that it has been handed down. The accuracy had to deal with how well each individual who was given the prophecy maintained the exactness of the prophecies. Those given the prophecy met at least once, sometimes twice a year, in the Kiva, where they would actually sit down and go back through them. One person would talk about the prophecies, and if he ever added something to it or left something out, the rest of the group would know that part of the prophecies was missing. So, they would tell him, "Well, you didn't say this one here," or, "You added this to it." This way it was kept exactly as originally given.

The Hopi believe that fulfillment of the Hopi prophecy will be a new brotherhood of mankind. In the course of their communion with the Great Spirit, Native Americans have received many visions of the destiny of North American civilization. The largest number of such prophecies have been preserved by the Hopi in Arizona. Their community of Oraibi is the oldest continually inhabited settlement (about 1,000 years) in North America. The Hopi believe that the human race has evolved through three world stages of life since its origin. Each of these worlds was destroyed in turn, and human life was purified and nearly ended by the Great Spirit because of man's corruption and greed. In the Hopi belief, the universe at first was only infinite blackness in the mind of Taiowa. Taiowa made Sotuknang, the first man, and commanded him to order the cosmos. On the first day, Sotuknang divided the universe into nine worlds. One world was reserved for Taiowa, one was for Man, and seven were for future worlds. The present is the Fourth World. Topkela was the first and most beautiful of the worlds. There, humanity thrived in harmony with nature in the company of animals. But the Snake spoke and seduced Man away from Taiowa the Creator. Seeing this, Taiowa ordered Satuknang to destroy Tokpela and its inhabitants, except for a few "children of pure heart" whom he sheltered in the center of the Earth when he rained fire upon the planet and burned the sky. The people stayed underground while volcanoes erupted. Afterwards, the people emerged and moved into the second world, Topka, which was less beautiful than the first. There, men lived in huts, learned crafts, and drew apart from nature. Eventually they became greedy, materialistic, and insatiable as before. Taiowa again ordered Sotuknang to destroy the humans and the world they had ruined. The faithful few again hid underground with the Ant People. The earth rolled over twice, and everything on it was destroyed by ice, which covered everything. After the ice had melted enough to make the world inhabitable, the survivors emerged into the third world, Kuskurza.

There, man built cities and tall buildings, and departed further still from the Creator's nature, becoming very evil. Kuskurza, in turn, was destroyed by flood. When the Hopi's ancestors emerged from the underworld, they met the demigod Maasaw, who owns this world. Maasaw had been caretaker of the Third World, but because of his pride, he had been demoted to become the god of death. When Kuskurza was destroyed, Taiowa gave Maasaw another chance and appointed him to be the guardian of this world. The people asked Maasaw for permission to live in the new land of Turtle Island (North America). Maasaw said, "It is up to you, whether you are willing to live my poor, humble and simple life. It is hard, but if you are willing to live according to my teachings and instructions and will never lose faith in the life I shall give you, you may come and live with me. Now you look at me. I am a poor man. I have almost nothing: I have only my planting stick, my seed corn, and a jug of water. I live a simple life.

"If you wish to live with me, you must sacrifice many things. If you want me for your leader, your chief, you must prove that you can live this way of life. Now look around. See this land. It is poor land. There is not much water and very few trees. But this is the richest land. There is great wealth under. But hear this warning: You are not to disturb this land and take this wealth out as long as there still is war going on. If you do, these things will be used to destroy life and this will not be your salvation… Never disturb this land. Do not cede your land to anyone; don't ever give it away. Above all, it is to provide your nourishment. Hold this land dear like a mother as long as you live. If you sell it you will no longer reap crops. Be prepared. One after another people will approach you and put you to the test in this matter. If, in addition, you are willing to adopt the religion which I practice, you will derive further benefits for your life. But you have arrived with great ambitions and expectations. When you fall into your evil ways again, you will make me weep.... All right, you have settled in a desert, yet the land is filled with riches.

"You reside on the very backbone of the earth. All kinds of precious things are buried in this earth. There exists a storehouse of treasures underground but you must not dig them up yet. Three times big wars will rage. Should you excavate these treasures while the killing is taking place, powerful weapons will be forged from them and people will be slain by them. If you act on your own in this matter, you will do wrong. Not before the day of purification has been completed, may you unearth these things. At that time people will benefit from them. However, if these wars ever take place here, don't pick up your weapons, and don't engage in the business of killing..."

The people asked Maasaw to be their leader, but he declined. "No," he said. "A greater one than I has given you a plan to fulfill first. When the previous parts of the world were pushed underwater, this new land was pushed up in the middle to become the backbone of the earth. You are now standing on its west side slope. But you have not yet made your migrations. You have not yet followed your stars to the place where you will meet and settle. This you must do before I can become your leader. But if you go back to evil ways again I will take over the earth from you, for I am its caretaker, guardian, and protector... So go now and claim the land with my permission." Maasaw then placed four different colors and sizes of corn before the leaders of the four different racial groups, and had each one choose which would be their food in this world. The Hopi were the last to choose, and they picked the smallest ear of multi-colored corn. Pleased by their choice, Maasaw said: "It is well done. You have chosen the real corn, for all the others are imitations inside of which are hidden seeds of different plants. You have shown me your intelligence; for this reason I will place in your hands these owa tutuveni, symbols of power and authority over all land and life to guard, protect, and hold in trust for me until I return to you in a later day, for I am the first, but I am also going to be the last." One of the three Bear Clan tablets describes the land from the Grand Canyon to the Rio Grande, which was granted by Maasaw to the Hopis.

Another tablet is inscribed with mnemonic symbols of prophecies. A third tablet maps the allocations of farmland to the various clans, and delegates leadership to the Bear Clan. The fourth tablet is a very precise map of the location of the Sipaapuni, the great underground city where the Hopi ancestors hid during the destruction of the past worlds. The symbols on the front of the tablet now held by the Fire Clan show the mask of Maasaw and the swastika pattern, which represents the Hopi migrations. One corner is missing. The back of the Fire Clan tablet shows the figure of a headless man, which symbolizes the following prophecy:

In a time to come, the Hopis will be forced to develop their lives at the dictates of a new ruler. They are not to resist, but must wait for their Elder Brother, Antsa Qoetsapava Powatanica.

A corner of the Fire Clan tablet was broken off and given to the Elder Brother when he left on his migration. He hid it in the Sipaapuni city because he did not want to risk losing it in the course of his travels and reincarnations. He will retrieve it when he returns. In due time, the tablet will be split open to expose interior inscriptions which will reveal the origin and identity of the Hopi. Fitting the missing corner piece to the tablet, the Elder Brother will thus identify himself to the Hopi. The tablet will be split open to expose interior inscriptions which will reveal the origin and identity of the Hopi. Then Pahaana will proceed to deliver them from their persecutors and develop with them a new and universal brotherhood of man. But if he accepts any other religion, he must assent to having his own head cut off. This will dispel the evil and save the Hopi people.

The chief of the Bow Clan led the faithful Hopi to this new land, but he fell into evil ways. His two sons rebuked him for his mistakes, and after he died they assumed the responsibilities of leadership. Then Maasaw sent the Elder Brother to the east and across the ocean. Upon reaching his destination, he was to start back to look for his younger brother, who remained on Turtle Island.

The Elder Brother's mission was to help his younger brother to bring about Purification Day, when evil people would be punished and destroyed. Afterwards, real peace, brotherhood, and everlasting life would be established. The Elder Brother would restore to his younger brother all the land, which the Evil One among the white men had taken. The younger brother (the Hopi ancestor) was instructed to travel throughout Turtle Island and mark his trail with the petroglyphs we see today. This was done to claim the land, and to record and preserve the history of the Indians throughout the reign of white men. The whites would destroy most of the Native Americans' oral history and culture before destroying themselves also. A great white star would appear when the Elder Brother reached his destination. All people were to settle wherever they happened to be at that time, and there they were to remain until the Elder Brother returned. The Hopi settled in Tuuwanasavi, the area now known as Four Corners, where the state lines of Arizona, New Mexico, Utah and Colorado meet. This area is the "heart" of Turtle Island and of Mother Earth, and it is the microcosmic image of the entire planet. There, the Hopi lived a simple life as stewards of the land, which produced abundant crops despite being a desert. Their katsina ceremonies serve to maintain the balance of natural forces and to reaffirm their faith in Taiowa, in Maasaw and other spirits, and to show respect for all life. Maasaw told the Hopi that after a time Pahana,

White Man, would come and take their land and try to lead the Hopi into evil ways. Life would be Koyaanisqatsi ("World out of balance"). The Hopi were told that they must hold to their ancient religion and their land, and they must do it without violence. Maasaw promised that if they succeeded, their people and land would be a center where the True Spirit would reawaken. Maasaw said that after many years the Elder Brother might change the color of his skin, but his hair will remain black, and he will wear it long, in a braided tail. He will wear a red cloak or a red cap which resembles the back of a horned toad. He will speak the Hopi language, and he will be able to write. He will follow no religion but his very own. He will bring (or come to recover) the missing corner of the owa tutuveni, and he will correctly interpret the tablets. The Hopi are to meet him on the trail on the east side of Oraibi if he is on time (on the last day of Soyal, the winter solstice ceremony), or on the trail to Sikya'wa (Yellow Rock), at Chokuw (Pointed Rock), Nahoyungvasa (Cross Fields), or at Tawtona (Where the Sun Ray Goes Over the Line) below Oraibi if he is 5, 10, 15, or 20 years late. Then, great judgment and punishment will take place. The Elder Brother will help the younger brother obtain justice. In one day he will gain control of the whole continent. Even the Hopi people must beware. "If he comes from the East, the destruction will not be so bad. But if he comes from the West, do not go up on your housetops to see because he will have no mercy." It is said that the Elder Brother will bring with him two great, intelligent and powerful helpers. One will have a sign of a swastika and the sign of the sun. The first helper can be interpreted to represent the German-Japanese Axis of World War Two. From the Hopis' perspective, these enemies of the U.S.A. were doing the Indians a real service. The second helper will have the sign of a Celtic Cross with red lines between the arms of the cross. In the Hopi symbology, this form of a cross represents women, and the red lines indicate their menstrual flow. The symbol represents their liberation and the revival of matriarchal power after ages of suppression. Maasaw warned that if these great beings failed, terrible evil would befall the world and great numbers of people would be killed. However, they would succeed if enough Hopi remained true to the ancient spirit of their people. Unfortunately, there are very few traditionalist Hopis remaining today, so the situation looks very bleak.

Hopi prophecy states that World War III will be started by the people who first received the light— China, Palestine, India, and Africa. When the war comes, the United States will be destroyed by "a gourd of ashes", which will be thrown to the ground. The rivers will boil, the earth shall burn, and no grass will grow there for many years. It will cause a disease that no medicine can cure. This can only mean that nuclear weapons will be used against the U.S.A. Hopi traditionalist's believe that if many U.S. soldiers are sent overseas, they will be killed by atomic bombs, and then Turtle Island also will be bombed. "Men will fall from the sky," meaning that invading soldiers will parachute to earth.

According to another prophecy, "When the Blue Star Kachina dances in the plaza, the time of the great trial will be here… The end of all Hopi ceremonies will come when a Kachina removes his mask during a dance in the plaza before uninitiated children. For a while there will be no more ceremonies, no more faith. Then Oraibi will be rejuvenated with its faith and ceremonies, marking the start of a new cycle of Hopi life."

The following Hopi prophecy was first published in a mimeographed manuscript that circulated in 1959:

I am an Elder of the ancient Bear Clan. In my long life I have traveled through this land, seeking out my brothers, and learning from them many things full of wisdom. I have followed the sacred paths of my people, who inhabit the forests and many lakes in the east, the land of ice and long nights in the north, the mountains and streams of jumping fish in the west, and the places of holy altars of stone built long ago by my brothers' fathers in the south. From all these I have heard the stories of the past, and the prophecies of the future. Today, many of the prophecies have turned to stories, and few are left— the past grows longer, and the future grows shorter.

And now I am dying. My sons have all joined their ancestors, and soon I too shall be with them. But there is no one left, no one to recite and pass on the ancient wisdom. My people have tired of the old ways. The great ceremonies that tell of our origins, of our Emergence into the Fourth World, are almost all abandoned, forgotten. Yet even this has been foretold. The time grows short... My people await Pahana, the lost White Brother, as do all our brothers in the land.

He will not be like the white men we know now, who are cruel and greedy. We were told of their coming long ago. But still we await Pahana. He will bring with him the symbols, the missing piece of that sacred tablet now kept by the elders, given to him when he left. That shall identify him as our True White Brother. The Fourth World shall end soon, and the Fifth World will begin. This the elders everywhere know.

The signs over many years have been fulfilled, and few are left.

1st Sign: *We are told of the coming of the white-skinned men, like Pahana, but not living like Pahana— men who took the land that was not theirs. And men who struck their enemies with thunder.*

2nd Sign: *Our lands will see the coming of the spinning wheels of wood filled with voices. In my youth, my father saw this prophecy come true with his eyes— the white men bringing their families in wagons across the prairies.*

3rd Sign: *A strange beast, like a buffalo but with great long horns, will overrun the land in large numbers. These I saw with my own eyes— the coming of the white mans' cattle.*

4th Sign: *The land will be criss-crossed by snakes of iron.*

5th Sign: *The land will be criss-crossed by a giant spider's web.*

6th Sign: *The land will be criss-crossed with rivers of stone that make pictures in the sun.*

7th Sign: *You will hear of the sea turning black, and many living things dying because of it.*

8th Sign: You will see many youth, who wear their hair long like my people, come and join the tribal nations, to learn their ways and wisdom.

9th Sign: You will hear of a dwelling place in the heavens, above the earth, that shall fall with a great crash. It will appear as a blue star. Very soon after this, the ceremonies of my people will cease.

These are the Signs that great destruction is coming. The world shall rock to and fro. The white man will battle against other people in other lands— with those who possessed the first light of wisdom. There will be many columns of smoke such as I have seen the white man make in the deserts not far from here. Only those who come will cause disease and a great dying. Many of my people, understanding the prophecies, shall be safe. Those who stay and live in the places of my people also shall be safe. Then there will be much to rebuild. And soon— very soon afterward— Pahana will return. He shall bring with him the dawn of the Fifth World. He shall plant the seeds of his wisdom in their hearts. Even now the seeds are being planted. These shall smooth the way to the "Emergence into the Fifth World". But I shall not see it. I am old and dying. You— perhaps you will see it. In time, in time...

The signs are interpreted thus:

The First Sign is of guns.

The Second is of the pioneers' covered wagons.

The Third Sign is of longhorn cattle.

The Fourth describes railroad tracks.

The Fifth is a clear image of electric power and telephone lines.

The Sixth Sign describes concrete highways and their effect of producing mirages.

The Seventh Sign predicts catastrophic oil spills such as the Exxon Valdez.

The Eighth Sign suggests the hippy movement of the 1960s and 70s,

The Ninth Sign was the U.S. space station Skylab, which fell to Earth in 1979.   According to Australian eyewitnesses, it appeared to be burning blue. Or, the Russian space station Mir may be indicated here.

Another version of this prophecy says that when a black ribbon (the highway) is built on the land, a bug (the automobile) will move on it, and this will be the sign for the first shaking of the Earth, World War One. The first shaking will be so violent that the bug will be shaken off the earth and will begin to fly (the airplane), leaving a trail of dirt behind it. Eventually the sky will become so dirty that it will cause diseases that will become worse and worse. This may refer to the current controversy about "chem-trails", the aerial web of chemical sprays that are beings spewed over America.

Another Hopi prophecy warns that nothing should be brought back from the Moon— obviously anticipating the Apollo 11 mission that returned with samples of lunar basalt. The Hopi warned that it would disturb the balance of natural and universal laws and forces, resulting in earthquakes, severe changes in weather patterns, and social unrest. All these things are happening today. In 1948, Hopi spiritual leaders met in Shungopavi, the Indian pueblo, on the high mesa in Hopi Indian Reservation and chose four representatives to approach the United Nations. Because of their prophetic knowledge, the Hopi leaders felt it was time to go east to the edge of Turtle Island, where a "House of Mica [glass] would stand at this time, where Great Leaders from many lands would be gathered to help any people who are in trouble". They were to go there when the lands of the Hopi and other Indian brothers were about to be taken away from them and their way of life was in danger of being completely destroyed by evil ones among the white men and by some other Indian brothers who were influenced by the white race. This is a clear and present danger, because the infernal meddling of Christians, the betrayal of treaties by the federal government, the sale of tribal lands by Indians, and the ecological disasters caused by coal and uranium mining, are destroying the Hopi land and people, and all native Americans.

According to prophecy, at least one, two, or three leaders or nations would hear and understand the Hopi warnings, for they too, should know the ancient instructions. Upon hearing the message of the Hopi, they were to act immediately to correct many wrongs being done to the Red Man. However, the Hopi might find that the doors of the Mica House would be closed to them. "When Great Leaders in the Mica House refuse to open the door when you stand before it that day, do not be discouraged or turn about on the path you walk, but take courage and determination, and be of great rejoicing in your hearts, for on that day the White Race who are on your land with you will have cut themselves from you and thereon lead themselves to the greatest Punishment at the Day of Purification. Men shall be destroyed for their sins and evil ways. The Great Spirit has decreed it and no one can stop it, change it, or add anything to it. It shall be fulfilled!"

In 1959, another delegation of six traditional Hopi elders traveled to the U.N. building. Their prophecies foretold that if the Hopi's request to address the House of Mica was refused after knocking (visiting) four times, mankind would surely be destroyed. Hopi elders knocked for the fourth time in 1991, and were permitted to address the General Assembly for a few minutes during the opening ceremony of the United Nation's International Year of Indigenous Peoples. They were the last to speak, and only a few U.N. delegates remained to hear them. They said, "We have made a sacred covenant to follow Maasaw, the Great Spirit's Life Plan at all times, which includes the responsibility of taking care of this land and life for his divine purpose. Our goals are not to gain political control, monetary wealth, or military power, but rather to pray and to promote the welfare of all living beings and to preserve the world in a natural way." They then told the Hopi story of the previous worlds which were destroyed because of human greed, and warned that this world, too, is near its end. They said, "This is now a time to weigh the choices for our future. We do have a choice. If you, the nations of this Earth, create another great war, the Hopi believe we humans will burn ourselves to death with ashes. That's why the spiritual Elders strongly urge that the United Nations fully open the door for Native spiritual leaders as soon as possible. The Native peoples of the world have seen and spoken to you about the destruction of their lives and homelands, the ruination of nature and the desecration of their sacred sites. It is time the United Nations used its rules to investigate these occurrences and stop them now."

They requested that the U.N. protect the Four Corners area, because it will have a special purpose in the future survival of humankind. They asked that the UN keep its doors open for spiritual leaders of all peoples "to come to speak to you for more than a few minutes". They also invited world leaders to visit the Hopi country and "sit down with our real spiritual leaders in their sacred kivas" and learn their "ancient secrets of survival and balance". The UN has failed to respond.

Between 1975 and 1986, a group of traditionalist elders and English-speaking Hopis cooperated to produce 44 issues of a newsletter called Techqua Ikach (Land & Life), totaling over 200 pages which outlined their prophetic message in great detail. In 1993, Thomas Mails was selected by Dan Evehema (then 100 years old) to represent the authorized prophecies. The resulting book 'Hotevila' was written in complete secrecy to prevent interference from the Hopi Tribal Council. One day Hopi children with short hair or bald heads would be the ears and mouth for the elders, and in time become the leaders. So the Hopi Tribal Council was formed... "The Bahanas' government will gradually cease their responsibility in caring for the Native people... Any mistake we make will be our own doing. The Bahana government would not be held responsible.

Their influence would linger on in making sure we run our government the Bahana way, not by our own... traditional ways... If we link ourselves with a culture not of our own... it will be difficult to regain what we discard in the name of progress. Of course we can continue to practice what we lose, but it will have lost its value. What happens at the end will be the consequences of our carelessness."

According to the prophecy, the Hopi are to be the last target. "We are to be conquered, not by the army and their weapons, but by our own people; by our sons and daughters without us lifting our hands. Their weapon will be what they learned through the education so kindly taught by the Bahana... The Bahanas will pat the back of the conquerors while cheering and applauding. They will be satisfied that they are not required to finish the task which they set out to accomplish. It is our own people who bring this about and the Bahanas, therefore, cannot be blamed. The conquest will be over and all Native People will be finished. This is a sad ending and it is a pity that we must end this way... It is said if purification does not come, our Great Creator will take the land back because we do not care for the land and we don't deserve to be on it. The above subject, to our children, is soundless and has no meaning... One day our own children may become our enemies. Schools will destroy the sacred balance of Hopi life. They will interrupt the traditions and people will forget the instructions of Maasaw. This destruction will reach much further than our village. The whole Earth could go off balance. As foretold, all of this information must come out into the open at the period when we are about to be overcome by harmful elements and can step no further... Just two or three righteous people will be able to fulfill the Creator's mission. Even one truly righteous would be able to do it... Three people were named who were to help the Hopi when we reached the crisis of no return. The Paiute Indian was to help according to his wisdom, but if he is unable the Navajo Indian will help also, according to his wisdom. If their efforts fail then Bahana will come to aid.

This is where we are now... So it was predicted that one day we would encounter the presence of people with ways different from our own; they will pose as good-hearted. Their words will be charming and they will multiply like ants. We must not be deceived by them, for the vines of their kingdom will spread throughout the land, diluting and dissolving everything that gets in its way. We must be cautious and not covet or adopt any of their ways, for it will forever be a curse upon our nation. It is said, among the Bahana the people of the Cross will appear on our land. They will be kind and helpful with good hearts. Beware, for they will be the instruments of Bahana's kingdom and will seduce you into forsaking the laws of our Great Creator. The wicked of our people will join their flock to clear their sins, but this will be in vain... One day a strange people will appear in our midst, people who will create man in his own image. Once given his language and knowledge, our people will become the instrument by which he will try to rule over us and carve the rest of us into his image. Our own people will become his tools, and he will make certain they do a good job. But if we remain strong and firmly rooted, we will not be reshaped, whereas others will slump because they are rootless. So when the tests come we must possess the strength to preserve ourselves... The Earth is like a spotted fawn, and each spot has a duty to make the body function. Hopi Land is the center of the earth's body. It is the spot of power with the duty to foretell the future by comparing the actions of mankind with the prophecy told to them...

One of the traditional Hopi elders emphasizes that most of the events predicted by their prophecies already have happened, and that the Great Purification is imminent:

Life has become out of balance. When people are so out of balance, someone will hear our voice and our White Brother will answer the call and clean away the evil ones. According to prophecy, when the purification is over only a handful of people will survive in every nation overseas. Then they will come to this continent, which we call heaven. This is where the Creator first lived and that's what he called it.

He sent his own son from Oraibi to Bethlehem in order to be born there. The Hopi already knew that the morning star would rise one day and someone special would be born... In our prophecies there are two brothers, one dark-skinned younger brother and the light-skinned elder who we call the White Brother. Together they will decide how the purification will be accomplished. The two brothers were with us when we first came to this continent. When their father passed away, the elder brother went out in the direction of the sunrise and the younger brother stayed here. They had agreed the elder brother would go, but would not stay away too long. He would return when people would travel on a road built in the air. At that time we would know that the earth had been corrupted to the point that it must be purified. We've come to that point now. Everything has been corrupted. Because we are out of balance, we don't obey the laws... It's too late now for gradual voluntary corrections... As Hopis, we are calling for the purification because it is our obligation. We're ready. We want it to happen... We've already gone over the time limit that was given to us in the prophecy...

Hopi prophecy also warns that there will be three divisions among the Hopi. The first division was in 1906 between the traditionalists and the modernists. The traditionalists were forced to leave Oraibi and move to Hotevila. The second division took place in the aftermath of a spectacular UFO sighting in August 1970. The third division is occurring now as the Tribal Council has forced the installation of electric power and other modern inconveniences upon the unwilling traditionalist residents of Hotevila. During the Hopi Hearings of 1955, many elders spoke forth to remind people of the ancient prophecies. One elder said: "Then the sun won't be as hot any more, and the summer season will grow shorter and shorter. One day the weather will no longer get warm. You will experience snowfall at the height of planting time. Then you will have to sow wearing gloves and long underwear. To sow, the farmer will have to push aside the snow, dig a hole, and then plant his seeds.

It will come to this if you extract those precious things from the earth. And all the grasses across the land, which many different animals feed on to raise their young, will not grow as before. In the future the animals will suffer great hardships. Then the grasses will not sprout.

There will be no point in having rain; nothing will grow as it used to. Gradually your corn plants will produce only tassels and then everything will freeze. And when you replant, only tiny, stunted ears will appear, and then they, too, will freeze. The third time you sow, the stalks will still be short before the frost strikes. By the fourth time the plants will barely have pierced the earth before freezing. All of these predictions Maasaw made to the Hopi."

The newsletter Techqua Ikach warned, "When the end is near, we will see a halo of mist around the heavenly bodies. Four times it will appear around the sun as a warning that we must reform, telling us that people of all color must unite and arise for survival... We were warned the ice will grow again. Should the [Flute] Clans with the controlling powers vanish or stray away from the great laws of the Creator, there will be no way of stopping the ice buildup. So the time will come when we will experience late springs and early frosts, this will be the sign of the returning Ice Age...

"The time will come when from the Earth will arise a mystic fog which will dilute the minds and hearts of all people... A sudden eruption will explode in the midst of their follies, and this will creep over the earth. Then men will destroy each other savagely." According to prophecy, the day will come when people in high places will be hunted and vice versa, the lowly hunters will be hunted. This will get out of control. The hunting will gather strength and spread far and wide... The period of this age will close by the gourd of ashes, which will glow brighter than the Sun. The earth will turn over four times and mankind will end up in the lowest level of darkness. There they will crawl around on all fours forever.

Then the spirits of our Ancient Fathers will return to reclaim the land. They will mock the lowly man for he will no longer deserve or be worthy of the land. Only those who are obedient to the guidance of the Great Creator's laws will survive... the true brother and sister will give a rebirth to the Earth and renew its life. It is also said elsewhere in Hopi prophecy that... "Turtle Island could turn over two or three times and the oceans join hands and meet the sky." (Since 1931, geophysicists have detected nearly 500 shifts of the north magnetic pole, moving northwest.) "If corruption of nature becomes so thick and pollution so thick, we will be in darkness, and if we don't change things, the animals... they're going to yell at us. Pretty soon the eagles flying over us will be going to cry at us; when you walk in the woods, the trees, some will cry at you— because human beings are supposed to take care of them also, through prayer, meditation, and ceremony instead of destroying them with machinery and inventions that you have made."

In the 1950s the elders also predicted the development of genetic engineering, saying that, "You're going to see a time in your lifetime when the human beings are going to find the pattern that makes us. They're going to cut this pattern. They're going to make new animals upon the earth, and they're going to think these things are going to help us. And it's going to seem like they do help us. But maybe the grandchildren and great grandchildren are going to suffer. They will release these things; they will use them. You will see new animals, and even the old animals will come back, animals that people thought had disappeared. They will find them here and there. They'll begin to reappear."

After the Great Deluge several thousand years ago, the survivors split up into four groups, who migrated north, south, east and west. Only one group completed their journey— to the North Pole and back— under the guidance of a brilliant 'star' in which Maasaw traveled.

When he landed, Maasaw drew the petroglyph on Second Mesa, showing a maiden (with the traditional "butterfly" hair arrangement) riding in a wingless, dome-shaped craft. The petroglyph tells of the coming Day of Purification, when the true Hopi will fly to other planets in "flying shields".

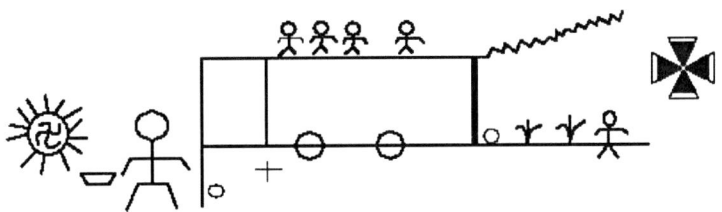

Hopi Life Plan

The famous "Prophecy Rock" petroglyph is known as the Hopi Life Plan. The following explanation, which was provided by the Hotevila faction, has been approved by the traditionalist Hopi elders: In the figure above of the Life Plan, represents Maasaw pointing to the earth from which the Hopi emerged. The short lines between his right hand and foot represent the Hopi clans. In recent years, the Hopi added a bow to the right of Maasaw to illustrate his instructions to lay down their weapons and live in peace. With his left hand, he is touching the path of Life Plan which the Hopi are to follow. The circle near his left hand represents the Hopi's stewardship over Turtle Island. Point (where he's pointing in the picture) indicates the time when, as Maasaw predicted, the Hopi would digress from the True Path and follow another trail. The square at this point is supposed to represent Oraibi. The two lines leading from Oraibi mark the split that occurred in 1905 between the progressive Oraibi and traditionalist Hotevila factions. The upper line branching from the square is the false path of the wicked people who strive to dominate Nature and rise above other people without the guidance of God. The three human figures on the false path are the generations of wicked people who walk that way. Hopi elders claim that in recent times, heads were added to the symbols. The lack of heads would represent the punishment of death that will befall the wicked. Two zig-zag lines branch from the false path. They represent carelessness and different paths to the final destruction pursued by the wicked people. Each zig and zag is another evil intention that eventually will be exhausted, which is indicated by the drooping symbol for turning around or sagging down at their ends. The lower straight line is the true path of life leading to everlasting life, symbolized by the masked figure of Maasaw.

He holds a planting stick in one hand while touching a corn stalk with the other. He stands waiting at the end of the True Path of Life because, as he says, "I am the first and I am the last." The True Path is interrupted in three places by arches (m) which might have been complete circles at some time in the past. These are said to represent gourds, symbolizing three great "shakings" or wars that will rattle humanity before the Life Plan is fulfilled. Hopi elders say the third gourd is the "final war of purification" in which all evil will be destroyed. Line, which also resembles a corn stalk, connects the false path with the true way. It offers a last chance for the wicked to repent and return to the Path of Life. The two dead-end zig-zag trails indicate complete and permanent destruction of body and soul, since they continue for only a short distance beyond the point of no return. The symbol is obscured by scratches, but the Hopis claim it is a crucifix, added to the petroglyph after a bloody 17th century encounter with the Spanish. The symbol was at Maasaw's behest to show that Christianity is incompatible with the Hopi Life Plan, and should not merge with it. The three figures on the upper path also have been interpreted to mean the white man's inventions of the wagon and automobile, the train, and the airplane.

THE MYSTERY OF THE TRUE WHITE BROTHER
an interpretation of the meaning of the Hopi Prophecy

A few words about the People of Peace:
The Hopi live on three mesas in the northwest corner of Arizona. They number slightly more than ten thousand, and their particular reservation is totally surrounded by the much larger reservation of the Navaho Indians, whose numbers are over ten-fold greater. Besides their unusual language, the Hopi are noted for their ceremonial life, which is very complex and rich, and which is tied in its timing to the equally beautiful rhythmic movements in the heavens.

Their way of life is now somewhat modernized (itself a problem causing internal dissension, a division between so-called progressives and traditionalists). Their life appears simple; the main element of diet was once corn. Water, until modern times, had been very scarce. The central thesis of the religious teaching is that if the Hopi carry their responsibilities, continue to enact correctly the ceremonials, then the world will be kept in balance.

Yet, this same teaching tells them that the time will come when all this will be endangered. Their way of life will be on the verge of destruction, and with it the whole world. Late in Grandfather

David's life, a power struggle between the progressives and the traditionalists, ensued, and he was poisoned. While he survived this attempt on his life, there was still a struggle because of various issues facing the Hopi concerning their relations with the surrounding Navaho, and the disposition of valuable mineral rights on the Hopi reservation (coal and uranium ore). As the Prophecy becomes better understood by the reader, the significance of the above matters will become clearer. Hopi prophecies, which date back about 3,500 years, are meant to be shared with the public. The Hopi prophecy is an oral tradition of stories that Hopis say predicted the coming of the white man, the world wars and nuclear weapons. And it predicts that time will end when humanity emerges into the "fifth world." The Mayan calendar predicts a similar end in 2012; some Hopis have said their prophecy roughly coincides with that time. The tradition says the years after 2012 could be a golden age with humans at peace. It also says the world will go through a time of trial, suffering and purification before a time of "one-heartedness."

The late Edgar Cayce, considered the most documented clairvoyant of the Twentieth century, spoke of earth changes. He predicted that the years between 1958 and 1998 would indeed be a period of great global transformation. He believed these changes would not lead to the end of the world, but in time, to the dawning of a New Age of hope and community for all humankind. Today, many organizations continue to predict major cataclysms and the approach of inevitable change. These groups fail to realize that change is all about us. There are wars and conflicts around the globe. Ethnic cleansing is rampant. Floods, famine and hate crimes occur, gang wars, drugs and our inhumanity to one another run rampant. This information has become so commonplace that we simply shrug our shoulders, change the channel, or turn the page. In spite of the evidence, many individuals continue to wait for the Big One. As the Hopi say, "It's time for us to wake up and realize that the changing times are happening now. Our world, our civilization, and our individual lives are all undergoing dramatic personal and collective change. Yet, this is sometimes hard for us to recognize because the changes have not been a single event. They have been a process. Cayce's predictions for the future were not about earthquakes; instead, they are about the fact that a new world is being born. The challenge of the times is for us to come together as one global community. The purpose of the changes we are experiencing is not for the changes themselves; rather it is so that we will undergo personal and global transformation. Only in this way may we usher in the dawn of a New Age. From Cayce's perspective, the future offers the chance to transform the world as we work together, building hope and community for all of humankind. But now is the time to start. Actually I believe it's really late to start, but better late than never. The Hopi believe there was only one God or Creator, Taiowa. All else was endless space. There was no beginning and no end, no time, no shape, no life. Just an immeasurable void that had its beginning and end, time, shape, and life in the mind of Taiowa the Creator. Then he, the Infinite, conceived the finite... The Hopi Creator, Taiowa, is not the "father", but an "uncle" whose first creation was a nephew, Sotuknang.

To Sotuknang he gave the task of manifesting the finite out of the infinite, of transforming vision into reality. Sotuknang created nine universal kingdoms: one for Taiowa, one for himself, and seven universes for the life that was to come. Each of these universes was composed half of solid and half of water, and surrounded by air. To these three elements, earth, water, and air, Taiowa then instructed Sotuknang to add the fourth and final element, that of life and its movement. To carry out this task of creating life, Sotuknang went to the First World and created a woman to help him. Her name was Kokyangwuti, or Spider Woman.

When she awoke, Spider Woman asked, "Why am I here?"

"Look about you," answered Sotuknang. "Here is the earth with shape and substance, direction and time, a beginning and an end. But there is no life upon it. There is no joyful sound or movement. So you have been given the knowledge, wisdom, and love to bless all the beings you create. That is why you are here."

The first people were among the many beings that Spider Woman created. She created the first people in all the four colors of black, red, white, and yellow. Each of the four races was given a different language to speak, and the "pristine wisdom" to understand that the earth was not to be dominated and conquered but was, rather, their mother. The corn that sustained them, because it became a part of their flesh, was the earthly manifestation of their mother. The sun, which gave life to the whole universe and served as the "face" of the Creator Taiowa, was perceived as their father. In the First World, the people created by Spider Woman lived together in harmony with nature and all her creatures. They were also in harmony with all their fellow human beings, and understood one another despite their differences of color and language. For the Hopis, the Road of Life is the journey through all seven universes created at the beginning by Taiowa's nephew Sotuknang. In the First World, children grew to identify themselves with universal citizenship, in harmony with all creatures and with the earth. The living body of man and the living body of the earth are constructed in the same way.

Through each runs an axis, man's axis being the backbone, which controls the equilibrium of his movements and his functions. Along this axis are several vibratory centers that echo the primordial sound of life throughout the universe, or sound a warning if anything goes wrong. The First World of the Hopis was corrupted not so much by evil as by "forgetting". The people had been instructed by Sotuknang and Spider Woman to respect their Creator, and to use their vibratory centers to help them follow his plan. But as they forgot this, they began to quarrel among themselves. Finally, the situation reached a point where Sotuknang and Taiowa decided that the world had to be destroyed. Sotuknang appeared before those "chosen people" who still remembered the Creator and his plan, and told them that the doors at the tops of their heads would lead them to safety before he destroyed the world. They took refuge underground with the Ant People as the First World was destroyed by fire, and a Second World was created for their emergence. The Second World was almost as beautiful as the first, with the significant difference that the animals no longer trusted humans and remained separate from them. But here, too, people began to forget the plan of the Creator, until finally this world also had to be destroyed. Again, those who had 'remembered' were saved, and taken care of by the Ant People. Once they were safe, the twin guardians of the poles were told to leave their posts so the world would spin off its axis and out of control. As it traveled through space, it froze into solid ice, until the twins took up their stations again and restored the Earth to life, creating a Third World. Now in this Third World, the people multiplied in such numbers and advanced so rapidly that they created big cities, countries... a whole civilization. This made it difficult for them to conform to the plan of Creation and to sing praises to Taiowa and Sotuknang. More and more of them became wholly occupied with their own earthly plans. Some of them, of course, retained the wisdom granted them upon their emergence.

With this wisdom they understood that the farther they proceeded on the Road of Life and the more they developed, the harder it was. That was why their world was destroyed every so often to give them a fresh start. When this world and its advanced civilization was finally destroyed by Sotuknang, this time with great floods, the people who still remembered took refuge inside the hollow stems of the bamboo. Then came their emergence into the Fourth World. In the Fourth World, the people had to search long and hard for a place to establish themselves and start over again. They journeyed by boat, paddling uphill from place to place. Whenever they found a beautiful and bounteous place to land, they would be told by Spider Woman that they must move on: this place was too easy, and soon they would fall into evil ways if they stayed. Finally, completely exhausted from their efforts, the people 'opened their doors' and let themselves be guided. The water carried them gently to a sandy shore, where they were greeted by Sotuknang and given further instructions. They were to separate into different groups, each heading in different directions, to claim all the land for the Creator. Each group would have to "follow its own star" to a place where the earth met the sea.

They would complete such a journey four times in all, to cover all the four directions, before being guided back together again to settle permanently. The people who eventually settled together in the Hopi desert mesa homeland had spent many generations of time apart, living in different clans, developing their own traditions and ceremonies. But throughout their journeys they left signs of their passage, and these signs reveal the common threads that bound them even as they went their separate ways. By looking at these symbols, they can tell how many rounds of their pilgrimage the clan had completed at the time, what direction they were moving in, and how long they stayed. There are four clans who carry out essential ceremonials throughout the year. Each of these four clans also represents one of the four directions.

These are the actual directions from where these clans originally came to settle in the village of Oraibi, the central, spiritual heart of the Hopi homeland. Traditionally, the Village Chief of Oraibi has been a member of the Bear Clan. It is generally agreed that the Bear Clan was the first to complete the cycle of four migrations and settle in Oraibi. The Bear Clan arrived from the west. The 'mother' of Oraibi is represented by the Parrot Clan, a clan that arrived from the South. The other two points of the compass in the sacred ceremonies are represented by the Badger and the Eagle clans, occupying north and east respectively. The Badger Clan holds special knowledge of the powers of the spruce trees, whose upturned branches provide a "throne" for the clouds and attract the precious rain. The Eagle Clan contributed feathers for the paho, which carries the remembrances and prayers of the people to their spiritual father, the sun. All through their migrations, there were prophecies that the Hopis would make their final home at an austere place where life would be difficult. But their guiding spirit promised to watch over them if they led decent lives. The Hopis were not supposed to accumulate wealth, but to be generous with everything. When they settled in their desert country, they said, "Life will be hard in this place, but no one will envy us. No one will try to take our land away. This is the place we will stay. We feel that the world is good. We are grateful to be alive. We are conscious that all men are brothers. We understand that we are related to other living creatures. When you go out of the house in the morning and see the rising sun, pause a moment to think about it. The sun brings warmth to the things that grow in the fields. If there's a cloud in the sky, look at it and remember that it brings rain to a dry land. When you take water from a spring, be aware that it is a gift of nature. If you meet a person, greet him. If he is a stranger or someone you know, it is all the same. If someone comes to the village from another place, even if he belongs to a different tribe, feed him. Keep your mind cleansed of evil thoughts against people... Be generous with whatever you have."

Before the newcomers to the Fourth World set out on their migrations, they were given a tablet containing symbolic representations of their journey and final resting place, and events that would confirm their adherence to the Creator's plan. The tablet today is held by members of the Fire Clan in the village of Hotevilla. This tablet has one corner missing that, according to legend, is in possession of a 'lost white brother' called Pahana. Pahana's return with the missing corner will signal the beginning of a new brotherhood of mankind. "See," said Sotuknang, "I have washed away even the footprints of your Emergence; the stepping-stones which I left for you.

"Down on the bottom of the seas lie all the proud cities, the worldly treasures corrupted with evil, and those people who found no time to sing praises to the Creator from the tops of their hills. But the day will come, if you preserve the memory and the meaning of your Emergence, when these stepping-stones will emerge again and prove the truth you speak."

The fulfillment of the Hopi prophecy will be a new brotherhood of man. Hopi elders explain that it makes no difference whether your spirituality falls in line with an organized philosophy or religion, or if it is something that you have come up with and practice on your own. "Practice your spirituality, whatever it may be, like you have never practiced it before. And realize that your consciousness affects the outcome. Your consciousness affects everything."

Grandfather David Monongye stated:

We Hopis believe that, after three other attempts for spiritual evolution failed with global destruction, when human beings came into the fourth world, it was on the mesa now called Oraibai. As some of the human beings went off to the east, they vowed to come back with technology and inventions that would make life easier. The rest of the human beings were to stay in Oraibai and keep the ways of the heart and live as good human beings.

But while discovering these technologies the human beings of the east would be guided by their heads and lose their hearts and the ways of human beings. They would be known as the two-hearts and this is what we call most white people today. An exchange would occur when they would meet again. The human beings of the east would bring the inventions that make life easier in the physical world while the Hopi at Oraibai would teach them the ways of the heart. Then all human beings will transcend to the next dimension, the fifth world. The Hopis evolved from profoundly simple truth and still live planting their sacred corn today in remove villages in Northern Arizona. Their message is based on a series of remarkable prophecies they were given thousands of years ago. Their elders tell us that their tiny village, Hoteville, is in fact a sacred microcosm of our world, that it holds the promise and the possibility of mankind's future on the planet. The shield symbol with its four circles in four quadrants means:

These Hopi Traditionalists have been keepers of a faith and culture for more than 22,000 years, [according to carbon-dated prehistoric rock recordings]. They are the only native people of America, perhaps the world, to have sustained virtually their entire culture, though it is highly threatened today. Hotevilla reveals the Covenant the Great Spirit of the Earth made with the Hopi 1,100 years ago and the prophecy that it involved. The Hopi were to understand themselves to be the microcosm of all of humanity and keepers of the world's balance. Time would spiral down toward a climax. This information was to be released at a special time in history (our time) when they, their tradition and wisdom would be threatened with extinction that, if it were to happen, would be catastrophic for all of humanity.

It is obvious to many of us that we are in end times. Tsunamis, earthquakes, earth and temperature changes, man's inhumanity to man, the extraordinary greed that dominates our country are all indicators of end times.

Those who live their lives in loving, take responsibility for their loving and share with the less fortunate, have nothing to be concerned about. If it is true that what we put out returns to us, what goes around comes around or karma (as ye sow, so shall ye reap), cause and effect, then we do have control over our futures! Every present act will return in the future. Unlike doomsayers, I don't believe life will end on earth. I do believe we are entering an era where people will learn to take responsibility for their loving, or be removed. It is almost time. I'm not worried, are you?

I grow Hopi Orange Squash and it will be one of my main staples if the system shuts down. Only in the southwest are the blossoms of squash and pumpkin important as religious symbols as well as food. They appear as sacred symbols in many Pueblo ceremonies, and gave rise to a popular design worked in silver. There is also Patung and Wuya for the Hopi Pumpkin Clan. The Hopis and Pueblo farmers gather large quantities of squash and pumpkin flowers to use in their sacred ceremony, at the end of the growing season, when these flowers can no longer make fruit.

MESSAGE FROM THE HOPI ELDERS

You have been telling the people that this is the eleventh hour.
Now you must go back and tell people that this is the hour.
And there are things to be considered:
Where are you living?
What are you doing?
What are your relationships?
Are you in the right relationship?
Where is your water?
Know your garden.
It is time to speak your truth.
Create your community.
Be good to each other.
And do not look outside yourself for the leader.
This could be a good time!
There is a river flowing very fast.
It is so great and swift that there are those who will be afraid.
They will try to hold on to the shore.
They will feel they are being torn apart, and they will suffer greatly.
Know the river has its destination.
The elders say we must let go of the shore,
push off into the river,
keep our eyes open,
and our heads above the water.
See who is in there with you and celebrate.
At this time in history, we are to take nothing personally.
Least of all ourselves.
For the moment that we do, our spiritual growth and journey comes to a halt.
The time of the lone wolf is over. Gather yourselves!
Banish the word struggle from your attitude and your vocabulary.
All that we do now must be done in a sacred manner and in celebration.

We are the ones we've been waiting for.

THE ELDERS
ORAIBI, ARIZONA

Author, basic training, 1954
Author owned photo

M48 tank

Amphibious Truck (Dukw)
Author owned photo

Author's Demolition Derby car
Photo by author

Author on milk bench, Meher Baba on wall
Photo by author

Two Gallon a Day Devi with Cabrito
Photo by author

Meher Baba, 1949   *Meher Baba, 1956*

Meher Baba and Agnes Barron at Meher Mount, 1956

Lama Dome

Lama Kitchen
©Photos by Frank Cox

Entrance to lama Fd.
prayer room

Prayer Room

Lama Fd. High Hermitage
©Photos by Frank Cox

Author next to Lama kitchen
©Photo by Frank Cox

Peyote
Photo by author

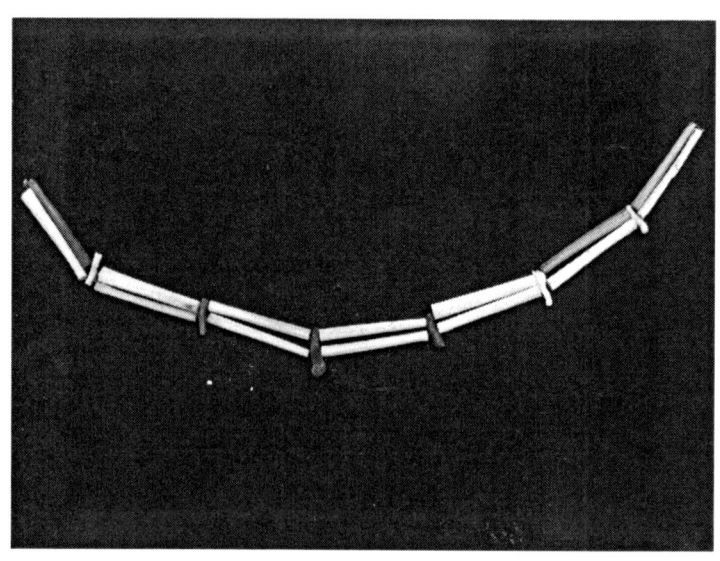

Author made coyote shinbone necklace

Author made concha belt
©Photos by Mary Kay James

Author's Teepee

Author in teepee, 1975
©Photos by Meridel Rubenstein

Hippy Gathering, Lama Mt., NM, 1972
Author in striped shirt
©Photo by Carl Fritz

Cowboy author

Author with red rail hawk

Tellus Good Morning and wife Pauline, 1975
©Meridel Rubenstein

Little Joe Dancing 1967
©Photo by Lisa Law

Grandfather David
Lama with the Dali, 1975,
fulfilling Hopi and
Tibetan Buddhist prophecy
©Photo by Marcia Keegan

Dr. Hunter, 1970
Photo by T.D. Thompson

Dr. Hunter, 1972
Photo by T.D. Thompson

John-Roger,
early 1970s

John-Roger,
early 1980s

Hari Dass, late 1960s   *Hari Dass, early 1970s*

Arati, 1972

Zalman Schacter, 1992   *Zalman Schacter, 1998*

Ellevivian, 1945
Used by permission of Barbara Power Martin

Ellevivian, 1990
Used by permission of Barbara Power Martin

Sasaki Roshe, Zen Master, 1993
©Photo by Don Farber

Neva Dell Hunter

*These roses under my window make no
reference to former roses
or to better ones;
They are for what they are; they exist with God
today.
There is no time to them.
There is simply the rose; it is perfect in every
moment of its existence.*

EMERSON

AFTER MY MIRACULOUS HEALING, (COVERED IN THE Ellevivian Power chapter) I was determined to find out more about this amazing work. I started commuting the three hundred miles from my home to attend classes at Quimby center every month. On one of these visits, Dr. Hunter asked me to join her for lunch. She informed me that my aura had turned white and she wanted me to move into her home to be her right-hand man. Wow, I was stoked! She obviously set my ego up and I bought it hook, line and sinker.

I agreed and suggested it would take approximately two weeks to put my affairs in Taos in order. She suggested I move in A.S.A.P. As I had a small dairy goatherd, I made arrangements with a commune to take care of my animals, placed my stuff in storage and moved to Alamogordo. As my hair was very long I decided to cut it short. I was assigned a bedroom, and one of her assistants told me the house rules. She showed me exactly how all the dishes were to be put away. She told me if I put one dish in the wrong place, Dr Hunter would go ballistic. Occasionally she would change the order and not tell us, then scream at us. It took me a very long time, probably way after I moved out, to understand she was teaching us to live in the moment, to accept what's in front of us now and deal with it from that place. Heaven help anyone who told her, in a whiney voice: "Well, yesterday you said," etc, etc.

I had only been living in Dr. Hunter's house in Alamogordo, New Mexico, a couple of weeks when she told me to rake the leaves in the backyard. I was so angry at myself for agreeing to live with this nasty, rude, disrespectful, sarcastic dictator. What had I gotten myself into? For a moment I thought, "What a fucking asshole she is." That thought barely flitted through my mind when she was out the back door, minions in tow, clapping her hands rapidly screeching at me, that "while living in her house, I was not allowed to have thoughts like that." Christ, I might as well be naked! She always knew what I was thinking, what I did the night before and what I would do tomorrow. She had the ability to see things that are veiled to most of us.

After I moved there, I would occasionally overhear her counseling people. I would watch her time and time again. She just knew too much. She would ask them things about their lives that they hadn't said anything about and she knew all about it. She definitely had a clairvoyant ability. I was with her only a few days when strong feelings, fears, anxiety and a sense of disorientation and being unconnected to things that had been familiar to me started to come up. I believed it was her influence that was causing this. There are few spiritual teachers that have this presence and what they emanate from their own energetic field is so powerful that when we come in contact with that, it has the effect of hitting all those dark areas within us and pushing them up into awareness for us to deal with. I was constantly in overwrought emotional flux. One day she went to Las Cruces, sixty miles away. Thank you! Finally! A day off! I decided to settle in her favorite chair in her bedroom with my feet up on her desk and watch television, when she walked in the door. She and I both knew I was dead, waiting to be buried. "What are you watching? Looks like a good show!" she sweetly remarked. I was emotionally incredulous. Then she again left for Las Cruses.

I couldn't sleep all night waiting for the morrow and the ensuing guillotine. It never came. She never said a word about me being in her bedroom.

She was the master of emotional manipulation. Once her chiropractor friend from California was visiting. She was talking to a group of women in the living room while I was in the kitchen with Dr. Hunter. She asked me if I was still having back problems and advised if it was so to ask her friend to adjust my cervix. Without thinking I went into the living room and when appropriate I told her Dr. Hunter suggested she adjust my cervix. Everybody laughed. I had no idea I meant cervical. She was always fucking with me. And from a thirty-five year retrospect, it was exactly what I needed. I had enormous blocks of emotions lodged and locked in my aura and she always had the key. For the first six months I knew her, she treated me lovingly and sweetly, like I was her best friend, while screaming at her staff, then when I was hooked, the hammer fell. I was really in love with her, not like a lover relationship, but more like a son to a Mom. She was brutal. I've heard her being described as "six tough truck drivers rolled into one." Being around her was very uncomfortable, as she took away everything in your consciousness that seemed to have permanency until you were floating in a void with nothing to hold on to.

From what I now know about consciousness, there's a name for it: Cognitive Dissonance. And it's typical of the growth process. In order to build new reality, you have to let go of the old reality. She just did it in a very heavy-handed and very shortcut kind of way. Over the years, it was like she was compressing it down by intensifying the experience. I have a lot more respect for what she was attempting to do now, than I did then. She worked with people by breaking down their belief structures and then put them back together again with a metaphysical reality. She believed we were stuck in consciousness, as the personality is a composite of the mental and emotional level. The mental levels are fixed ideas, called definitions of reality. But every one of those definitions of reality has an emotional tag that goes with it. For example, if you feel something is wrong and you see it going on, you don't feel good about it.

You feel bad about it because your definition of reality has defined it in the bad category, and so you're going to have a negative feeling about it. What she did was to begin to break down all of these definitions. Plus she violated a lot of the definitions of reality that we were told about appropriate care and behavior.

So, if I have a definition of reality that says that people should be considerate of each other, when inconsideration is being demonstrated or I am in the presence of it, the negative feeling is going to come up associated with that. So, by treating people that way, she would surface a lot of negativity inside of them because we all have rules that say don't do that, don't be that way. And with her ability to know what we were thinking, there was no place to hide. If you stayed with her long enough as a student, her heavy approach would start to shatter your definitions of reality. Consciousness is largely made up of definitions of reality that we hold; kind of like the glue that holds it together. This tactic of berating people, of breaking them down, had the effect of taking apart those structures of reality. It made you very malleable inside.

Another thing that she did was sleep deprivation. She would keep you up very late at night and get you up very early in the morning.

These are all classic tactics of teachers working with apprentices down through the ages. This is nothing new. And she was really very, very good at it because she was so powerful. She would talk about different kinds of people that had to make adjustments to the tracks in their consciousness. Some of us had to rip up entire tracks and start all over again. It appears that from a spiritual sense when one makes a commitment to study with a spiritual teacher, a master teacher, if you will, one has to open all the psychic doors. You've made yourself vulnerable and available to do that work and on some level in the collective unconscious there is ability for the teacher to have an awareness of what is going on with you all the time. For me it was brutal, as she always knew what I was thinking.

She was beauty, grace and love except when she was angry, which appeared to be quite often. Then she was brutal and sarcastic and would rage. I thought she was the most tyrannical dictator I had ever been around. And one of the most effective spiritual teachers I've ever met. And from a thirty-five year retrospect, exactly what I needed at the time.

Neva Dell Hunter was born May 11, 1903, in West Branch, Michigan. Her mother passed on early in her childhood. Her father was a psychiatrist who studied with Sigmund Freud. She had a very typical upbringing except she was raised by a father who was searching for answers in terms of the unconscious. She grew up around her father's colleagues, and the constant talk of the sub-conscious. She was very close with her father, and on many occasions, he took her to Europe to meet Freud during his study trips. She attended Ohio State University choosing Journalism and Advertising as a career. Marrying in the early thirties, she soon became pregnant. The death of her husband, Harry, in 1935 and then her daughter soon after, left her heartbroken.

After spending many years in advertising, she sought a new direction for her life and found it through hypnosis. In 1949, under hypnosis, she went into an altered state, another level of consciousness, and was contacted by an inner teacher, a being from the other side, who taught her how to put herself into a trance state where she was capable of channeling "karmic life readings" for people. These "channelings" were read from the akashic records. Phineas Parkhurst Quimby was the inner teacher, he was born in New Hampshire, February 16, 1802 and passed away on January 16, 1866.

PHINEAS PARKHURST QUIMBY

TWO-THOUSAND, THREE-HUNDRED AND SEVENTY-SOME years ago, in book seven of his Republic, Plato gave us the allegory of the cave. In the cave were a captive people whose only knowledge of the world was their understanding of shadows they saw on the wall of their cave.

These shadows came from a puppet show that mocked reality. In their ignorance they supposed these shadows and the echoes of their sounds to be the truth. One of the captives found his way out of the cave into the sunshine. He was at first blinded by the light, and then slowly learned the truths of the real world. He returned to the cave to tell his friends.

Upon first re-entering the cave, he was blinded by the darkness. Seeing his confusion, and then hearing his assertions about the falsity of the shadows, the cave dwellers laughed at him and scorned him. They determined never to go from the cave and to kill anyone who tried to lead them out. (Plato had in mind the killing of Socrates.) All great thinkers and observers have encountered cave dwellers. Dr. Quimby's healing work dealt with one problem, false beliefs. These shadows or false beliefs, not wisdom, he found to be the cause of disease. Quimby often told of his experience with the opposition of the cave dwellers of his day. He lived almost all of his life in Maine, was a clockmaker, daguerreotypist, and inventor who obtained patents on a lock, chain saw, and steering gear for ships. But his most important contributions followed his investigation of mesmerism and the interpretations of it given by several of its practitioners, who might be called America's pre-Socratic philosophers. In 1830 Park Quimby entered his career as a healer through the study and demonstration of mesmerism. A true scientist, he experimented and observed. He rejected mesmerism as a deception, but these experiments and his later studies taught him the true nature of disease and the true method of healing. After twenty years of healing practice in Portland and Belfast, Maine, he began to write notes recording his observations and his knowledge for an intended book. His notes are a daily journal, repetitive and disorganized. Because his notes were not published until sixty years after his death, and were incomplete and difficult to read, Quimby is little known even to those who acknowledge him as the origin of their beliefs.

Quimby believed: "Make man responsible for his beliefs and he will be as cautious in what he believes as he is in what he sees or does." He also believed that women contain more spiritual wisdom than men, and their wisdom is not of this world, but of a higher power. He further believed the mind of the female contains more of that superior substance required to receive the higher development of God's Wisdom. Doctor Quimby had a clairvoyant gift and a strong ability to empathize. He had the ability to "clearly see," to clearly sense, the feelings of his patients. It was his great power of empathy, coupled with his analysis of false beliefs that made him a miraculous healer. All opinions of the world opposed his science: the church, the medical faculty and spiritualists. In this too, Park Quimby was united with the great thinkers of all ages.

He gave many demonstrations of mesmerism, including to some extent, its healing powers. Quimby came to question accepted theories of what was happening in mesmerism and eventually developed his own system of spiritual healing, in which the emphasis was on the action of God, rather than merely the influence of one human mind on another. Quimby believed that he had rediscovered the healing method of Jesus. Quimby received almost no formal education, but was far from unaware of philosophical thought, especially common sense realism, which was important in his day. He referred to his outlook by various names, including "Science of Life and Happiness" and "Science of Health and Happiness." Occasionally he referred to his work as: "Christian Science." His spiritual relationship with patients centered about the conviction that man is spirit, created into the image and likeness of wisdom, with an unchanging true identity to be summoned into activity. Thus the creative phase of his work was outstanding. He had a true religion to offer to his patients, displacing the 'false identifications' of the old order of things in the churches.

He believed that powerful intuition was latent in each of us, but more so with women, therefore there is some common ground of spiritual powers in our primary self. He felt there must be some way to arouse the latent primary self in the patient. This could not be accomplished by a word of command (as in hypnotism). The real self could not be aroused by mere suggestion. It must be appealed to by Truth, by what Quimby called Science. The power of this spiritual appeal can be nothing less than Wisdom (God or Spirit). Quimby was led to this conviction because of the uplifting advancements and insights of his inner experience when sitting by the sick, inwardly seeking to heal them and set them free. He found that the life or power with which his spirit came in contact on the higher activity level was not an energy he controlled or tried to control. His objective was to rise from the level of natural mentality to the level of divine creation, so that the imagery and efficiency of perfect health should utterly dispel the disturbing patterns, repressed emotions and the other adverse mental factors. The greatest step made by Quimby in developing his technique was in realizing that the primary self— created and reared in the image and likeness of Wisdom for health and freedom, spiritual living and spiritual progress— is not sick, does not sin, is not really the slave it appears to be. Quimby believed that many religious beliefs of his day were at the bottom of much illness, so he had to help his patients escape from theologians as well as physicians. The whole process at work in the "silent treatment" was indeed silent because Quimby found that he could work directly with the patient's subconscious, could address himself to the spirit within, in fact that he must do so before the patient could cooperate. He learned how to bring spiritual light into a patient's subconscious in order to heal. On this level there is the peace, which knows no disturbance, fear or illness. On this level there is only love. Then the efficiency is not in the finite thought, the human will, not even in the imagery or suggestion which helps to make the realization definite: the power rests with God as Wisdom.

For there is no strength in anything human that is not in deepest truth a sharing of divine power. He found that beliefs create disease. His ability to heal every form of illness was extraordinary. People by the thousands came from all over the country as word of his healing powers spread. He truly believed that happiness is determined by belief and that life responds to our beliefs; and that disease is due to false reasoning in regard to sensations, which man unwittingly develops by impressing wrong thoughts and mental pictures upon the subconscious spiritual matter. He further believed that disease is due to false reasoning, so health is due to knowledge of the truth. To remove disease permanently, it is necessary to know the cause, the error which led to it. "The explanation is the cure." Many times he stated that to know the truth about life is therefore the sovereign remedy for all ills. Jesus knew how to cure and Dr. Quimby, without taking any credit to himself as a discoverer, believed that he understood and practiced the same great truth or science.

One of Doctor Quimby's woman patients, an intensely interested student of his science, was Mary Baker Eddy, founder of the Christian Science Church. She publicly stated, "Without Quimby there would have been no Christian Science; Dr. Quimby was not only a philosopher but a brilliant scientist who discovered the true cause and cure of disease after long years of diligent laboratory experiments."

In the beginning of her channeling, Dr. Hunter would use a loud ticking clock to put herself into a trance, but eventually she found just by clapping her hands twice she could achieve the trance. Initially this form became her main spiritual work. While under this self-induced trance, where Dr. Hunter would appear to be asleep sitting up, Quimby (he referred to himself as Ralph Gordon, his name in his next re-embodiment) would "take over" and speak through her.

Every reading started out:

Date: —
Location: —

We're going to have an appointment with, and I'm going to let them speak their own name. We're going to surround ourselves and this room and everyone in it with the pure light of the Christ. So that nothing, beloved Father-Mother God, shall enter but that which is for the benefit of each and all.

And so, as we come into this great court with thanksgiving and enter into these greater moments with pride, we bless you and thank you for the privilege of sharing with this our beloved son, and with all that are present.

She would then clap her hands twice, very loudly. Then another voice came out of her, louder and masculine, "Alright, beloved one of the light, this is the inner consciousness of Dr. Ralph Gordon and I'm going to speak to you from the 5th plane, and the 17th chair. Now, beloved Son of the Light, as we are entering into your life stream: (He would then relate pertinent information from your past lives.) It was really weird. When she gave a reading, she would appear to go to sleep with her eyes closed and her head and hand would droop. All of a sudden, she would sit straight up and Dr. Gordon would speak through her. If you closed your eyes, you would swear it was a man speaking. He obviously used her vocal cords, but the diction, and everything was different. He would apparently read from the akashic records, and these readings would go on for about an hour. Then at the end he would say something like, "Now Gordon, returning my child to awareness..." Dr. Hunter, once again, would slump over, and then she would say, "Come on, wake up, wake up, wake up. And she would wake up. It was an incredible experience for people because they knew this was information that pertained to them; it was real. My reading helped me focus my spiritual direction. The information he gave me about my lifetime during the time of Jesus was not only invaluable, but I still hold it dear to my heart. Every morning Dr. Hunter would have inner meditations with Dr. Gordon before she got up. Occasionally her staff would request her to ask Dr. Gordon a question.

Then later, she would have the answer for them.

Settling in Detroit, Michigan, she attracted around forty students of all ages who attended her metaphysical study classes. In between her school sessions she traveled the country to anywhere there were meta-physicians or new-age conferences, lecturing, holding classes and offering Karmic Life Readings. Many people who received readings set up classes and readings for her in their part of the country. An assistant always sat in on the reading to turn on the reel to reel tape and for protection and to hold the light. She charged $35.00 for each reading. She was proficient in Numerology, Astrology and natural health practices. Known all over the country as a "Spiritual Psychologist," she was in demand for lectures and readings and drove from state to state, usually with students doing the driving. In 1964, Dr. Hunter blended Quimby's science with her understanding of the human energy fields (aura and chakras), and with another healer, John-Clarke McDougall, under Dr. Gordon's tutelage, incorporated aura balancing, an ancient Lemurian technique. The main focus of McDougall's collaboration was the use of crystal pendulums. This made possible a transformation of energy at the precise location of the block or distortion in the chakra area in the aura. This technique cleared negativity and karma within the psyche and the aura itself without the need to touch the physical body.

At one point Quimby Center balancers were doing six to eight balancings a day. People would fly in from all over the world for a balancing. At one point I was asked to drive to El Paso International Airport to pick up the wife of a governor. She flew in with terminal cancer and after the balancing, left without it.

Dr. Hunter's astrological chart clearly showed who she was: Through Chiron relating from her descendent, combined with her big Taurus heart and deeply emotional personality, she could tune in on the emotional and psychic state of anyone.

Taurus, the natural physical healer of the Zodiac, was the persona that shone out into the world (11th house) teaching unconditional spiritual love (Through Pisces Jupiter in the 9th house.) Once the mental aspect of her work was communicated, she showed a powerful authority (Mercury trine Aquarius Saturn) that was at odds with the gentleness of the healer.) The power which poured through her (Pluto in 12the house quincunx Scorpio Moon) combined the authority and gentleness to bring about transformative healing through the Chiron, and assisting humanity's move into the Age of Aquarius through teaching freedom as an adjunct to taking full responsibility. Her words could have been like a sword of criticism (Virgo Mars in 3rd House). If one can take the step in humility to speak of her soul path (Moon's Nodes), she was using her innate courage to stand in the world (Aries 10th House), to create a sense of balance in her own life (Libra 4th House) relating to individuals in her own home, balancing, and finding the beauty in them. Her approach was to care for others, with a tendency to take responsibility for them (Cancer/Capricorn horizon); her personal aim would have been to go it alone, in spite of the spiritual need to relate deeply, lovingly with others. (Astrological information from www.soulastrology.com)

Many of us saw her phenomenal caring as an enlightened spiritual teacher. And many more, to this day, harbor ill feelings toward her. She was a master at forcing students into completing unresolved issues. She appeared angry most of the time, but it was years later that I realized she used anger as a tool; that she probably wasn't angry. It was just an act. What was interesting to me was her ability to keep students "in" their unresolved issues, one of the reasons it was so difficult studying with her. She was relentless. She kept everyone in constant emotional flux. To outsiders we must have appeared masochistic, as she screamed at, berated, made fun of and put us down. She did anything she had to do to get you through whatever you were going through. In retrospect, there's no doubt in my mind how much she loved us.

And she had a wonderful sense of humor. Those not on the proverbial shit list, got to experience it often. And if you didn't like it, there was the door. Her ability to "be in loving" was always consistent, as she couldn't care less what anyone thought of her. Her main agenda was your completing your unresolved issues. She rarely slept and everyone had to stay up with her late at night, sometimes beyond 2 A.M. On many occasions I would walk into the center late at night and there would be a half-dozen people dozing around the living room with her holding court. She never minded the sleepers as long as they were in the room. With her ability to see spiritually, she always knew when her student balancers got into egotistic places, where occasionally they thought they were doing the work rather than spirit. Then she would take them out of the balance room until the proper adjustment took place, from days to weeks. Many students shared that when they finally got from anger and resentment, and started taking responsibility for themselves, and stopped denying who they were, they were able to get to the love and gratefulness they had for her. Some of her former staff felt that here was a person who finally understood them, who loved and supported them. Obviously, it was tough love also. It was senseless attempting to be anything other than what you were around her. If there was something you were hiding, she always knew it. There are spiritual teachers that have a presence and what they emanate from their own energetic field is so powerful that when a person comes in contact with it, the effect is one of hitting all those dark areas within us and pushing them up into awareness for us to deal with. She had absolutely no need for approval. She had this solid awareness of who she was and what she was here to do. She couldn't care less whether you liked her or not.

Once, one of her students told her, "I feel like running away."

And she said, "I'm not your mother. I'm not your friend. I'm your teacher."

But she did function in those other roles also, and the bottom line was, "I'm your teacher and don't run away." She was also always feeding people, making meals or chicken soup.

To this day I have trouble with people calling Dr. Hunter, "Neva Dell," probably because I was so intimidated by her. In Michigan in 1973, she informed her staff, "it is disrespectful to call me Neva Dell, so from now on you will call me Dr. Hunter."

Besides training certain staff to balance auras, most of them also functioned as light bearers, during balancings. They helped provide energy in a non-judgmental space. Learning to remain neutral and hold their loving, light bearing was a teaching tool to learn to be in a neutral place. With new balancers Dr. Hunter always came in after a balancing to check. She had a certain ability to see if there was some part that was not complete and she would just say a couple of words and finish it up if necessary.

After creating Quimby Center, there was a two-week metaphysical conference in her home every year. There were always many attendees and lectures.

In the beginning of her Southern New Mexico work most people were interested in one of her karmic life readings. That really was the main attraction. She had a large reel to reel tape recorder. Students would be in the room with her while she was doing the reading so that they could turn the tape over and also function as a light bearer. On the road they had two rooms in a motel and she would do karmic life readings in one room and the staff would do balancings in the other.

Just prior to my tenure with Dr. Hunter, I was accepted into a prestigious craft show in Las Cruces. I had thousands of dollars of my silver work for the show and very little cash. Rather than risk losing the opportunity to study with Dr. Hunter, I cancelled my participation in the show. During a Quimby Center conference, Dr. Hunter set time for me to demonstrate my silver work to her captive audience, with the possibility of my selling some of it. She called me up front and introduced me, then stood next to me waiting for me to begin. I turned to her with a big smile and kiddingly said, "You're excused!" Lord would I ever learn!

I knew immediately from the daggers piercing my thick cranium that she didn't think my remark quite as humorous as I did. She reluctantly left the stage. Too late, I realized she would patiently await the appropriate punishment.

Shortly thereafter she told me to attend an evening meeting in the dining room. When I arrived, she was sitting with one of her staff. She told me to sit. Than she proceeded to tell me I was worthless and impossible to work with. She wanted me off the property the next day. As I was leaving the room, she casually remarked, "And your truck is going to blow up!"

I was actually quite relieved to be leaving and for the first time in a long time I had a good night's sleep. Next day, as I was packing and getting some of my tools out of the garage, she introduced me to a man who was there for a reading. During the conversation he shared that he lived in Oro Grande, south of town, a small mining town on the El Paso, Texas highway and he was a silversmith. I shared my dilemma with him and he invited me to stay at his house and use his silver shop.

Finally my '54 Chevy panel truck was loaded and I was ready to go. I turned the key in the ignition, the motor kicked over and a valve spring broke, forcing a valve down onto an upcoming piston which ended in the oil pan in a hundred pieces. I was pissed. I really thought she had done it. I loaded all my stuff into his car and we drove to his place. I had a bunch of jewelry and very little money. Oro Grande with one bar, one restaurant, and one gas station, was probably the all-time most desolate place I've ever been. The town was two blocks long with a handful of houses. Dry, hot, flat, rattlesnake-laden desert. Mining activity in the Ore Grande area goes back several hundred years when Indians would mine turquoise. In 1898, a 6 ounce gold nugget was found near what became the Nannie Baird Mine. A smelter was built at the town of Oro Grande. It ran off and on due to lack of ore. Principal ores were gold, copper, iron and a good deal of turquoise. Other valid minerals from the Nannie Baird were calcite, chalcopyrite (a major source of copper) garnet, hematite, limonite, pyrite and quartz. The mine consisted of several 150-foot-plus vertical shafts.

My new friend and I eventually worked part-time at the old turquoise mine in return for stone for our silver work. My friend's house sat two blocks off the main highway.

The only restaurant in town served mostly greasy-spoon type food. Toward the end of my stay in Ore Grande, as I didn't have transportation, I took a part-time job as a dishwasher in the place in return for meals. I had been into healthful food for years and these meals were borderline painful heart attacks on a plate. I believed until I could stop judging this food, I might be stuck there for a long time. The people who were taking care of my goat herd in Belen, New Mexico, agreed to tow and store my Chevy panel truck, until I could move up there and overhaul it.

Sundays, I would hitchhike to Alamogordo to participate in Dr. Hunter's Sunday class. She told everyone not to let me in their house as I was a thief. No one was allowed to talk to or have anything to do with me. I was like the leper with the bell around my neck, and was allowed to sit in the corner of the back row. In the Sunday class, Dr. Hunter would channel Dr. Gordon from the other side. As I had made friends at the center, my isolation was even more difficult, for no one would dare disobey her, except perhaps me, but I was the designee.

In retrospect, this isolation was perfect for me. From a childhood of abuse, I had major trust issues, was a loner and pretty much stayed by myself. She put this pattern right in my face and I didn't like it. Finally, after approximately seven months, I was ready to leave purgatory, overhaul my truck and move back to Taos.

A few years after I left Dr. Hunter I was married on Lama Mountain north of Taos New Mexico. An old Quimby friend contacted me and asked if I was angry at Dr. Hunter, as I didn't invite her to my wedding. I thought about that for a while and decided to write her and thank her for all she had done for me. Her return letter was tear stained and one of her staff told me she wept as she answered my letter. She shared with me that there was only room for one spiritual teacher at Quimby Ctr. HUH?

It took me over thirty years to understand what she meant. At the end of this chapter, there are two channelings from Dr. Hunter from the other side. The McNames channeling is amazing as Dr. Hunter apologizes for being such a bitch and explains why.

Dr. Hunter passed away January 27, 1978 and I was told inside that I had inherited her two main aura balance crystal pendulums. The keeper of the crystals Ellevian Power (next chapter) laughed and said, "No way!" So I forgot about them.

Twenty-five years later, after being prompted by my inner spiritual team, I called her and reminded her that Dr. Hunter's two crystals belonged to me. She again stated "No way!" I told her she wasn't getting that information from spirit. She was quiet for a while then said, "Oh my God, they do belong to you." Thank you! She asked if she could keep the smaller one until she passed to use in her work and she would mail the large one. Fine.

After her passing her son mailed the oval one. I use both in my balance work. They are beautifully faceted and powerful.

Dr. Hunter from the Other Side

THE "PREFACE" FROM DR. HUNTER'S 1960
BOOKLET: "WHY A KARMIC LIFE READING?"

WE CAN BEGIN TO UNDERSTAND MAN'S POSITION IN *the divine scheme if we consider what the modern physical and metaphysical sciences are demonstrating today in the search into karma and reincarnation. When we understand these thoughts sufficiently, we undergo a mental transmutation so that our lives become oriented to new values and new powers in attunement with the New Age. Our minds are such that once we have fully grasped without prejudice the interdependent ideas of karma and reincarnation; we have a buffer for life's problems. When we reach the point where we accept a Karmic Life Reading, we embark on a fascinating exploration.*

A person's Karmic Reading always indicates his home planet, and suggests the impulse, which sent him on his journey to earth. Much of mankind's present day confusion has been created by separatism from the planetary system. However, when man became expressive of self, moving toward universal love, he made a reversal to his true nature. We are on the way toward a regenerated humanity, toward a different world. A Karmic Life Reading suggests to all individuals a picture of a scientifically practical and spiritually approved future. With a new way of thinking and living, we will enter the gateway leading to the Heaven on Earth, which lies within us!

DR. HUNTER, FROM *THE OTHER SIDE*, 1978

THE SPIRITUAL BOUQUET FROM THE ASCENDED
LADY MASTERS CHANNELED
compiled and published by Samuel George Partridge

DEARLY BELOVED BROTHERS AND SISTERS OF THE LIGHT
*Eternal. I am here, and really delighted, because in your hearts
you have asked for me. There is a beautiful orange candle, which
has just been lighted in my honor; it is truly symbolic of what
had just recently happened to me.*

*I am the Ascended Lady Master, Neva Dell Hunter. And
have so recently joined the Heavenly Father in his realm of
Spirit. The orange candle represents my victory, and truly it is a
victory, to gain the ascension into the light, after a lifetime of
striving, overcoming, and trying to serve humanity in the best
way possible.*

*I am very happy here in the Spirit realm, but I was also very
happy while living upon planet earth, working in the vineyard of
the Father. I had lived many lifetimes before coming to planet
earth, and during that time, accumulated knowledge and
wisdom, which I brought with me to planet earth. I knew when I
reincarnated upon planet earth; it would be my last incarnation.*

*Therefore, I made of my life all that I possibly could. Along
the way I had my heartaches and sorrows. With much to
overcome, because it is not an easy task to go on serving in the
light, trying to enlighten others, trying to bring to them the truth,
the knowledge, the wisdom of which I had gained. Not only in my
lifetime upon earth but also in other lifetimes, because there is
always attached to a mission like this, the negative force, the
darkness, which tries to obliterate the light. I found this situation
many times in my long life. But with the help of the beloved
masters and our God Eternal Father-Mother, I was able to go
right on through and rise above many situations.*

*The reason I am here today is because I do have a bit of
wisdom to share with you, something, which is very close to me
at this time. It is the situation in your world at this present time,
of so many, many people clambering, searching, reaching and
indulging into the black arts of psychism. There is black magic;
there is white magic! There are good psychic phenomena and
there are bad psychic phenomena. So many channels are trying
desperately to find the truth, that they are accepting too much of*

the negative side of this aspiration. They aspire to reach the heights of glory, to reach the realm where they can find real truth, but unfortunately so many are confused at this time, they are frustrated because of their anxiety to make up for lost time, make up for the times when their lives have been wasted, for they have ignored many things which they are now beginning to believe are important. This is why they will grasp at the least straw for this opportunity, and dearly beloved ones of planet earth, you who are aspiring to be channels, truth bearers, teachers, please be careful. Do not test the spirit; do not be taken in by everything that seems to be attractive to you.

This is because there are the lying spirits loose in the world today, and there are also the false prophets. They can appear most interesting, most fascinating, but I am here to tell you that there are so many pitfalls around this pathway.

In my lifetime I did encounter much of this myself. You have to live in the pure, divine light of the heavenly father. Your vessels must be clean, your hearts must be pure, and your thoughts must rise above all negativity of the chaotic conditions in the world. You can do it, although it is a task.

For those of you who sincerely desire to make your Ascension into the light and to rise above any human condition existing around you, you have to be truly a dedicated heart. Those of you who just participate partly in the pattern I have described, will be misled. You will be blocked from reaching purity of the high truth. That is why, if you have binding habits, or if you do not follow the golden rule of loving your neighbor as yourself, or if you do not feel that is the goal, the true pattern of life, then you must change. You must change because you cannot be a true messenger, or a channel for light and wisdom and truth, unless you have prepared your complete physical being, body, mind, spirit, and soul. All of the bodies of your human existence must be ready. You must care for your etheric bodies, as well as your human physical being.

I traveled many places during my lifetime, meeting wonderful people, and I know each time I visited a new place, there was someone there who was lifted and helped. My work was done through channeling. I was a channel and able to help many people in this way. For all of those whom I have known and met, I send greetings and love and I know, if you are one of the ones whom I have told through revelation, you are one of the 144,000 souls, I am here to tell you again, it is true. Believe it, it is true! What a wonderful, glorious thing to know about yourself!

You especially must become leaders in this light work, because all of you are Masters; both the Masters and Lady Masters. This is why you are a chosen one- to belong to the 144,000. I have told you, this was one of my duties, to discover who you are.

My work along this line was interrupted, but only for a short while because I am still doing this work, and still working with people of planet earth. I work with you beyond sleep to quicken your minds and hearts to many things. I made my transition very recently, but only to come into another new dimension. I am working just the same as ever, and it is most delightful. Here I do have advantages, which I did not have while living in a physical body on earth. We are needed. We who have arrived are in a higher existence of service. Those of you who are working toward this goal shall one day live in this exalted place with the father, but I say, only if you live properly, only if you follow through the golden rule, the teachings of Beloved Jesus Christ. Then you can have the pattern for living, which will place you right into the realms of spirit one day.

There are so many wonderful ones whom I have met. The only way I can say it today is to send you blessings and love. There are many whom I am extremely proud of, for their progression in their lifetime, and many of you are doing exactly what you were told to do through the higher spirit, which came through me as a channel. This truly gives me joy because this channeling can be for a wonderful purpose. You channels of earth, you pure channels, are divinely chosen, you are doing the work that is so needed. One day there will be no other way in which to have contact with the divine ones, the masters on high, the higher ones, the heavenly father. You will be the only ones who will be able to bring forth truth from the masters or the ones whom God chooses to come through as earth channels. So, my greatest message today is pertaining to just this; the wonderful channels of planet earth who are needed to do the father's work. Be sure it is the truth; be certain that you are qualified to receive the truth and do not exploit anything just because it seems to be phenomena. This, too, could be great, and this, too, could also *be harmful. I lovingly tell you this, because there are many pure, channels upon earth and they are truly special.*

It is indeed an honor to be contained in this new book, "The Spiritual Bouquet from the Ascended Lady Masters," which is being compiled and published by my friend Samuel George Partridge whom I have met.

We did not know each other long upon planet earth, but we are kindred souls in spirit, and I know he is doing marvelous work. I know he is a living master upon planet earth! He is to be Beloved and Blessed for all of these wonderful things which he is doing through the media of his press, and the media of the books written by those channels who have something to be portrayed to the world and shared. This indeed is his work to do, which he is doing nobly at this time.

Dear ladies, I am happy to speak to you now and to honor you, because you are the divine creation of the family of the world. I know you as women, mothers and wives who stand alongside your beloved husbands more in the future than ever before, because in the days long past, ages past, the women and the men worked together in love and unity and this is meant to be. It is not meant to have this separation, which is so prominent in the world today. This is a phase. This is something people are working out through their own frustrations, and it will all be solved harmoniously one day. It has to be. Otherwise the plans of the Divine Source, will not be finished. You must live together in peace and harmony among all peoples, not just your families but among the whole world. And it is true; the time is getting shorter. The change is going to be upon you, and in this change there will be so many chaotic conditions, but only to those who are not prepared, only to those who have become laggards in the search for truth and light. They will have to pay a karmic debt for their carelessness, for their lack of interest to live in pure light, love and harmony.

Good afternoon, I do have a flower to present to the bouquet, so that you will remember me better, with this token of my love to all of you wonderful children of light wherever you are. I present to you the Delphinium flower, which had always been my favorite.

This is my way of saying how much I have enjoyed being with you. Know that I am standing by to continue my work with all of you.

You will know, if you have an inspiration from on high, that you, too, are one of the 144,000 chosen ones. Think of me, because I no doubt have been able to prompt you from where I am at this time, the same as I did when I was upon earth.

With blessings, and much love.

I am the ascended lady master, Neva Dell Hunter

Dr. Hunter Apologizes After Her Passing

Dr. Neva Dell Hunter
Reading from Lucille Sari McNames
April 23, 1978

THAT PART OF ME THAT WAS NOT MADE KNOWN TO YOU *at the Center, can now flow through... It's true that I learned discipline on other planes, but I carried discipline too far at the center. I see things more clearly now. I now think it's a good idea for all instructors to teach more than a rudimentary grasp of the meaning behind disciplinarian measures. You see, discipline prevents human emotions from surfacing. I felt that because love IS, love need not be demonstrated the way physical love is demonstrated in Earth consciousness.*

I was in a human body myself and I see that the reason for being cantankerous and difficult to live with is due to the fact that I, too, needed to express spiritual and human love, as well. Well, I couldn't do it.

I still can't apologize. I can explain, though. I felt that at the center, I needed only to give service to the father and I was indeed expressing love for "HIM." However, I should have shared the love for "Him" by letting IT flow to my staff! This was my error on Earth. I now realize that I should have called "Quimby" our Center instead of "my" Center. After all, a center should be a reflection of center of spirit. Spiritual love IS and therefore beyond the five senses. When the five senses are emphasized rather than the Spiritual connotations of the father's gifts, I feared that all at the center would suffer more pain, as you have previously. By discipline I felt I was protecting you from further grief and pain, but I now see that I caused more pain. I love all at the center but as explained herein I was unable to tell you. Before coming to earth to primarily teach discipline, I should have taught all connotations of love as expressed in earth consciousness along with expression in spirit consciousness. Until one can let love flow through their being and allow others that flow, you progress little...

I always felt on earth that if one allowed human emotions to surface, this hampered the souls development. Well, that's just not so. It involves human emotions to teach the soul. I knew this but couldn't express this. It was primary in my consciousness that discipline cushions disappointments after one has placed too much emphasis on human emotions. I desired to prevent my staff from further grief and pain, yet cause emphasis on same. Well, I couldn't yield because of my own disciplinarian training that is so very strong in me. Love in me was like the crystal embedded deep within me. So love was closed in the earth cycle.

Listen: I have long known that love is BEING LOVE and I thought love need not be expressed except through loving service to the Father. I dared not allow human senses to interfere with what I'd learned in higher planes.

I see now that to have expressed love...shared love at the center, which would not have interfered in any way with spiritual love. You see, the teacher also learns lessons. It was not until I viewed my earth sojourn that I clearly saw these things, on "film" for what they were worth. Now Quimby Center is a reflection of an etheric center and this is why it must continue to be successful. It shall succeed. Quimby is firmly established and you know it would not be such a successful center without your help, et al. Then too, nobody should feel favoritism. We are all of the ALL and ALL should be shared, equally.... All of you listen. When love finally flows outward, love washes out all of the accrued hostility patterns. This is what you must do. Feel love. Be love, then, let IT work for you, collectively. I am to blame for some of your negative patterns that lie in your subconscious mind area. I want them washed clean for your benefit and for my benefit. Being clairvoyant, I spent too much time on higher planes. Well, a channel can never neglect those with whom he/she is affiliated on earth planes. A team should feel spiritual love and it is OK to express love by touching, or a pat or a hug.

For the most part, this was denied you. As to balance, I am very pleased with the methods. You are succeeding with the balancing. I joined your class one day and your high selves helped to balance my own auric emanations. I did not realize that they needed balancing. Isn't that amazing? You must, all of you, balance with discipline, for lasting results.

I no longer claim Quimby center as "mine," I share it. All belongs to the Father and Centers are reflections, so how could I think it was my very own? I shall help to direct the Center two more years, than I shall be about my Father's business. I sign this message with the Father's seal of love. Accept my love now. Your acceptance of my love now and always is for my own growth as well as for you own growth. Let love glow now and forever through the all. Blessings, blessings. I pour my love upon each of you from the All to the ALL.

I am Dr. Neva Dell Hunter.

Ellevivian Power

In 2003, I FLEW TO ALAMOGORDO, NEW MEXICO for one of my spiritual mentors, Ellevivian Power's, ninetieth birthday. It was wonderful being with her as for over twenty-five years she was instrumental in my work in "Facilitating Spiritual Healing". She was one of Dr. Hunter's lead aura balancers. Although nearly blind and needing a walker, she was still offering her spiritual counseling. Prior to my trip, I had sensed I had earned another initiation and knew Ellevivian could assist the process. The third day of my visit she asked me for an aura balance. I felt honored. One of my assistants participated as a light bearer. We were amazed at the number of angels in the room. The next day she said to me, "Your turn, 3 P.M."

When I entered the light room, she was sitting in the corner in her usual counseling chair. She had me lie on my back on a massage table and told her assistant to open my aura. This technique is accomplished with a crystal on a silver chain swung in a circular motion all around the body. When this process was complete, Ellevivian told the balancer to make a pattern around my body about four inches out with the crystal. She called it a "mantel." When complete she said to me: "Receive the Mantel of the Christ!" Instantaneously, a huge bolt of lightening crashed through the window near Ellevivian's chair and in less than a split second later, an ear-deafening crash of thunder followed. I was momentarily blinded and deaf. Obviously the balancing was over. The next day she told me she brought the mantel into this incarnation and gave it to me.

She wouldn't tell me anymore, she said I'd figure it out. I haven't!

In 1973 I spent a month in the Taos, New Mexico Hospital with a disease never before seen by medical science; my weight was around a hundred pounds and fevers up to 108 degrees. Upon discharge, my doctor told me I was dying and there was nothing medical science could do for me.

He shared that the Mayo Clinic in Rochester, Minnesota wanted to fly me to their facility to check me out. I decided to go home. I was living in a commune teepee. A few weeks later, some friends asked me to come along to Southern New Mexico to a healing center for an aura balancing. Leery of New Age healing, I called my doctor. He had never heard of aura balancing, but felt I didn't have long to live and if it were him, he would go. I come from a lot of abuse as a child, physical and emotional; lots of guilt and lack of self-worth. I believed I was no good and didn't deserve to live, that I was truly a bad person. And when the doctor told me there was nothing medical science could do for me, that I was dying, I was okay with that. Normally people don't want to die, but I was fine with it. I wasn't consciously aware that this death wish was the crux of my problem. So off to Southern New Mexico we went.

As I was so weak and could barely walk, my friends assisted me into the center, a home in a residential part of Alamogordo, New Mexico. I settled on the living room couch to wait my turn. I looked like a hockey stick with hair. Then I was introduced to Ellevivian Power, the person who was going to work with me. At one point, as we were quietly chatting, she said to me in a very loving, motherly way, "Billy, don't you want to live?" and I said, "Uh, I don't know."

And she screamed at me "Then get out!' I thought she meant get out of the house and started to get up, but she didn't mean that. What she meant, I found out later, was:

You have life. If you don't want to live, then get out and let someone else that wants to. That was the essence of what she was saying. I think she was also setting me up because she really got my attention. Then they schlepped me back to "the balance room" (a back bedroom with a massage table in the middle) and they lie me on my back on this table. I thought it really weird. There were also two other people, called light bearers, functioning as neutral channels for the Holy Spirit to flow through to assist with the balancing. They were going to hold the light for me.

I didn't know what the hell they were talking about, I mean, there were no flashlights or anything. There was a candle but no one was holding it. She said a prayer calling on the Holy Spirit, and Jesus. Then she swung a crystal pendulum around me for about ten minutes. Through her direction, I was considering the possibility that, "Maybe I was okay." I didn't understand the purpose of all this self-forgiveness. I experienced energy sensations and feelings moving in and around my physical body, and a mysterious resolution of inner conflicts. At one point, and I'll never forget this, because this is a sweet old lady, it got so difficult for me that I got a little jive, and attempted to avoid some painful issues, So she punched me on the shoulder, really hard. That definitely got my attention. The whole balancing ended with more self-forgiveness, as she tied in some Bible stuff like, "The Kingdom of Heaven is within, and God lives within that kingdom," and, "You're created in God's image." If all of that is true, then how can you be unworthy? It was the first time in my life where I started looking at the possibility that maybe I was OK. I didn't understand the purpose of all this self-forgiveness stuff we were doing, but I went along with it because I didn't want to catch another punch.

After the balancing, I was able to walk back to the house. That evening I had spaghetti for dinner. The next morning when I got on the scale, I weighted 116 lbs. Overnight I had gained sixteen pounds. I didn't eat sixteen pounds of spaghetti. So I'm observing this energy increase, appetite return, weight gain, normal temperature and overall feeling of well-being. Within a few months, I had all of my weight and strength back and the disease mysteriously disappeared. Whatever happened, was working. I was around forty when I met Ellevivian, and I had been drunk for over twenty-five years because I couldn't stand the way I was. So we were dealing with all of that dynamic, all of that lack-of-worth stuff. To this day, they don't know what the hell that disease was. They've got the blood sample. Ain't nobody else got it— because I created it! It was an astonishing experience.

In 1975, I brought Elle Vivian to Taos for an aura-balancing workshop. At lunch we all went to a local pizza parlor and the twelve of us sat around one long table with Viv and I seated at one end. We were all looking at menus and I quietly asked her if we should get a beer. There was a quiet gasp around the table. I had the menu positioned between the two of us and the other participants. I asked her if she was aware of their reaction. She said: "Fuck'um. Let's get a pitcher." She didn't really drink, but I loved her feistiness.

In 1945, Elle Vivian was in San Francisco awaiting her husband's discharge from the Navy. Since his enlistment during World War II, Elle Vivian had become involved in her spiritual quest, studying with her first spiritual teacher, Josephine Taylor. In September of 1945, Ms. Taylor channeled an inner plane document called "Special Recordings of Plans for World Improvement" or more commonly, "The Fifty-Year Plan for the Earth," and gave it to Elle Vivian. She was advised not to share it with anyone until the time was right. In the forward by Robert D. Waterman, Ed.D., one of Dr. Hunter's students states: "It is a little known document that was given to Elle Vivian Power as a means of focusing—as a means of anchoring ideas, magnetizing awareness in popular consciousness, and promoting action." When she met Dr. Hunter in 1963, she knew the time was right to share the plan. Copies were made and sold and given away throughout her life. (Complete plan at end of book)

Elle Vivian and her husband moved to Alamogordo to be full-time members of Quimby Center in the mid-60s when she began her balancing training. Over the years she would talk about Quimby Center being a bridge between the times of the Piscean Age and the Golden or New Age. She saw the Piscean age starting with Christ's saying that the kingdom is within but everyone still saw God on the outside. She would say that people come to healers to have them tell you what to do (God on the outside again). Facilitating people within is the way to show the New Age and the purpose of this new form of education (Quimby Center, now Southwest College of Life Science in Santa Fe, New Mexico) is to honor the inner knower and allow God on the inside to inform one of one's journey. She also taught about the mystical marriage, the true meaning of the experience of the Christ light within, when the polarities are united through working out our separation with mother/father God that symbolically are illustrated to our personality through the wounds we come to take on from our parents whom we mistake for mother/father God. After moving my family to the Alamogordo area to be near this work, my wife and I built an 18-room home on a small ranch, which was eventually licensed as a Children's Residential Treatment Center. Elle Vivian was on our Board of Directors. (See author's first book *Friends of the Children.*)

As I was intrigued with the aura balancing process and as Dr. Hunter had passed away, I asked Elle Vivian if I could apprentice with her. No! But she told me I could occasionally hold the light during balancings. Thus began a twelve-year silent apprenticeship. Three or four times a month she would call and ask me to hold the light. I was in awe of how she would simultaneously direct one eye at the client and another into the inner planes to get the information behind the scenes where the problem had been created. She knew that like a "cut down" tree, if you didn't get to the "roots", it would grow back, shrub-like.

She could always see exactly where the problem was created, whether in this or another lifetime. I felt traditional counseling dealt mainly with "effect" while this work dealt with finding and eliminating the "cause". So by observing her work over the many years, I learned the process. I've known all along that no one can teach a student "how to" listen to spirit. We all must learn this one on our own.

One day, after a few years working in the balance room with her, after the pre-balancing counseling, she handed me one of her chained crystals and said "Open the aura."

"Huh? What?" I sat there dumbfounded.

She asked me, "How many years do you need to sit here before you get it?"

So, I took the crystal and, as I had seen her do countless times, opened the aura. When that was complete, she said, "Nice crystal work." From this point, she would occasionally bring me into her work. While reading one of the Austrian anthroposophist Rudolf Steiner's books, I came across an entry that intrigued me. Steiner believed that many emotionally disturbed children were not completely incarnated, and the work to bring them fully here is done in their sleep. We decided to work with two of the younger children in their sleep. After the younger boy was asleep, with Susan as light bearer, I gently held the chained crystal near the child's stomach. It started moving in a clockwise circular motion. The energy was so strong, I knew something was happening, though I had no idea what. When the crystal came to a stop, an astonishing thing occurred. An invisible hand wrapped gently around my wrist and moved my arm over the child's heart. Then the crystal swung in a large arc. At that moment, I became aware of another presence in the room. I looked at Susan, and she said two words, "Guardian Angel." Simultaneously, we both knew an angel had appeared to be with this child. This humbled us, and we were eager to work with the older brother. The next night, while working in the same form with the sleeping sibling, the experience wasn't as powerful, but we were aware that something extraordinary was happening. I had much to learn about this healing form.

The following week, when their caseworker arrived for a site visit, she was astonished at the change in the boys.

Special Recordings of Plans for World Improvements

As presented to Ellavivian Power by
Josephine Taylor, September 1945

I AM MOTERLIN, AND HAVE RECENTLY BEEN ASSIGNED *to duties relative to the Earth Planet and the New Order that is now being born upon it. I came here from a very large Holy City located much nearer to the Planet Jupiter than to Earth. A group of about five thousand of us have been studying and preparing for many years for this assignment. We knew that when the Earth Planet reached this place in her evolutionary experiences we would be assigned to her. Our group consists of scientists of every kind, artists, specialists in economics and continental and intercontinental organization. It is our special assignment to work out system and order international understanding and cooperation among the various races and countries upon the Earth Planet.*

Due to the conditions we have found, it will be quite necessary for us to use speedy and drastic measures. We must keep before us continually the ultimate accomplishment desired and not be affected by the seeming destruction as we force old systems aside and bring in the New Ones.

This will entail the rushing into strategic positions of danger and authority of many people who have been prepared for this moment. Many of these people will meet with what you call death. But they will perform their destined tasks. It is essential now that many people be brought from seclusion and be placed in active public service.

There will appear many seeming tragic and destructive schemes— but they will be used as tools in the hands of Destiny.

During the next fifty years we have an assignment to accomplish certain definite results regardless of outer appearances. This we intend to do.

The TEACHER writes:

The entire personnel of assigned workers for this fifty-year period are now in their places, having accepted individual and collective duties, which will result in a really beautiful and peaceful Planet.

Many of the new workers are functioning in bodies of great density— quite close to the human levels of people living in physical bodies. In order that this program may function with as little friction as possible, it is necessary that hundreds of earth-dwelling citizens, who have been prepared for this time but are now unknown and unheard, be placed in positions of their destined authorities. These people are going to be protected from interference by guardians who will never leave them so long as they have need of Earth bodies. This type of guardianship differs considerably from that of power and light radiation from Teachers and from special power centers. The guardian takes on a special kind of body and functions in the strata of his world much as you do. There will be three guardians assigned to each person so qualified. They will work in shifts so that each has a rest period at regular intervals. These guardians have come from special training schools located in various parts of the universe. They have known of this assignment and have been studying the entire history of the Earth Planet from every conceivable angle. All have had its geological, astronomical and astrological history. They know the over-all pattern of destiny for the nations and races, the destiny of the key peoples who are now being moved into positions of special action.

The political, economical, industrial, educational and cultural trends are well known by them.

This sure knowledge that they bring into the atmosphere of the human brains of Earth will add impetus and power to the advancing program in every way. This type of guardianship does not interfere with the freedom or free will of the individual. They remain free to act in the strength of their own talents and natural genius. The guardian makes a condition in which it is impossible for the person's freedom to be suppressed or his valuable and vital avenues to be used for any other purpose by entities of selfish or unprincipled inclinations. Then, as I said, the presence of such guardians within the human family will be as light and love to the whole.

The executive headquarters for both the planet and the universe remains in the holy city located above the Mt. Shasta area. Many of the friends you know are still there. There very special area has been cleansed and purified in atmosphere immediately over the Pacific Ocean just a few miles out from San Francisco, where entirely new "Islands in Space" have been created and upon which living facilities for all guardians working this side of the Rocky Mountains have been built and supplied with all the needs for their comfort and existence. A similar place has been created over the vicinity of the Great Lakes for guardians working on the other side of the Rocky Mountains. These two take care of the United States only. There are others for each continental area upon the planet. They are located and distributed in relation to the populations of the various areas. You can readily see what powerful centers of protection these "Space Islands" are. They constitute protective screens for all countries within the radiance of their atmosphere. There were many reasons and many strategic points to be considered when choosing the locations for these "Islands". Now every one is completed and inhabited. By the first day of October every member of these "Islands" will be on his or her assignment. This entire project has been kept in the darkest secrecy until August 1st this year. It is one of the greatest of the kind ever attempted. We believe it to be the most valuable contribution toward establishing planetary unity.

Basically every human being really desires planetary unity, but the various pressures and problems of daily living obscure the ways and means of attaining it for many. You will receive papers on the various working plans and systems. We are desirous that you and your kind know as much about what is being done as possible. Later when the new global maps are completed, we will be able to show you many things of vital interest.

MOTERLIN writes:

With the help of the guardians about whom your teacher told you, we hope to gradually spread a network of power over the entire Earth that will hover so close to the human brain that no destructive or mean plan or idea will find lodgment there.

The humans upon Earth today can be, roughly speaking, classed in seven major groups or gradations of intellectual advancement. (I use the word "intellect" here in its past tense.) This does not, of course, include those who are dwelling in physical bodies who are the great ones functioning on special assignments. These seven gradations represent some in the very lowest scale of evolution to the very highest, who can be permitted physical bodies. It is the present plan to locate the members of each of these seven gradations throughout the planet, whoever they may be, regardless of race or color. The planet has been divided into seven major localities or divisions. (When you get the new global atlas, I will mark the divisions for you.)

There is a group of our workers, including guardians, assigned to each locality. The number of people in each will be carefully studied and listed in the seven gradations of intellect. From this report we can quickly know exactly how to adjust the needs of that locality. Each locality great one who is responsible for making the reports will have a listing of all kinds of production and of all kinds of needs for his locality; also a list of talents of the people and their desires. These talents will be those natural to the basic creative lines of the people, not necessarily surface inclinations. Same with desires.

All of these locality-working groups will report to the one great planetary center in the holy city over the Mt. Shasta area.

This center is the highest in space of them all; also the highest in power, authority and love, and stands as a tremendous pure star from which all of our communications with each other take place. Imagine the large seven-pointed star at the top, and going out from each point is a great number of communication lines to the smaller stars which represent the seven localities or area divisions. From each of these there flows to the ground level of the earth, innumerable lines of communication to the guardians and other assigned out of these control centers to the people of the earth. This gives you an idea of the working base.

As the destined people are found on earth, they will be quickly moved into positions of power line anchorage. This is one of the most important things now. Because, as you were told before, the new world order is complete and lying now within the auric atmosphere of earth. Gradually, this New Order will filter through into the minds and hearts of people. We must find honest and pure-thinking people in all lines of scientific research and endeavor so that they may be the ones to give expression to the new discoveries and new formulas. We must prevent, at all cost, the releasing of these great new truths by unprincipled or selfish people.

The New World Order is divided into seven major cycles of releasement or revealment through the human race on earth. It is so arranged that all phases of human action and organization should experience changes in balanced proportions. It is the imperative and unswerving purpose of our assignment to guard and direct this "filtering through" to avoid unnecessary destruction and chaos. We know there will be much opposition and attempts to blast huge openings into the artic circle of the earth in order to create confusion and try to cause the humans to lose faith in the great signs of the future. This will not happen. All purification of brains and human forms will take place in the areas lower than the artic circle of the earth.

We have already created a powerful magnetic band of such depth around the earth that nothing at the present time can reach through or beyond it that is functioning at a rate of vibration lower than what is safe for the new world order. And that includes no selfish, mean or destructive motive, I assure you. We have tested this new protective band many times and know it is solid.

So, because of this arrangement, all evil and out of place motives and desires will have to be fought out and cleared below this level. It will be a great comfort for you to know that even if there are some things on earth that look pretty bad— that is the worst. It gets better the further from earth you go.

The principles of the atomic bomb were purposely released and applied. Now an entire new group of young scientists are being gathered around the whole basic idea, and they will release the applications of the principles for advanced, peaceful living which are the principles of the basic foundations for the new world order.

Upon the principles of Radar will evolve the first recognition on Earth of possible planetary communication. Now that we have the New World Order for the Earth protected from attack from beneath and also from attack from above, we know that the handling of the purifying and organizing within the human races upon the earth will be but a matter of stern discipline and efficiency. San Francisco, California is now the magnetic center of the planet. From there will originate and go forth the major part of Laws and Principles of Procedure for the New World Order. Out of what is now called the United Nations Organization will evolve the Planetary Congress, and the members of this group will eventually appoint or ask one to act as Planetary head. All peoples of the earth will have an opportunity to vote for this one. He will be an American. He, with the aid of the Planetary Congress, will select a body of twelve people to act as his council. Under the Council of Twelve will be the United Nations. Eventually every country on the Planet will belong to the United Nations.

Destiny decrees that the United States of America act as the guiding spirit of freedom to the rest of the Planet. Knowing this, the President and every state official must do all in their power to cleanse the area for which they are responsible. There is an immediate need for every alert citizen, especially the young ones, to urge and insist that all the all-over pattern of national behavior be improved. There must be immediate education all over the United States, by propaganda and the purest kind of nationalism and idealism, for the purpose of building such a high degree of respect and love for the principles upon which the United States was originally based, so that every citizen of the

United States will feel himself personally responsible for the character and moral standing of the nation. This love must be real and true, yet firm and unwavering, but with a simplicity that permits of no swaggering or selfish boasting. The United States cannot miss her present assignment. She must accept this tremendous task of leading and guiding and loving the Planet into one harmonious working unit. Many of these countries will be difficult. There will need be the greatest understanding and tolerance ever known on a planet. Some countries will be similar to catching a large fish – there will be need of relaxing the line many times and with and with steady patience and kindness leading them step by step to an understanding of cooperation. The young people of the world must be permitted to hold many strategic positions of international responsibility. They will be more willing to devote their lives to selfless idealism than the older ones. There has never been a time in the history of the Planet that offered so much to so many. No greater thrill was ever offered the human race than to bring into being this great new world that is here. Every possible effort must be put forth to help the young people see and feel this beautiful opportunity. Enthusiasm endowed with pure imagination will bring through the essential wisdom for every day's needs. This enthusiasm and eagerness to sustain the new world in freedom will completely dissolve evil and all its attributes when applied in love and true recognition of every person on the planet as an essential member of the blessed human family.

MUDOLA writes:

I am a member of the new group now in charge of the Earth Planet for the coming fifty years. My division of the work is entirely with the young people fifteen years old to twenty-five. In making the seven major divisions we segregate the age groups also. All people over twenty-five years of age, unless otherwise assigned, will be scheduled to leave the planet sometime during the next fifty years. Of course, there are many who are scheduled to remain for special work and study. I am speaking of the majority. All people twenty-five years old and under are being given very special care and training. The people who are now fifteen years old will have to hold lines of balance and anchorage for the human race during the closing of this fifty-year cycle and the beginning of the next.

The children under fifteen years of age will be given special guardians and helpers. They will be channels for many new and revolutionary inventions and organizations. They will usher in many systems of human relations that will be startling to their parents and grandparents. Also the children under fifteen now will be the parents of a wonderful race of people. During the next twenty-five year period there will be the farthest intellectually advanced children born into the Earth that the Earth has ever known. People who are now twenty-five and over will give birth to many children during the next five-year period. These children will be the parents of the pre-destined ones who are even now in the great light cradles awaiting human birth. Many hundreds, yes thousands of people from fifteen to sixty years of age will be taken from the planet during the coming five-year period. The numbers will be so much greater than the usual natural turnover that you will be remembering this recording. These will be people who do not fit into the progression pattern and will be taken to other locations more suited to their state.

There may be epidemics of a strange disease that will affect the hearing and the heart. It will be given a name— but there will be no cure on earth— because it will be the result of change of the vibratory rate of the bodies, purposely done to loosen the bodies from the seed atom and give it protected freedom. This changing of the vibratory rate will be done by special Great Ones who are assigned. The lists of names of those destined will be given them in each of the seven localities. One of the most important tasks of this period is the controlling of birth and death of the races upon the earth. It is imperative that this be carefully and accurately done, otherwise the entire program would be endangered. There is a huge Light Candle filled with predestined seed-atoms located in each of the seven localities. These are completely protected and can in no way be attracted to Earth out of time or place. The Seed-Atoms who are leaving the Earth are being cared for according to a definite plan and are not permitted to wander aimlessly or to cling to former possessions or friends. All helpers and guardians for earth people, beginning on September first, 1945, are assigned by us –

no matter what you may hear to the contrary. We are now working diligently to bring about a rapid and world-wide action through the various law and court organizations of the world, to locate and either imprison or put to death all people who are so obsessed by evil forces that they are now beyond hope of salvaging in time for this New World Order. As rapidly as such people are found and taken care of, they will be brought to a healthy state. This can be done much better and more quickly without the physical body. As we have said before, every possible means will be used now to cleanse the races upon the Planet. All young people between the ages of fifteen and twenty-five are being carefully checked and guarded throughout the Earth. This does not mean that every one of them will be an outstanding person or that each one will do a spectacular work or be recognized beyond the limits of an ordinary life.

But it does mean that each one will be given an opportunity to live a life according to the best that is possible considering his background or former existence, his talents and present opportunities. By carefully checking, we will locate many whose condition in time will permit us to use them in our present plan of procedure. We are desirous of these young people bringing in new methods of education and also many new topics of study into the school rooms. Because of the recent rapid trend toward planetary unity, it is most essential that emphasis of all education be placed upon preparing people to become more useful world citizens rather than concentrating upon the limited scope of citizenry for one nation. There must be an entirely different method of teaching Geography and Languages. What we want to happen as quickly as possible is for huge air transports to take groups of Children twelve years old and over, all over the world. These trips should be planned and supervised by adults especially qualified for such work. Children from every country on the Earth should be traveling continually, learning the customs, crafts and languages of as many other countries as possible.

Children who see other countries and know something of the people by meeting and visiting with them, will make intelligent world citizens and will decide whether or not they wish to engage in international service and what parts of the earth interest them most.

We are now holding a series of meeting with Great Ones from all over the planet formulating a plan of procedure for this exchange of child travelers. The children who are given these journeys must meet certain definite requirements in character and scholarship. They must be accompanied at all times by sufficient numbers of adults to assure their health and safety. We prefer that this entire work be managed and handles by some non-political group; preferably by a committee set up within the educational and cultural departments of the United nations; that the representatives from the various countries on this committee arrange for such traveling expenses and arrangements with their individual governments. It would really evolve into a very simple matter to plan such international study groups.

There will be large groups of visiting students of older people, college age and older, very soon. This, too, is important, but it is much more important to take the younger children. Children should have the joy and thrill of trying to prepare for eligibility to such educational travel groups as soon as they enter school. Then by the time they are twelve years old, they would have a good idea of what would be expected of them. Particularly, should artists and scientists of all countries become acquainted with each other. They are always in the front ranks of the builders of nations.

Every year, beginning just as soon as it can possibly be arranged, there should be people representing the educational institutions of every country on the planet meeting together and exchanging ideas and plans relative to building this international education project. Out of such group meetings should evolve great and beautiful international festivals of beauty and music. All kinds of outdoor pageants and festivals should be encouraged. With air transportation as it is today and with group leadership developed to such huge proportions as have been evidenced in the Great War – tremendous festivals on land and water could be produced and people from all over the planet could attend easily. World Unity makes possible tremendous activities in every creative line.

These new productions should be based upon new ideas and not be patterned after something in the past. There must come new forms in drama, dance, music, design and all the arts that will be in harmony with the enlarged scope of world action and world citizen participation. The basic need right now is for all people to enlarge their individual scope of thinking and imagination to the circumference of the planet instead of just their own country. The entire approach to child education must be changed. Just as soon as we can impress upon the minds of people (especially scientists and students of the physical body,) the basic truths of its fundamental structure and its relation to the planet and the universe, we will be able to instill an entirely different attitude toward the body and life in general.

But for the immediate moment we are hopeful of bringing a new method of physical education into practice. We believe that through the practitioners of Light and Radio Therapy we will reveal the major electric and magnetic centers of the body and their close alliance with the brain. Then through this, gradually release the idea of using thought as the greatest tool for physical education, instead of exercises of the muscles with no understanding of the basic reasons. There will be classes of instructions on the meaning and value of flexibility and body coordination with the brain and other vital centers. Instructions will be given on the vital power centers of the physical body and how to use them, so the physical education will be a scientific study of the physical body for use and maintenance, and not the blind senseless thing that it is today. With the above discoveries established in acceptance by the human brain, the next step will be recognition of the great lines of communication with the great source— the origin— God. During the period of transition from the present methods of so-called psychological study and research to the new method of opening original lines of communication with the great reservoir of all wisdom, there will be many children and young people discovering these avenues for themselves. They will have no fear of their new experiences because the assigned guardians will maintain an atmosphere of safety and confidence. In such an atmosphere, growth and expansion will continue naturally. As the young people grow and take their places in the mechanical and industrial world, they will establish new methods based upon their personal experiences. With development and clarification of the microscope and other highly sensitive instruments, it will be possible to photograph the power and light centers of the physical body. This discovery will usher in the new era treatment for all body and mental ailments. We intend that the present medical standards of practice be completely exposed and many new treatments introduced within the coming five-year period.

The attitude of the majority of young people toward God and Religion will be quite disturbing to many of the older ones. But it will be a healthy and welcome improvement over the past senseless and inadequate religious practices. One of the extremely valuable improvements that will be recognized in the new education of the physical and mental equipment will be the clarification of sex. The children will be instructed regarding the sexual organs, what they are, why they are, when, how and for what purposed they were created and to be used. With true, intelligent and unrestrained education regarding the sexual functions, the greatest dangers and avenues for evil destruction of the human physical body will be eliminated. This paper is not the place for teaching methods or material regarding sex to be recorded. There will be a great one who is a member of our working group in the educational field who will record a special booklet on the subject. Because of the false interpretations and artificial attitudes that have been created around the whole idea of sex, it has become one of the most difficult subjects to clarify within the human consciousness. Of course the immediate major problem confronting us regarding the education and teaching of children is the establishment of an adequate system to inspire adult teachers to better and clearer understanding of what the teacher really is.

Our plan of procedure of accomplishing this is not yet completed. We see the difficulties to be over come very clearly – but – the method of overcoming them – and staying within the laws of courtesy and safety – is another story. At the moment we believe the quickest and best solution is to select certain flexible and dependable people who have adventurous inclinations and by means of continual impressions upon their brains and hearts, inspire them to establish private schools in thickly populated communities; there to carry on these new and revolutionary methods of instruction. From the recognition of their satisfactory results, their methods would be adopted by the public schools and other institutions.

It will take several years we know to accomplish this change, but we are beginning now with the above plan and know that revealment will come to us as needs and opportunities arise. Included in our plans for improvements in the coming era of education of children are many ways of helping them to discover their talents and desires for adult life. Handcrafts, work shops, laboratories, machine shops, electric and magnetic units of experiment and research will be universal and standard equipment for every school. Just as soon as a child starts to school, he will be made familiar with these things to the degree that he/she is able to grasp it. The majority of children, even now, are capable of much more advanced training than they are receiving. Mathematics and all calculus should be taught while the child is doing crafts that prove to him the need for it. The same with most other studies. All study and learning should be accompanied at all times with as much physical action as possible. All kinds of home crafts should be taught in the very early school years, including chemistry of foods and their relationship to the body. All studies should be harmonized to the needs of the community in which the children live. After twelve years of age, they should be able to know the things in which they wish to specialize or concentrate on, then formulate their educational program to conform to the fulfillment of the plans. Every community will have branches of higher learning under the immediate supervision of the educational committee for the district. Smaller working groups under efficient leadership bring much smaller results than schools that are too large. There will be many large schools, too; these will be world colleges where men and women who are preparing for world positions will study the cosmic or universal laws. These schools will be very much like the temple schools of an earlier period in the earth's history. We will not write in detail here as you have had a description of a temple school. The pattern of study and dedication to world service will be similar to all such schools.

Simultaneous with this advance and change in educational methods will be the rapid releasement of thousands of inventions and discoveries that will be used in educational processes and, by their very existence, force new methods as well as thousands of new trades upon the people. Sometime within the coming ten-year period, before Monal and his group leave, the study of the body based upon the premises of mechanics, electricity and magnetics will be the custom instead of the crude studies of today. The greatest contribution to the human race that will result from the recent discoveries about splitting the atom, will be conscious construction and destruction of the basic atoms that compose the human physical body. Within the coming five-year period there will be very little, if any, study of the human physical body based on lifeless tissue. With discoveries and perfecting of the various electronic and magnetic instruments that are already in development process, there will be no need for such. With these new, highly sensitized and perfectly safe instruments, the vital, living body can be observed and photographed even to the change that takes place in brain cells and nerve tissue under the various types of thought and experiences. All of the foregoing also opens entirely new methods for studying natural phenomena of every kind. Botany and the study of every living, growing thing will be completely free to reveal their innermost secrets to all who seek in wisdom and truth. This entire era of scientific progression will teach the human race the basic working laws of natures. People can then work in harmony with these laws instead of wasting time and effort trying to overcome them or break them down. The great ones destined to become embodied upon the earth and lead the races to their illuminated fulfillment, can live and teach in such an atmosphere.

NALUNO writes:

I am a member of the new working group assigned to the earth planet for the next fifty years. My special work is to guide, direct and inspire the people who will till the soil of the earth and be responsible for supplying the natural food for all of the races of people upon the earth. As with other departments of this fifty-year assignment, we have a working group in each of the seven localities. In each locality all soil is being tested for chemical and mineral analysis. The food needs for the type of people living in the locality are listed. The probable changes in land, climate and people are carefully taken into consideration when planning food production. Many of those whom Mortinion and his staff have trained will be born to be active in physical bodies within the next twenty-five year cycle. In localities where the climate is warm enough to eliminate the need for hot food, for comfort, uncooked diets will be encouraged and impressed upon all people. In the colder climates a certain amount of cooking will be essential. It is the present— and analysis of signs for the future indicate— that many people will take advantage of community cooking and serving facilities and will do no cooking in their homes at all. In fact there will be many homes where there will be no cooking facilities, except for small units for an occasional hot drink or something. Even this will be procurable at any time for a very small fee and a phone call. As we speak now of such things as cooking and eating and having practically all labor performed outside of the home, we are aware that it is a little shocking to people of today.

They immediately feel that much of their family and home life is disappearing, but such will not be the case at all. In fact there will be a much closer family relationship than at present. The family will be brought together in different types of interests than now. It will be a very simple thing for families to have their food sent to their homes and eat there if they wish. The present plan is to locate the very best facilities possible in each of the seven sections for providing raw foods. In some countries soil will be tilled and food grown in the ground. In others, there will be vast projects where foods will be grown in chemical and mineral vats. However, due to the efficient and rapid transportation systems, large land areas that are especially suited to the purpose will grow the major part of such things as grains, fruits and vegetables for most of the planet. The World Congress will arrange the production facilities for all supplies to be calculated in world needs, and always the approach to every problem will be from the premise of the earth as a single unit. In this way, the best localities and climate will be utilized for each need, regardless of what race may be occupying them at the moment.

There are many thousands of synthetic products sold as foods today that will be completely eliminated when there is not advantage in monetary gain from its manufacture. We have been quite amused at some of the present food practices of the people. In the coming years— when people learn more about physical bodies and how they function— they will eat food for use. This will in no way detract from the joy of eating. The sense of taste was given man to enjoy, but he has lost the finer flavors and aromas as he has adjusted to bodies of greater density resulting from the cooling and aging of the planet. Now, as the planet ascends into finer atmosphere, and the industrial and scientific progression makes possible a life of great leisure and culture, the human races will again experience much keener appreciation of all the senses. Many excesses of the present day will be eliminated and a balance eventually attained. The eating of flesh in every form will be completely eliminated. In fact, the gap between human beings and animals will widen continually as the new order becomes more freely expressed in the lower strata. Many animals that are used for food today will exist only in menageries and museums to complete the historical records. People will not wear clothing that is made from any part of an animal. Milk, butter and eggs will remain as food the longest of any animal product.

But these will eventually be replaced by new fruits and vegetables that will supply all the body needs. One reason why flesh eating of all kinds will stop is that people now living on the earth who are evolving up the evolutionary path, will either be beyond the need of eating flesh or will be removed from the planet in time to keep from retarding the rest of the people. The members of the human race who originated through the Royal race as human beings practice an unnatural custom, for them, when they eat flesh. They can stop it at any time without harm to their bodies and to great advantage to all body equipment, especially to sensitive communication lines and intuitive perception. As people become more accurately attuned to the higher strata of consciousness, they need lighter foods and less volume. Except in cases where special lines are being anchored deep within the heavy material layers of earth, as the present, then people, through whom releasements are being made, need to eat oftener and will consume a greater volume of food than when they are free from heavier earth vibrations. It is seldom advisable for people to overfill the food capacity. A much better way is to eat at shorter intervals and take smaller amounts at a time. There is a vast difference in the kind and amounts of food that various people need. Bodies vary greatly in their chemical and mineral needs. This is first caused by the composition in the body seed from the parents. This body seed is then influenced by the various atmospheric and planetary conditions surrounding it during the first twelve years of its growth. Mental surroundings and material food consumed establish basic body qualities during the first twelve years. Given a good, healthy and well-balanced twelve-year-old body, the person may withstand many hardships during the next twelve-year period with little damage to the body.

The above is a general statement— as the physical body is greatly influenced by the type of consciousness of the seed atom inhabiting it.

All parents should understand the extreme importance of the first twelve years of existence on earth for the physical body.

When the child is being reared in a well-balanced, quiet, mental atmosphere, it is invariably quite safe to let it choose the foods it ears from the very beginning. Parents should exercise care and judgment regarding the amount and elapse of time between feedings. Of course, there are some children who inherit bodies that are not quite comfortable to live in at first. Sometimes the vibrations from the mother's blood and nervous systems are not quite in perfect attunement with the seed atom who inhabits it. In such cases, the child may be restless and complaining until such time as its own powers, plus foods, succeed in changing the first imbedded vibrations to harmonize with the individual mind that inhabits the brain. When such a condition exists, it is well to feed the child much oftener than the usual habit until it finds peace.

There exists within the consciousness of every living thing, whether vegetable, mineral, chemical, animal or human, a sure knowledge of the correct food for its sustenance and growth. Many people have created artificial tastes and false mental concepts within their body cells and by so doing have buried the natural basic knowledge so deep that only rarely does it have opportunity to come to the consciousness in the brain. When people who have used these artificially created tastes over many years and then have awakened and begin to seek freedom and use of the basic natural knowledge, they usually have conflict within the body until the cellular desires for certain wrong foods have been dissolved. By making the changes and adjustments gradually, much distress can be avoided. Balanced diets of good wholesale foods that are pleasing and satisfactory to the body will play a vital part in establishing permanent peace and neighborly actions between the peoples of the earth in years to come. The best method of arriving at what are the best foods for the body, for an adult, is to consider if the thing desired could have real value or if it is a habit or a whim.

Could it do real harm to the body, brain or nervous system? Is it a builder, a destroyer, or just a pleasure? When the physical body has been properly fed, there should be an all over feeling of contentment; no crowded feeling, no feeling of being over stimulated or a feeling of desire for more food. One should be totally unconscious of any body need regarding nourishment or any body reaction to the food except the natural experience of forgetting it completely. All natural functioning of the physical body is meant to be happy and peaceful, so people should not try to deprive the body of food that they enjoy if they are not injurious or outside the natural trends of body foods. The very fact that a person especially enjoys some particular food is possible proof that the body likes it and assimilates it easily. I'm sure that every adult human being can arrive at a true and accurate decision regarding the proper diet for his body if he is absolutely honest to his conscious guidance. All the foregoing paper will be released in both simple and expanded form into the minds and hearts of the races upon earth.

ALOHA writes:

I am a member of the group who is assigned to the earth planet for the next fifty years. My department is for the purpose of establishing planetary unity in all types of creative arts and to arrange for exchange of artists and their works in all countries. I was aware of your surprise at my signature. It is my true name for the assignment and means understanding in love. As the others who have recorded through you for this group, I am headquartered in the holy city above Mt. Shasta. This department is also represented in each of the seven localities. There are many branches to our work.

The following have the most valuable influence on world unity for the future:

- *Planning departments for teaching basic philosophies of creative arts in public and private schools.*
- *Applying the experimental work to creations and*

activities of daily life, such as buildings, roadways, parks, gardens, designing of all kinds.

- *Establishing world-wide systems of travel and study for all types of creative artists.*
- *Building special galleries and exhibit spaces that will be used to house exhibits and giving musicians, dancers, actors and all types of artists ideal surroundings and facilities for their displays and performances in every locality.*
- *To find and study the natural talents for creative arts in each locality and inspire ways and means of contributing these talents to the world unity program.*

Our method will be to work in direct communication with the special guardians in every locality. They will report to our representatives when they find people, especially children under fifteen years of age, who are equipped to come under our guidance and supervision. After having observed and proven their value— special guardians from our department will be assigned to help them. In a general way, the following system of impressions will be released to them, mainly during hours of sleep. Until they reach an awareness of communication lines vital enough to permit a closer relationship.

- *Close observation of the world around them.*
- *Analysis of form, color, movement and sound.*
- *Vital desires to reproduce what is seen, heard and felt.*
- *Desire to know basic impetus behind all change.*
- *Feeling for size of creation.*
- *Inner urge for silent contemplation of brain action, heart*
- *Action, life forces and nature forces.*
- *Adequate background of techniques underlying all creative arts.*

Out of an adequate recognition of the inter-relationship of all arts will grow the great desire to express their particular work.

At this point their individual lines to the great source will be sufficiently active to let the guardian be only a guardian of the lines and protect the earth-dwelling person from too much interference from individual bigotry or ego, or any quality that would interfere with his destined work. Of course all departments are so closely allied to every other that exchange of materials and instructors is essential. Particularly is this true of chemistry of minerals and metals, light and color, the science of air currents and control of sound and movement of materials.

This method of study, research, practice and application will result in an extremely simple basis for all creative study. There will probably be a period of artistic expression that will appear chaotic, that is, a mixture of many types of experimentation before clarification comes. At no time is a guardian permitted to reveal the answers or results to the student. The guardian may impress upon the students mind a direction of effort or a method, but the answers and results must be left free for the student to discover. The student must be allowed free will at all times. He may be shown the path, the formula or method, but he must never be forced to make a decision, for that must be done of his own complete free will. Only when a student has an especially assigned teacher or master with whom he has completely dedicated his life to a special work or service can he be told at all times what to do and how to do it. Even then he is left with free will, unless in a crisis where his wrong decision would either be dangerous or delay the greater work. The object of all life existence on the earth is to give the person experience and expansion in consciousness.

Out of the program from this department will gradually evolve a much greater appreciation for all beauty. Because of the method used for releasement, all people have access to all that is released from all departments. The type of consciousness and brain of the individual person will determine what kind of wisdom he attracts and to what degree.

A natural inclination toward, and vital desire for, any particular activity will determine, to a great degree, how much the person discovers regarding it. Also, the more a person uses the information he gets and the more he applies the principles to his daily life, the greater will be the inflow. All over the earth planet, in every place where people dwell, research is now in *progress to discover and record those who are equipped to be catalogued in this and other types of training. This research department is permanently established and will operate continually, checking and recording all who are born upon the earth. The inspiring of people for creative action is a most delightful task. At no time are the guardians of earth-dwelling people permitted to be active within the lower strata for long periods of time; that would allow them to become weary or exhausted. They must remain continually at a high peak of joy and efficiency; only so, can we be sure of complete success. When humans learn the art of treating their physical bodies and brains with enough respect to give them proper rest and nourishment, changes of view and atmosphere, pleasing recreation and interest, they will be surprised at how quickly and smoothly adjustments will be manifested that will place them in positions of complete harmony and happiness with their surroundings, their friends and themselves. These are the first basic requirements for correct creative endeavor in the new age. The old human theory that the greatest drama and the greatest creative urge is born within experiences of tragedy and sorrow and deprivation of physical needs is false. It is an untruth released and established by forces whose very existence has been dependent upon such false teachings. The greatest creative urge is always born out of great ecstasy, experienced from the awareness of great beauty, in consciousness. It may be beauty of color, form, sound, feeling, etc., but only from such experiences with beauty can sufficient heights be reached to contact the most powerful constructive forces of creation. It is absolutely necessary for every person to feed their consciousness upon beauty as it is to give the body food.*

The human race must come to realize that time spent in the outdoors communing with nature and time spent in contemplating beauty in any form is not time wasted. Nor should it be considered that such experiences are luxuries – but essential and necessary parts of correct and sensible living practice. The commonly used example of lilies growing out of the swamps, jewels being developed under stress and extreme changes of temperature are all true – true for the things portrayed. These experiences are natural to their growth and development. The human being who is progressing on the evolutionary path has gradually unfolded beyond the necessities. As he reaches a stage of freedom and moves in the finer realms, he leaves behind him the attachments of former laws and experiences. He is born into a different species, a different set of principles. Here he controls the lower influences; they no longer impose their pressures upon him. Man must come to accept these basic truths and strive to maintain his true status upon new heights, and by contemplation of the beautiful strengthen his new lines to the great future. Upon arriving at these heights, he need not expect a life of monotony or of sameness. Always, he lives in the midst of the great ocean of life. Mind and power. The mighty waves carry him into vast peaks of vision and acceleration, into the valley of quiet and seeming inactivity, but to the enlightened one there is always eager expectancy to behold the varied beauties and accept the experiences and expansion natural to his state. These basic principles man must accept and use if he ever intends to experience the greatest ecstasy of creative expression. Through deep inner silence man contacts lines of high vibration over which he feels the unalterable conviction of the truth of the above statements. By accepting this conviction, even if he lacks understanding of its working, he immediately begins this conviction, even if he lacks understanding of its workings, he immediately begins the severing process of his ancient lines to the heavier strata and his former beliefs.

At every attempt to gain workable understanding of his new convictions, his foundation in the new life becomes stronger and the magnetic pull to the former beliefs and resultant acts is weakened until he eventually severs all old lines and he is truly born free into a new world of beauty in which he is a master of the physical expressions about him. The great power lines of attraction to this new world are created from desire for expansion and vibrated by alertness of mind that tries to observe and understand all that surrounds it. They are made strong and unbreakable by the power of love for all beauty. People advancing along these power lines have joy and music in their minds and hearts. The great radiance from such joy and the tones from such music dispel every ugly and destructive movement. In mighty ecstasy the human race upon the earth advances into the new world, there to accept their inheritance of godly beings and contribute their actions to the illuminations of this universe. As the human races upon the earth progress into the greater consciousness of higher strata, it will be possible to exercise very different methods of all teachings that are available now. With the present system of purifying the earth's surrounding atmosphere in operation, there will be no need for special individual guardians for people who are outside the physical body. They will be perfectly safe and free to travel and congregate wherever they desire. The areas beyond the earth's atmosphere are being especially organized now, and great and mighty artists and scientists of every kind are building light and power centers in preparation for the reception and control of the new communication and transport facilities that will be operating within the coming one hundred years. All of the cities, or centers, are much too fine and rapid in their vibratory rate ever to be visible to the physical eye. But they can radiate and control powers that will influence and control areas of safety for those who will be destined to pioneer the outer strata as science and art progress.

We believe that now, in a comparatively short time, possibly in fifty or seventy-five years, cosmic photographers, who will operate special high powered cameras from great heights, will catch the light radiance and forms of some of these centers being built now. At first they will believe them to be just light reflections of the lens, but when they develop and enlarge the plates, they will discover definite form, and from there will be born the new step in photographic research that will prove the existence of great cities in what in now accepted as power-filled space. One of the most interesting "Cities" is now being constructed just outside of the earth's gravitational circle, above where the North Pole is located, during most of the time as the earth makes its journey around the sun. There have been erected tremendous power centers for the releasing of thirteen rays into the earth over the magnetic lines that form the axis. From this center will be sent into human consciousness a vast amount of cosmic science that will be the basic premise for all artistic and scientific calculation and experiment. You will remember that in 1940 Utillergon came from the planet Jupiter and brought the great light sphere that was anchored above the North Pole. Shortly thereafter the scientists of earth noticed strange phenomena there that had not been seen before. This was the real beginning of preparing the Earth for the great city that is now being built. The great light sphere that Utillergon brought acts as the receiver and distributor for these thirteen cosmic power rays. As research in air transportation continues over these northern routes, many new phases of the district will be discovered.

At this time, we are not quite really certain what affect these Power Centers and Cities will have upon the climate of the Earth as a whole. We will not be at all surprised if the cold climates and much of the areas now covered with ice and snow become much warmer, at least at certain times of the year.

There was a time during the ancient days of the Earth, when the most secure places and only secluded places for the great teachers and temples were in otherwise inaccessible mountains. This condition will gradually change. As the ancient members of these orders and temples expand into the strata beyond the Earth, the centers of balance will be completely changed and the chief centers of learning will be located where the greatest numbers of people live. The necessity of keeping the existence of the great ones in Earth secret, will lesson with the incoming of the new world.

Science and art will advance sp rapidly that the natural laws underlying the present "Mystic," "Esoteric," and "Exoteric" teachings will be common knowledge and practice. The great ones, who will be holding the wisdom for the next stage of advance, will have no need to live as the holy men must today. From this time forth, there will be greater and greater revealment, less and less mystery. All things will be proven naturally and there will be a basis of World Unity built upon the elimination of space in time, the understanding of the futility of holding material things as individual possessions, the over-all existence of life, mind and power and the inseparable unity of all races as citizens of THE ONE FAMILY – THE ONE PLANET.

This ultimate condition must begin in the hearts and minds of those in the Earth today who are capable of grasping the vision. It must be held by them with the enthusiasm as a Sacred Trust. To each person so blessed this ultimate condition must be finished and true today; not something to look forward to in a far away time – but here and now – finished and complete. Only so will the anchorage hold without wavering. To you who can grasp this recording with understanding is also given the responsibility of anchorage. These are mighty and beautiful gifts. Hold them in dear and sacred love, knowing that therein are you serving your time and race as few people today are privileged to serve.

RULADA writes:

My committee has complete responsibility for directing people living upon the Earth to locate and bring forth the new metals and minerals that are now within the body of the Earth, that will be needed for the many inventions and high precision tools and instruments of the next cycle of advancement for the mechanical age. As with the other committees, we, too, will concentrate our efforts through assigned representatives in each of the seven localities. Most of our work will be done in the rough and mountainous sections of the country. Some work will be done in sections where recent upheavals have thrown old mountain material to the surface. Due to the work that has been done in recent years with the Sun Rays upon the earth, there has been a gradual drawing and forcing process in action that brings much valuable material near the surface. Much of this has been working up toward the tops of mountains for many centuries. In several of the great mountain ranges of the earth, there is a material that was at one time the original soil of the planet and lay much closer to the Earth's center than now. When the great upheavals came forcing the high mountains forth, this land was raised and for centuries since has been passing through the necessary changes that have created metals and minerals unknown in any other place. We are not permitted to disclose these locations at this time. They must be protected until the proper time for their revealments. These new metals and minerals are of such great value that we are not assigned to expose them until the economic and industrial conditions of the planet are greatly improved. However, there are some very useful chemicals in many of the desert countries today that will be discovered and developed within a very short time. Just as rapidly as we can inspire men to locate and mine them, they may be used. These chemical elements will be found most valuable in mixing with soil in which grains and food stuffs will be grown. It will add the required values to the foods that will help the bodies to be content and healthy in higher and finer vibrations.

With irrigation by water from the air – many of the dry desert areas will become flourishing farm lands. This will probably be within the next twenty-five years. I believe I am correct in telling you that there will be an experimental colony of people located on what is now a dry, arid region. They will build a community and by their combined efforts will have water flown in by air and sprayed over the land like rain. Trees will be grown and in an amazingly short time the trees and shrubs will begin to attract some moisture of their own, and in this way climate in that locality will gradually be changed by the efforts of man. During the next one hundred-year period, there will be more changes wrought by man than in any similar period in history. There will be many large excavations in and through mountainous and hilly countries. While working on these, the new minerals and metals will be found, seemingly by accident. One of these minerals will be extremely useful in the manufacturing of building blocks, which, when heated into a basic formula, will make the block practically indestructible. Pillars and foundations built of these will form the basic skeleton structure for many large buildings and temples. The substance will be poured into moulds while in pliable form. It will take any shape and can be made any color. When it has hardened and "set"— it will be unaffected by the elements or by any ordinary degree of heat from fire. Architects and builders will invent and design new ways of construction and of putting the blocks together. There will be other similar minerals come forth when a stratum of rock is opened that in the ancient of days formed the inside rims of the original canals when the first great expansion of the planet took place. It was not yet soil at that time. There are many of these strata of rock that are to become accessible to man within the coming one hundred years. It is deep within these layers that innumerable kinds of minerals, chemicals and metals unknown to man now, will be revealed that will contribute the necessary steps in man's great expansion upon the future great path of ascent.

By the time these ancient strata of rock are uncovered, there will be people in the earth sufficiently prepared in geological wisdom to recognize their historical value. Instruments will be perfected soon that will amplify the vibrations in rocks and hard packed substances sufficiently to reproduce some sounds. When ancient strata of first rock are uncovered, these instruments will be applied to them. Man will learn much.

There was a very particular and secret work done by the Royal family during certain development periods of planets and universes. When the cooling processes had reached the cracking stage and areas began to solidify, great ones were assigned to make historical recordings in the rapidly hardening substances. Some of these records were spoken into especially prepared and selected places. Upon every planet that has evolved from the great source in any way, these records were made. When the planet and the beings dwelling upon it reach a certain stage in their development, these sacred records are revealed to the people. From these revealments the people know the entire history of their planet and their own destiny. Instructions are also given them from these ancient records regarding their actions, their type of governments and their necessary human relations. These ancient sacred records are never revealed until the planet is completely cleansed from all possible evil tendencies. Never in the history of creation have the sacred records of the ancient day of any planet been refused or abused or doubted by the people. Never have such records met with ridicule, destruction or distortion. If there is a faint possibility of such, the people are not ready to have the great revealment. The place of concealment is never known by anyone dwelling within the planetary circle; only in the records of the most holy place on the great central Sun is the location and approximate time for revealment recorded. The plan for this world group that is now assigned to earth for the next fifty years has been outlined and registered in the great central Sun for many hundreds of centuries. This plan has been followed while we were being trained for this assignment.

When Moral and Mateo began their ten-year assignment last year, they really started the program of Preparation for the reception and application in the lower strata of Earth for the new age.

Mortinion's coming to America with his laboratories and workers prepared for them.

The work done from November 12, 1939 to the time of Mortinion's coming prepared for that event. The law operates in *the same way – the tiny stream high in the mountain becomes a rushing river in the valleys. Always the smaller opens the way and prepares for the larger. As we mentioned in another paper in this series, we expect radical changes in climate. We expect much of the great ice areas to be thawed enough to reveal the rock and soil underneath. Then the work that has been accomplished from the long frozen state will contribute its value to the planet. This will consist of huge areas for cultivation and mining. A shifting of population will take place and thereby cause many planetary adjustments. About when the great ice areas melt, it will change the moisture content of the air that there will be a shifting of large land areas that now border on oceans. Some land areas that are now under the ocean waters will come to the surface again. This land will be greatly renewed and purified by its long sojourn under the sea. It will influence all who dwell upon it to be sincere, honest and simple.*

These many changes of which we write will not, we believe, take place in cataclysmic shock, but will be gradually happening over an approximate five-hundred year period.

Each group of Great Ones assigned to the Planet will perform their special work preparing for the next group to come until the Earth is clean and free and securely moving in an aura of her own purity. The mining of metals and minerals will take one of the most important places in the industrial world in a very few years, much more so than now. During the next fifty-year period, there will be such an improvement in the methods of mining of all kinds that complete changes in the organizational methods will be necessary. The plan of operating on a planetary scale will have to come.

Regardless of the location of the deposits, they will all be mined and distributed to the manufacturing centers where they are to be used. Before this fifty-year period comes to a close, you will recognize many signs of the elimination of present monetary and commercial systems and see very clear signs of the planetary trends. From the discoveries and experiences of people in positions of authoritative responsibility, man will learn the futility and destructive dangers both to himself and the races, in the present inadequate systems of commercial procedure. As the lines of power releasement and communication from the great source to the Earth expand, many people will hear within their brains just as you do now. Many people will see with their inner vision facilities Beings of Light who will instruct them regarding their work and their destiny. These experiences will be so indisputable and so real to them, and so beautiful that from the first time they have the experiences nothing else will ever be as important to them. It will be their most ardent wish to obey in order to maintain the active contract. In this way the New Age will manifest firm and happy anchorage in the most difficult channels. The reason that the New Age is destined to reveal so much that is new in metals is that are particularly equipped to the needs of extremely high vibrations. Gold and silver will be used when fortified by other ingredients, for fine wiring and various parts of high precision instruments. There will be many mechanisms of very small dimensions for individual use. These will require extremely lightweight metals of lasting strength.

Construction metals for the coming air machine will have to be very different from the present. One metal alloy that must come into use will be one that has fine hollow wires of gold alloy, woven into the sheet metal in such a way that when sheets of it are fastened together the wires will match and high-powered currents of electricity be permitted to run through unhindered. This metal will be used for air machines that will explore the strata outside the Earth's atmosphere of influence. The electrically charged metal will be used in various ways.

By being attuned to a certain mechanism, it will neutralize the electrically charged air about it. By being used in the interior, it will heat the inside of any desired areas. Gold alloys in hundreds of variations will be found indispensable during the peak of the mechanical era. There are very few woods that are hard enough to retain high and rapid vibrations without shattering. Very little wood will be used in any kind of architectural construction after the coming fifty-year period. The synthetic products that are entering so successfully into the industrial world today are the first opening wedges into a synthetic flow of products of all kinds. Basic new minerals will be discovered that will form permanent "bases" and "binders" for so many synthetic fabrics and materials that practically the entire domestic and industrial needs will be filled without using a single product from the botanical or animal worlds. At some time within the next one-hundred-year period, all metals, minerals, precious stones and chemical elements, all natural resources that come from the Earth, including all that is grown in the soil of the earth, will belong to all people of the Earth and will be distributed according to the need for use. We fully expect the New Age to be functioning politically and economically by that time. This entire new way of life is so much simpler to operate and control than the present systems in use that it will be difficult for Earth-dwelling people to understand why the old system was practiced so long. The only really difficult thing about establishing the new way is the changing of the channels and habits of thoughts of the people. This will be largely the responsibility of the thousands of guardians who are working close to the people. There will be a gradual dawning upon the minds and hearts of leaders that they could sweep aside many bad and useless laws by using the powers given them in their positions of authority. This they will begin to do. After some of the useless methods are discarded and people experience improvement therefrom, they will be eager to have many others changed or discarded. In this way, the improvements will come rapidly once the few are brave enough to make the first decisions.

Some of the very first most radical changes will be suggested and carried to successful conclusion by representatives of some of the smaller nations on the United Nations Council for International Organization. That organization will thrive, grow and function. Many people will try to ridicule it out of existence, especially nations who may be affected seriously by any kind of international cooperation or control; but they will only harm themselves and their objections will expose their own limitations.

We intend to fulfill our assignment completely and permit nothing to impede our progress.

MULA writes:

My assigned responsibility, as a member of the new group who are assigned to the Earth for the coming fifty years, is to guide the religions and political unfoldment of the humans upon the Earth. I use the word "religion" in order to convey an impression in your language. Probably the phrase "spiritual growth" would be nearer. Due to the fact that there have been so many religions established upon the Earth as masks for evil and destructive forces, it is first essential that we investigate all very thoroughly. Whenever we find basic premises of value that seem desirable for the participants, we will cause them to be retained so long as they serve a constructive need. Members of various races on the earth now will not be returned to earth when their present sojourn is finished. During the time they do remain here, they must be permitted the organizations and customs necessary to their state. When such people are taken from the planet, their false practices will disappear.

Beginning immediately by means of the Guardians and their lines of operation, interest in and attraction toward a higher consciousness will be impressed upon all people. Basic truths and laws will be impressed upon the human brain and heart continually. Each race of people will interpret these impressions in vocabularies natural to their language.

Outward forms of spiritual application and practice will be natural to their surroundings and their needs, but upon careful investigation and translation, it will be found there is unity with all others and the basic teachings are the same. The basic teachings will be the same as you now have. THE ONE SOURCE – GOD – GOD IS ALL THERE IS – ONE SUBSTANCE – THE ONE GREAT RESERVOIR OF LIFE, MIND AND POWER – ONE CONSCIOUSNESS. Each branch of human activity and study will find herein a true, scientific basis for the philosophy necessary to teach the science of any craft or research. "Religion" in its true state can never be separated from the life and daily actions of a people. Religion in its basic meaning is really the recognition and acceptance of God. This needs no organization of people. It needs no building or ritual of any kind to either sustain it or to prove its existence. It is an act of consciousness operating through the brain. When people have never contemplated their source of life or consciousness and have not acted upon any inner decision regarding a belief, they have not yet a religion, but they unquestionably have life, mind and power. They have lines of inspiration, and often lines of communication with the great Cosmic Centers. They experience guidance and love, all of which is so real to them they would never give thought to it. Such people have no need for religion. The masses of people who are still functioning on planes of self-will and reason need to be inspired to reach higher. In many cases this requires experience that will give them desire for *clarification of causes. This, in turn, influences them to seek for something bigger and more powerful than their conception of individual faculties. Many times association with religious organizations acts as a clarifying medium. In the majority of cases the person is first inspired to commute with some inner feeling because of experiences with great beauty.*

Often it results from seeking God in fear. In such cases there is a much longer educational process necessary because the person must learn to approach God in love instead of fear. The psychology of fear is a very destructive path and is to be avoided at all times. When people, who have given very little consideration, if any, to God begin to feel the intuitive urge within their brains and hearts, there will be many simple and beautiful writings, songs, paintings, sculpture and poetry. This ecstasy and love will be almost childlike in its sincerity, and the deep beauty of little things will have a vital place in the art life of all people. "Religion" of the future will be the most simple it has been since the ancient of days. Gradually, people will discover that they are attuned to some great source from whence comes truth to them. They will learn to depend upon this source for everything until finally the expansion will reach the ancient beginning and the circle will be complete in love and wisdom. Simultaneous with the awakening in consciousness of God's and man's relationship to him, will come the understanding of the true meaning of freedom and justice. The loud preaching or missionary practices of zealots will not display this awakening to truths of religion and politics. It will be quiet, restrained and balanced. It will be revealed in the daily actions and attitudes of the people. There will be little need to speak of it. Over a period of twenty-five years, there will be continual, concentrated releasements into the deep consciousness of the races. The atmosphere in which they live and breathe will be saturated with words and visions of the new order. Channels will be opened through thousands of already prepared people for the releasement of power and God-love. People will expand to see with amazing clearness the futility and dangers in present political practices. People will insist that citizens of uprightness and intelligent understanding represent them in office. People will insist that the best people in the land hold the positions of great responsibilities and power

People will demand that conditions be made so that the best people and the most thoroughly enlightened ones will feel honored to represent them. Under such a regime of harmony between the people and their representatives, suitable avenues will be cleared for the incoming Great Ones who will lead the people of the entire planet into the new day with rejoicing, love and understanding. During the period of gradual awaking and expansion of the human consciousness, schools of every kind will include more and more teaching of the principles of international cooperation, how to organize and harmonize peoples of various talents and nationalities.

The young people who are interested in following political and executive careers will have opportunities to spend time in various

countries to learn the languages, the capabilities and heart-interests of the people. To live and study and work with any race of people long enough to gain understanding of them, their problems, their joys and their ways of living, is to love them. The most valuable method of developing ability to hold positions of responsibility in the world is to learn the languages and ways of people living with them. There will be new, simple methods of teaching languages so that a person will be able to spend a few months in any country and from careful observation and concentration acquire what is needed. We cannot over-emphasize this necessity for world travel and world study. The more people who do so, regardless of their talents, profession or destinies, the sooner will international relationships become smooth, and the stronger and more enduring will grow the foundation upon which the New World Order must be erected. The departments for political study in schools must not be founded upon the present false and inadequate conceptions of politics. The basis for study must be deep within and inadequate conceptions of politics. The basis for study must be deep within the consciousness of the race.

Politics must be understood as a principle of cooperation between human beings designed to produce harmonious action in leadership that will result in peaceful and progressive government. In such a state, individual and self-centered desires for personal attention or personal profit must be dissolved in the great understanding that to lose the personal profit must be dissolved in the great understanding that to lose the personal in the idealism of accomplishment of the greatest peace and happiness for the largest number, is to gain for the individual self, values that endure forever. The diplomacy, intrigue and underground workings of the new political teachings will be based upon the natural truth that the most valuable and permanent growth takes place in silence. Instead of a science that is used to conceal workings of questionable acts and attempts to undermine and destroy another country or organization, maturity of growth from silence will reveal beautiful surprises that prove to all people the constructive motives and plans being operated for the over-all good of the World, wherein evil will be destroyed and never used as a tool of accomplishment.

The ideals, desires and ambitions necessary to establishment of the foregoing are being planted deep in the consciousness of people. They are being nourished with Love and Light from the Great Source, Itself. Their blossoms of freedom and justice will beautify the gardens of humanity wherein Gods will walk and converse with man as together they ascend the Golden Pathways to mutual fulfillment.

MUDANLERO writes:

As a member of the Special Group assigned to the Earth Planet for the fifty years, I represent the work of unifying the Earth Planet with other planets of the Universe. We will work to educate the people of the earth in the history of the Earth's birth and its geographical and geological progression including the history of the human races upon it. Before the people of Earth can take their destined place among the inhabitants of other planets, they must know their own history and the history of the planet upon which they live.

The members of this committee will work continually through the assigned guardians to direct and inspire people to seek and locate ancient records and proofs of the past histories of people, places and occurrences that have caused many of the major changes upon the Earth. By means of highly sensitized instruments, particularly telescopes and cameras, radio and television, based upon a much finer wave-time than any being used now, man will discover great truths about the space around him and about the other planets in his own universe. When man has instruments of sufficient delicacy and sensitiveness to discern and photograph the forms of expressed life that dwell upon other planets, he will be able to establish a kind of communication with them. It will first be a series of Light signals, which will be changed into sound.

Eventually, a great one on each planet will be able to answer in the English language, and this interplanetary communication will be accepted just as naturally as the other mechanical inventions are today. Man on Earth will find out that even on the Sun there are people living in bodies just as harmonious to the atmosphere and conditions there as his Earth body is to Earth. Mind, life and power exist and function oblivious to the kind of material used to make the mechanical Instruments or focal points for consciousness. Every seed atom builds for itself a body out of the substance surrounding it at the moment in time when its individualized consciousness demands a body. This body is fed and sustained by the same values as those out of which it grew – regardless of the kind or nature of the surroundings or of its place in the universal plan.

Until the beings living on planets of lower degrees of vibration or density find some means of communication with the higher vibrations and finer densities, they have no facilities for making contacts outside of their own atmosphere. There are always people on every planet who can and do contact many others outside of their own planet by means of lines through highly sensitized radio-active brain cells.

These people can seldom disclose their activities or their discoveries because they are usually misunderstood or are in danger from the ignorance of the unenlightened, so in the majority of cases such destined ones are used by the great ones for line anchorage for the race.

In this mechanical age instruments of many kinds will be invented that will prove to man, beyond question, many truths about his body and brain equipment that he could not accept before. As has been recorded for you many times, the great one great purpose of this mechanical age is to teach the human being what his body and brain really are and how to use them correctly. When this is accomplished, the machinery outside of *the physical body will be unnecessary. There will be a continual releasement into the deep consciousness of the race, inspiring interest and a great curiosity to know how the universe is constructed. This will arouse desire to study the stars and interstellar space. From active desire is born discovery, and from discovery is born ways, and means for use. Within the next fifty years, there will be more people of all ages studying the various phases of astronomy than has ever been known before. This study will open great avenues of discoveries that will be useful in developing the necessary instruments for the communication systems. People will be amazed and thrilled to find many of the tiny formations in distant space inhabited. Within the next ten-year period, a most valuable series of recordings will be made that will explain, in very simple terms, the science of astrology and how it can be used by man in his research for both the past and the future. As man progresses along these avenues of expansion, he will live continually in the midst of finer and more highly sensitized surroundings which will influence the human brain to higher and finer facilities of recognition and selection. These, in turn, will help to discover and create new strata of action until the peoples of Earth are truly one in recognition, acceptance and understanding of one planet.*

Within the next fifty years, there will be seven major research and experimental centers built upon the Earth— one in each of the seven localities. These will be the seven major centers of magnetic anchorage for the Earth in space. From these centers, it will be possible to contact small, electronic propelled projectiles, containing instruments that will photograph all that passes before the lens. At first these projectiles will only go a short distance before returning to their base. They will be so equipped that when atmospheres beyond the control of either the base-line of power or the endurance of the projectile's body is reached, they will immediately return to their home base. From the recordings of the instruments within them and the nature of the photographs, scientists will learn how to strengthen them until they will travel unbelievable distances and contribute tremendous knowledge to methods of further research. In a very few years now, there will be an international research department built upon the exact spot called the North

Pole. Here will be used the most advanced electronic and radio-active instruments known. None of them will to be very large.

They will be contributed by the most outstanding and efficient scientists in astronomical research from every race. Here they will study and record the power currents striking the earth at that point. By following these power currents out from Earth towards their seeming sources, other important discoveries will be made. A location in San Francisco, now called Twin Peaks, will become another very vital research station. There also will be one upon one of the highest and most southern peaks of the Andes Mountains in South America. All of the country west of the Rocky Mountains on the North American Continent will become the most active and contain the greatest number of research scientists of any section upon the Earth Planet. This will be due to the strategic position of magnetic power lines that pass through the Earth and influence this section of land.

Just as soon as people have proof sufficient to convince them that other planets are inhabited, and that it is really possible to use the especially equipped cells of the brain for communication, they will seek out people who have such brains and with great earnestness listen to their teachings.

The Temple Schools will have many applications for entry in the departments for brain and body study. It would be dangerous and most unwise to permit such uses of the brain (except by the destined ones especially prepared) before the atmosphere surrounding the earth is cleansed and purified. Just as soil must be prepared for seed planting, so must the Earth and the people upon it be prepared for every cycle of new experience and discovery. During this fifty-year period the one great purpose of all our work is to prepare the brains and hearts of people for the tremendous discoveries and inventions that will be manifest around them. One of the first releasements being made from this department will be to awaken a desire in the brains of children to study the heavens to learn all they can about the present known facts, the location and present names of the stars and planets. We are now impressing upon the minds of some great astronomers to publish a series of six books in the simplest language about the skies and all that is known about the various stars and planets. We want these books to include photographic *pictures of the various types of apparatus used in observation. We would like to have groups of children and young people building their own apparatus and be interested in sky study as many are now in air travel and plane models.*

We are releasing impressions from every department to awaken greater interest in all phases of Natural Science. By becoming curious and interested in finding the causes back of the natural phenomena around them, people will reach beyond and draw to themselves new knowledge. The entire world of education must pass through simplification processes as well as purifying processes.

From the reports that come to us continually from the Guardians, we select and plan our strategic releasements for change and improvement in the daily lives of man.

The printing and publishing activities must be greatly changed. Selling and publicity organizations of all kinds must be cleansed and changed. These ideas are aside from my original topic— but are very important and will interest you. There has been a Special Committee of Guardians appointed to travel throughout the seven localities and concentrate on one idea to investigate and discover the organizations, methods and materials used to purposely influence the thinking and emotional acts of people. They will make an itemized list according to location, including the names of all people directing and operating such systems. When this information is in our hands, a committee of Great Ones will be given power to dwell close to the people and go to work to readjust the entire system and make it useful for the greatest possible good.

There are many such committees to be formed, and in this way faster and more efficient work can be accomplished over the fifty-year period.

You will probably have more from us— but these recordings have been made now in order to anchor these seven lines deep within the consciousness of the human races in Earth. This concludes our recordings for this assignment.

Signed: MUDANLERO
Channeled: September 1945

OBITUARY

ELLEVIVIAN (RICHARDSON) POWER, 90. LIFELONG *Spiritual Student & Teacher: Ellavivian Power of Alamogordo passed over Friday, July 16, 2004, at 11:15PM at a local hospital. She was born: August 8, 1913 in Marceline, Missouri.*

She moved to Alamogordo in 1964 and served in the administration of Quimby Center, a training school for spiritual teachers.

Survivors include a son, Donald Power and his wife Deborah of Houston, and a daughter, Barbara Martin of Garland, TX. and five grandchildren: Chris, Michele and Mandy Power, David and John Martin.

Ellavivian's love and teaching touched and helped many people. She was very grateful for the love and care she received from her dear friends and her long time housekeeper Sandra Swiger. She was preceded in death by her husband, Frank Clay Power, in 1988.

John-Roger (J-R)
Mystical Traveler

MSIA
(Movement of Spiritual Inner Awareness)

God comes to the whole world,
and the Movement of Spiritual Inner Awareness
comes to the whole world.
This Movement has not come only to one person,
and because of this it will extend into greater
and greater parts of the world.
MSIA has not come to say, 'Join us,' but to say,
'May you know Love and Light and freedom and
peace;
may God dwell happily in your household,
and may you awaken your Soul within you
so that you can know who you are
and awaken yourself and others
that we might all usher in a golden age.
FROM *PSYCHIC PROTECTION*, JOHN-ROGER

BY FAR, MY MOST IMPORTANT SPIRITUAL TEACHER! THIS has been a difficult chapter to write. I'm not sure anyone could do justice to what John-Roger has brought to this planet. An astonishing volume of love and work, in books, tapes and seminars and in person. True Practical Spirituality! Dogmatic teachings have never worked for

230

me. Fortunately I've never been able to be in lock step with any "spiritual or religious way" that I couldn't experience. "Do it my way, just take my word for it," never worked for me and I've always had difficulty with rhetoric. J-R has said on numerous occasions "There's no understanding without experience." The extraordinary tools I've received from John-Roger have changed my life. I don't have much in the way of material wealth, but the joy and peace I live with are priceless. Thank you, my friend, John-Roger.

My spiritual life, this last time around, hasn't been about seeking a Guru. Fortunately I've gotten beyond that. Until I met John-Roger in the late seventies, I wasn't consciously aware that I was seeking a teacher that could teach me about love and loving; not the sexual kind (although a bit more of that would work) but the kind that consistently lifts myself and others.

It is declared throughout the Bible in many passages, that man will be judged and rewarded according to his deeds and works. If this is true and I believe it to be, John Roger must stand very close to the Lord Jesus and the Lord Buddha, both of whom were Mystical Travelers, hence my feelings of inadequacy in writing this chapter.

Pauli Sanderson the author of the forward to John Roger's 2007 trilogy "Fulfilling Your Spiritual Promise" states, "I have studied with John-Roger— and, frankly, I've studied John-Roger— for forty years or so. In the late 1960s, I began working with him and assisting him to transform his spoken teachings into the written word, the better to reach people who were looking for a light in their life.

When I say I have studied John-Roger for forty years, what I mean is that he has intrigued me from the first day I met him and, after all these years, intrigues me still. He is an absolute original, one-of-a-kind masterpiece. Very Often, he is a surprise. He is a mystic and has lived a life profoundly grounded in Spirit and in service. He is completely spontaneous and unpredictable, which I have come to believe is the result of following a free and unpatterned Spirit. He is the most loving human being I have ever encountered and undoubtedly the funniest. His teachings are a curious blend of Eastern and Western thought. As you read his works, you will find teachings of reincarnation, the laws of karma (cause and effect), the evolvement of individualized consciousness through realms of Spirit, the grace bestowed on humankind by Christ, forgiveness, the power of working with the Light of God's sacred names, and the benefits of meditation all woven seamlessly together to create a tapestry and within that tapestry may be found a path that J-R calls Soul Transcendence, a path by which you may fulfill your spiritual promise.

I've heard John-Roger refer to himself as a spiritual scientist, meaning he is pragmatic and checks out everything he teaches to be sure it is workable. It is. And I've heard him say he teaches 'practical spirituality'. He does. One of his favorite sayings is, "If it works, use it; if it doesn't work, let it go" Through the years, I've heard him answer innumerable questions with one of his own: "Did it work for you?" Other times he shares— from the generosity of his loving heart— information that is both practical and liberating. Whatever his response, his answers are accompanied by an infusion of spiritual energy that is, in itself, transforming. I've sometimes not understood anything of what he said, but whatever bothered me disappeared. There is something mystical in the energy he works with that takes his words beyond the mind and into the heart and soul. I think of it as a little bit of magic, and it keeps me mindful that there is more to this than meets the eye.

Much of what you read by John-Roger is the result of his response to people's desire to get free, to break the bonds of negativity that hold them down, to realize the positive side of their nature.

Someone says, "I just keep doing the same stupid things

over and over." And J-R says, "Let me tell you about karma and how to break the cycle."

Another student says, "I am so angry at my parents that it affects everything I do," and J-R says, "I'll tell you about using forgiveness as a path to liberation."

Someone else says, "Here are some ideas about working with the Light." Add it all together and you get the science of Soul Transcendence, your practical guide to fulfilling your spiritual promise—and a bit of mystery to keep you intrigued.

From the altitude of the mystical consciousness, I believe it must be clear that each person is the embodiment of a divine soul and that each Soul knows its own destiny and path back into its true nature. I say this not from any mystical consciousness of my own, but from my observations that it is from that premise that J-R treats all of his family, friends, students, acquaintances, the guy at the carwash, the waitress in the local diner, and the down-and-out fellow on the street corner. On some level, we are all awarded the same respect, love and neutral regard. As a personal friend, student, and acquaintance of J-R's, and a sometime waitress and even occasional car washer for him (and maybe down but never out)."

In late 1983, I received a note from J-R. I believed someone in his office sent it to me by mistake and I stuck it away in a file. Eleven years later, as I was preparing to move to Hawaii, I came across it and knew it was meant for me.

Dear Billy;

In your expression of service, you have demonstrated an awareness of Spirit. By your doing for the joy of serving, you have reinforced your light a thousand-fold. I can only love and appreciate your growth in light.

John-Roger

John-Roger was born Roger Delano Hinkins on September 24, 1934, to a Mormon family in Rains, Utah. Rains is a mining town and Hinkins' father was a mine foreman. While growing up, the spiritual-teacher-to-be was more interested in girls and sports than in spirituality. The only unusual aspect of his childhood was that he could see 'auras,' the colorful energy fields that surround the human body. He held down a number of jobs, including a short stint in the coal mines. While in college, he worked as a night orderly in the psychiatric ward of a Salt Lake City hospital specifically to keep a closer eye on his brother who was in a near fatal mining accident. Later he held a part-time job as a PBX telephone operator and dispatcher with the Salt Lake City Police Department.

After completing a degree in psychology at the University of Utah in 1958, he moved to southern California and eventually took a job teaching English at Rosemead High School. In 1960 he earned a Secondary teaching credential also from the University of Utah and a California Secondary Life Teaching Credential. His graduate work was completed at the University of California, the University of Southern California and California State University at Los Angeles. In 2000, he completed a Doctorate of Spiritual Science from Peace Theological Seminary and College of Philosophy. In 2000 he received the Peacemaker of the Year Award from World Art Expressions.

The turning point of his life occurred in 1963, during what might be called a near-death experience. (Sounds familiar to me) While undergoing surgery for a kidney stone, he fell into a nine-day coma. Upon awakening, he found he had been given a spiritual initiation and was aware of a new spiritual personality inside--'John'-who had superseded/merged with his old personality. After the operation, he began to refer to himself as 'John-Roger,' in recognition of his transformed self. During the operation he was given the inner spiritual keys to the Mystical Traveler Consciousness. This Consciousness has total awareness in all realms of consciousness.

The primary function of the Mystical Traveler is to help souls realize their divine nature and establish their consciousness on the soul realm. When working with this consciousness an individual can more rapidly balance all their karma, complete the cycle of reincarnation, and become spiritually free.

After his post-coma realization, he didn't immediately abandon his career as a high school English teacher. It wasn't until some five years later that he began holding gatherings as an independent spiritual teacher, and not until 1971 that he quit his day job to become a full-time Spiritual leader. This core group of spiritual seekers was the foundation group that with J-R's direction created the Church of the Movement of Spiritual Inner Awareness, or MSIA. Early on in J-R's new consciousness/ministry he did "Light Studies." These were readings whereby J-R would read from the Akashic Records. I believe they were very similar to the information Dr. Hunter brought forward in her readings. They were offered to assist people in their spiritual direction and to offer suggestions in taking responsibility for clearing karma. Many early MSIA students consistently claimed that J-R knew more about them than anybody could have. MSIA developed out of a series of seminars in Santa Barbara, California. The first seminar took place in May 1968. Across the course of six evenings, the audience was modest with attendance ranging from 13 to 30 persons, depending upon the evening. A number of people who came to the early seminars drove from other cities in southern California.

As the seminars became regular ongoing meetings, these 'long-distance' attendees were able to persuade John-Roger to begin holding seminars outside of Santa Barbara. This expansion of J-R's activities continued until he was doing five seminars a week at different homes in different cities. The Church of the Movement of Spiritual Inner Awareness was formally incorporated three years later, in 1971.

An important factor for me was the position accorded Jesus Christ, who is viewed as the ultimate head of MSIA on this planet. Jesus embodied the Mystical Traveler Consciousness and holds the office of Christ for the earth (roughly like the "presidency" of this planet). I was raised Catholic in a family that for a time said the rosary after dinner every night and once a month on the radio. I attended Catholic school for a while, where the curriculum was bloody. I still have an indentation in my skull from Monsignor MacAvoy's black jack. As a Catholic raised and partially educated child, I don't recall hearing the name Jesus. Perhaps I was too pre-occupied with survival.

After studying with John-Roger, Jesus' teaching became important to me, not Christianity per se, which I find quite hypocritical. I believe the Christian take on having to go through Jesus to get to the Father is right on. And for whatever reason, probably control, centuries back, re-incarnation was removed from the Bible, making present day Christians believe that their loving God only gives you one shot, one lifetime, to get it or BURN IN HELL! Give me a break. What they don't realize is as J-R says, not one soul will be lost. Every spiritual quest, albeit Buddhist, Muslim, Hindu, et al is right on for those particular needs and through the process of re-embodiment will all finally come through the Jesus lineage. Throughout my spiritual quest, Jesus' teachings were rhetorical for the most part, until I met John-Roger. He has an uncanny ability to bring these teachings alive. Years earlier I had grown tired of Christian dogma and hypocrisy and yet here was a man, not a Christian per se, who just kept bringing these teachings alive. A man who truly walked the walk, as will be seen throughout this chapter.

Near the beginning of my MSIA tenure, I heard him say, "Check out what I'm saying for yourself. Don't take my word for anything and if it doesn't work for you, move on." I liked this lack of control.

In 1977 I went to a series of audio tape seminars in Taos, New Mexico. I was very judgmental and couldn't stand the attendees as my life had been full of the sub-culture and many of these people were of the so called "straight world." I knew John-Roger was an asshole because I saw a photo of him in a polyester suit eating a big Mac. My judgments were strong. I continued participating because whatever I was going through each week, I always felt better after the seminar, like something negative was lifted. This is true today, thirty years later. His ability to lift negative aspects from afar is amazing.

Despite the later proliferation of classes, workshops, and conferences, the home-meeting seminar remains MSIA's core gathering. The format of such seminars was also established in the early days, consisting of a talk by John-Roger, followed by individual sharing. As the organization expanded until J-R could not personally attend every meeting, a distinction developed between live seminars with John-Roger and taped seminars at which the group listened to a tape of a J-R talk. From these humble beginnings, John-Roger's activities gradually expanded. It was only after several years of steady teaching activity that John-Roger began to offer his students initiation into the sound current.

To be an initiate of the Traveler is to devote yourself to the God within you, to Spirit, and to returning to your home, the Soul realm, from which you originally came before you incarnated onto this earth.

JOHN-ROGER

As a prerequisite to initiation, and from the request of some of the early participants for reading material on the teachings, Soul Awareness Discourses were created and were mostly derived from seminar transcripts, ranging from

"Sending the Light" to "Overcoming Discouragement.

The earliest discourses were mimeographed. As MSIA developed, these were periodically revised and expanded, and more advanced levels of the discourses composed for long-time participants. The levels of initiation in MSIA correspond to the levels of consciousness:

- *Astral: relating to the imagination*
- *Causal: relating to the emotions*
- *Mental: relating to the mind*
- *Etheric: relating to the unconscious*
- *Soul: who we truly are*

The astral initiation happens in the "night travel" (dream state) after a person has in some way come in contact with a Mystical Traveler. For the four other initiations, the person meets with an initiator and is given an initiation "tone" (the name of Divinity on that realm), which the initiate chants during spiritual exercises (S.E.s). One of the primary ways that we learn to attune to and focus on God is through S.E.s. It's a form of meditation/prayer. I've always had difficulty with meditation. Sitting, listening to the endless mind chatter, blah, blah, blah. With spiritual exercises one actually leaves the body and travels the inner worlds. I liked the possibility thirty years ago and today it's one of the most important times of my day. During the initial two years of study in MSIA, the Traveler works with the person spiritually to help them clear karma and to prepare them for initiation. Discourses and S.E.s are two of the main ways the Traveler works with people in MSIA. Initiates or those studying toward initiation are asked to spend time each day for spiritual attunement through S.E.s and to do them often during the first two years of study in MSIA. Building a strong habit of doing spiritual exercises and spending time with the Spirit within can do much to help a person build a firm spiritual foundation. The Soul Awareness

Discourses—the basic lessons that Movement people receive on a monthly basis— originated from the request of some of the early participants for reading material on the teachings, and were derived from seminar transcripts. After the seminars started being taped, each tape would receive a name, based on the topic J-R had discussed that evening. In response to repeated requests for reading material, common themes and material were brought together from many different seminars to form the basis for printed discourses on particular topics, ranging from "Sending the Light" to "Overcoming Discouragement". The earliest discourses were mimeographed. As MSIA developed, these were periodically revised and expanded.

1971 was the year MSIA was formally incorporated and the first issue of the first Movement periodical, On the Light Side, was published. On the Light Side, which was not much more than an elaborate newsletter, soon gave way to The Movement newspaper, a true alternative magazine that reported on events and personalities in the larger spiritual movements, in addition to MSIA activities and concerns. In more recent years, The Movement was succeeded by The New Day Herald, an in-house newspaper focused on MSIA news and events. Most of the space in the early On the Light Side periodicals was taken up by transcriptions of seminar talks. The content of these transcripts provides a good sense of John-Roger's teachings in the early days.

The following passage from the first On the Light Side accurately captures J-R's, down-to-earth style:

First you learn who you are. And when you learn who the real Self is, the false images fall away rapidly. The person you thought you were, the religion you thought you were, the philosophy you thought you were may fall away. You may find out that all of these philosophies that you've been adhering to just don't work. But you may be afraid to throw them away because you don't know what will take their place. When you get rid of the things that don't work, you will find the true Self.

And the true Self doesn't have anger or jealousy or greed or lust or avarice. It doesn't have any of these things; it doesn't need them. But the false self has them and needs them and fights for dear life to hang on to them. If you could just once see within the true Self, if you could get that image just once in your consciousness for a fraction of a second, you could go on for the rest of your life using that as an inner guiding light

J-R's basic approach and style has changed very little over the years. He's an educator in the broadest sense of the word, helping people to become aware of the spirit in themselves and others and to make the most out of their lives. His teachings are full of wisdom, humor, common sense and above all, loving. He has led groups of up to one hundred and fifty people on Peace Awareness Trainings throughout the Middle East. John-Roger has written dozens of books, including best sellers, conducted thousands of seminars, and provided material for hundreds of hours of taped lectures over the past several decades, but comparatively little has been added to the basic themes laid out in the first few years of his spiritual teaching activity. At the same time, J-R has said that as the Spirit moves him with greater clarity, he also moves with greater clarity; therefore, the teachings are constantly undergoing slight revisions, and, from the point of view of participants, the teachings go deeper and deeper with time.

His journeys have taken him to such places as the former USSR, Yugoslavia, China, Israel, Egypt, Syria, Lebanon, and throughout Africa, South and North America, Australia and Europe. In the late seventies, John-Roger established Network Of Wisdoms (NOW) Productions, which has recorded over 6,000 of his seminars, and also produces his national cable TV show, "That Which Is". Besides his own show, John-Roger has appeared on other television and radio programs including CNN's Larry King Live, the Roseanne Show, and Politically Incorrect.

His influence extends into the educational arena, as he is the Chancellor and founder of the University of Santa Monica (USM). USM offers three Master's degrees all approved by the State of California.

He founded and is President of Peace Theological Seminary and College of Philosophy, which offers a Masters of Spiritual Science (M.S.S.) and Doctor of Spiritual Science (D.S.S.) degrees and whose headquarters is home to Peace Awareness Labyrinth and Gardens.

Peace Theological Seminary

For those seeking Spirit, all knowledge is accessible. In order to become available to the information awaiting you, you need to keep open the doors to your awareness. Peace Theological Seminary offers the keys. If you wish access to eternal knowledge, you must put your mind, body, and most of all, your heart on the line. The next step is up to you.

JOHN ROGER

IN 1977 JOHN-ROGER FOUNDED PRANA THEOLOGICAL Seminary (PTS) in Los Angeles, California. The name has since been changed to Peace Theological Seminary. This seminary is a non-denominational, educational seminary with classes, workshops and retreats, plus Masters and Doctorate programs offered around the world. In addition, PTS Distance Learning allows classes to be taken through the Internet, by electronic mail, and by correspondence. The purpose of PTS is to facilitate learning the lessons of the physical and spiritual worlds.

The Seminary's primary values include that each person is individualized Spirit, a Soul, on a journey of discovery of his or her true nature, which is divine. Seminary courses include releasing whatever stands in the way of a person's conscious knowledge of his or her divinity. All of J-R's teachings revolve around: "Loving is the essence of Spirit and is the most important to develop and nourish in the human consciousness." He also teaches that all knowledge exists within the human consciousness and this knowledge is awakened when information is presented as a living experience. J-R maintains that our primary relationship is with our own Soul and PTS provides educational opportunities that support students in becoming more aware of this. The beautiful mansion that is now Prana and houses the seminary was built between 1910 and 1913 for Secondo Guasti, who owned the world's largest winery at the time. He hired a local architectural firm and also brought in Italian artisans to fashion the Italian Renaissance interior. In 1937, Busby Berkeley, a Hollywood director and choreographer, bought the Guasti Villa and lived in it, adding an additional touch of glamour to the property's history. It changed hands several times until 1949, when the Los Angeles County Physicians Aid Association bought the villa and subsequently added two wings of rooms for retired physicians or their widows to live in. MSIA purchased Prana in 1974 and ownership was transferred to PTS a few years later. It became the headquarters for MSIA and PTS as well as home to many MSIA staff over the years. The Guasti Villa is described in the West Adams Heritage Association tour guide: "The imposing, nearly symmetrical main house dominates the neighborhood. Its graceful facade and European elegance connote affluence, power, and the aspirations of those who have lived there." The breathtaking entry hall has an inlaid marble floor, oak paneling with pilasters and garlands, and a carved cornice. The ceiling features a large and very beautiful figurative painting above a wood chandelier. The (former) dining room features dark paneling with seven-foot pilasters and inlaid hardwood floors. Appropriately, the cellar was originally well-stocked with Guasti wines but is now used for offices. The spacious rear gardens have four different levels and include a flower-rimmed courtyard with a fish pond, lawns (one of which also serves as a volleyball court), a beautiful rose garden, and an orchard with bountiful fruit and avocado trees.

One level contains the Peace Awareness hand-carved Labyrinth & Gardens where people can relax, meditate, find peace and quiet in the meditation garden, and walk the outdoor labyrinth.

Living in Grace Retreat

THE SEVEN DAY GRACE RETREAT COURSE GREW OUT OF AN inspiration that choosing grace is a process that takes practice— practicing forgiving ourselves and others, and developing an attitude of gratitude. The choice to love or not love is made in each moment. As students learn to choose more moments of loving in their lives, they can find themselves living more in God's grace and walking through life with the Lord.

Grace retreat is held at Asilomar Conference Center, Pacific Grove, California, every December. I've had the fortune to participate twice. 'Wow!' is truly the most descriptive adjective that characterizes this profound seminar. This course with approximately three hundred and fifty people, is a powerful step for the student in the eternal process of expanding inner peace.

At one end of the Grace room is a stage with the curtain drawn and on the stage are boxes and items for the event including some very inviting reclining lawn chairs.

One evening I decided to put on earphones, go behind the curtain and relax in one of those lovely chairs. As I had raised my hand earlier to be included in the microphone line to ask the boss some questions, when it came my turn, J-R said into the microphone: "Where's Billy Whelan?" I jumped up and still behind the curtain said to no one in particular, "Oh fuck, what have I done now." People sitting near the stage heard me, and they all loudly laughed. I stuck my head out of the curtain and said "You rang?" Again everyone laughed.

Then J-R said "What's so funny?" because if anyone loves humor, it's J-R So I repeated it and again everyone laughed.

As is probably apparent, my mouth sometimes gets me in a bit of trouble. I'm getting better at thinking before I speak. After all I am 73. After answering a few questions J-R mentioned that he and I had danced together in many lifetimes, metaphorically speaking, and I said something really stupid, prior to getting better at thinking before speaking: "You know J-R, if you had tits, I'd marry you." Everyone in the room was practically on the floor laughing. Too late I knew it was inappropriate.

J-R said something like "Oh, that's just the way Billy is." Yep! It was kind of funny though. During one meditation I was given another gift, the words

Hail Billy
Full of Grace
The Lord is with Thee

were seared on my brain. As an ex Catholic altar boy who prayed the "Hail Mary" prayer for years as a young person, this was shocking. Me and Mother Mary. Whoa! When I overcame my unworthiness, I thought yeah, me and Mary. Baby, why not? I have it framed in my bathroom as a reminder.

Then there are the Peace Awareness Trainings. (PAT) This series is the foundational course work for anyone studying MSIA Soul Awareness Discourses, because the primary focus of the trainings is to expand the student's awareness. Held in retreat, these trainings provide a gentle, natural setting, without the physical distractions of a city, in which students can awaken levels of awareness that come from deep within their consciousness. As their awareness expands, students discover and more fully experience their true selves. Each training builds upon the last, and completion of all three trainings is strongly recommended to gain the most value. The effects of doing a PAT can last well beyond the duration of the training, as students often experience a powerful, sustaining change in their consciousness that shows up as greater inner peace, clarity, and connection with Spirit. I took the first two PATs in the early eighties and I really didn't like them. Two solid weeks of finding out who I really was. Relentless! Silently being asked to give up illusion. The retreat was held at the MSIA property above Lake Arrowhead. Unlike Insight which is an educational experience designed to awaken the heart, etc. the PATs are designed to bring you home to the truth of who you are. Although not spoken of as such, the PATs were created to awaken one to their own Christed-ness.

This experience was so powerful for me I got sick. Really sick. So sick, I stayed on the property in my tent the weekend between I and II. But survive I did and I vowed I'd not take the third PAT. It took me approximately eight years to assimilate this powerful experience and be ready for PAT III. Many friends take all three PATs back to back with no problem. I'm kind of a slow learner.

On the third morning of the five-day PAT III, I was sitting in the middle of the third row calmly waiting for the seminar to begin. The night before, at dinner, there was a loud food fight. I decided not to participate, which was interesting, as I used to start them. But I thoroughly enjoyed watching the craziness.

This morning, people were sitting quietly talking as the facilitators were preparing for the day's event. Suddenly, I was given one of the most important gifts of my long spiritual quest, the realization that "I was the Christ." Many spiritual teachings speak rhetorically about the Christ being in all of us. I now knew! It wasn't a boo-hoo moment, nor one in which I would share with the group, as one might with an epiphany. It was the clearest inner communication since my time with Meher Baba. A moment later, JR walked in, looked around the room as if he were looking for someone (he was), caught my eye, and winked. We've never discussed it; it wasn't necessary.

Pat IV in Retreat: The Journey for Inner Peace

THIS COURSE IS BASED ON THE "PILGRIMAGE FOR Individual and World Peace," the seven trips to Egypt and Israel that the Seminary sponsored from 1984 to 1990. This course explores the qualities of the twelve disciples who worked closely with Jesus during his public ministry. Students focus on developing a fuller expression of the positive quality exemplified by each disciple and moving into the Christ within themselves, bringing forward greater forgiveness, loving, and peace for themselves and the world. A beautiful meditation that J-R recorded in the Luxor Pyramid in Egypt titled appropriately "The Luxor Meditation" is one I still listen to regularly. A beautiful meditation.

John-Roger is also the Founder and Chairman of the Board of Insight Transformational Seminars. He's a prolific writer, with over 50 books, 4 Bestsellers, including a #1 NY Times and a LA Times Bestseller. To keep up with his writing, he founded Mandeville Press, an independent publishing house that publishes books offering a contemporary look at ancient wisdom.

In all that he does, he encourages people to check out for themselves the information he presents, and through their own experience see how it works to bring them more abundance, joy and loving in their lives. He has transformed the lives of many people by educating them in the wisdom of the Spiritual Heart. He sure transformed my life.

In contrast to his simple, unadorned teaching style, another characteristic of John-Roger's activities has been a steady stream of unusual psychic-spiritual experiences among his students. These experiences have characterized his ministry from the very beginning. Some sense of this dimension of J-R's activities has already been conveyed in the preceding story of the early days of MSIA. These experiences have come to be accepted as what we might call 'everyday miracles' by many people in the Movement, including me. One profound "everyday miracle" I experienced: In the late seventies I was close to completing the structure for our 18 room children's home, built by volunteers and funded by donations. We were hoping to be licensed by Mental Health to operate a clinical Residential Treatment Center. This grant from the Mental Health Department was predicated on the completion of this structure. (See author's first book *Friends of the Children* at www.familypeacegroup.org.) We were asked to come to Santa Fe to the meeting where funds for projects like ours were to be decided.

The head of the Mental Health Department recommended not funding us for a variety of reasons. So did the head of Residential Treatment, who while visiting us in our uncompleted facility had promised his support. The Mental Health guy was married to the caseworker we had told about aura balancing and the other guy worked for him. Apparently they were concerned we were some kind of cult. The woman heading the funding team asked if we wanted to make a statement. We addressed each of their concerns and when we were finished, she said she was satisfied with our rebuttal and asked, "Would the department heads like to amend their recommendations?"

"No!"

Finally they decided to postpone their decision for a few weeks. I called John-Roger as I had already seen miracles in his work, told him the story and asked if there was anything he could do. He said he'd look at it from the levels he works from. Ten days later we were notified that both opposing department heads had left their jobs for greener pastures.

One had been promoted and the other was accepted into a Ph.D. program he had been wanting. One of their replacements knew of and supported our work. We were immediately funded. I was getting used to the power of spirit through John-Roger where everyone wins. This win-win attitude was new to me as, like all of us, I was used to a winner and a loser. I was beginning to realize I had found an amazing teacher.

In response to repeated requests for reading material, common themes and material brought together from many different seminars to form the basis for printed discourses on particular topics, ranging from "Sending the Light" to "Overcoming Discouragement". The earliest discourses were mimeographed. As MSIA developed, these were periodically revised and expanded, and more advanced levels of the discourses composed for long-time participants.

The Soul Awareness Discourses— the basic lessons that Movement people receive on a monthly basis— originated from the request of some of the early participants for reading material on the teachings, and were derived from seminar transcripts. After the seminars started being taped, each tape would receive a name, based on the topic J-R had discussed.

Besides the organization stated above, John-Roger has also created:

- *Institute for Individual & World Peace*
- *The Heartfelt Foundation*
- *Esprit Travel Corporation*
- *Windemere Ranch*

Two Ph.D. Clinical Psychologists from the Children's

home Board of Directors went to Los Angeles to take a new seminar titled "Insight Transformational Seminars." Upon their return, I was amazed at the change in them. This seminar was truly transformational. One of them had difficulty with my street attitude, and occasional crude demeanor and it was apparent at board meetings.

I had no idea what they went through in L.A., but the positive change in her attitude toward me was startling and I was grateful. I knew I needed to take this new seminar. I called Insight and explained because of directing my children's home, it was impossible to fly to L.A., and asked what would it take to bring Insight to New Mexico? They explained I would need to obtain 60 deposits and then a date would be assigned. So, I did and they did. I rented a large room at the beautiful "Inn of the Mountain Gods" on the Mescalero Apache reservation near Ruidoso, New Mexico and away we went. This seminar created by John-Roger and Russell Bishop, a long time friend and student, was one of the most extraordinary experiences I have ever had. This was the first time I met John-Roger in person, as he facilitated part of the training. To this day, thirty years later, since my initial participation, I have never met anyone work as effectively as J.R. His counseling gifts are truly amazing, and his obvious clairvoyance an extraordinary asset. He knew things about the participants that were impossible for anyone to know. I was in awe of his effectiveness and abilities, and knew I could learn much from this man. Little did I know how much. I'm aware I probably don't owe him anything but in light of how my life has dramatically improved since I started studying with him, I could never re-pay him. As he was leaving after the seminar ended, I got on the microphone and asked: "Who was that masked man?"

This commenced a long affiliation with Insight and John-Roger where I participated in all the seminars including the month-long Facilitator Seminar. I eventually worked three Insights as an apprentice facilitator before realizing that this wasn't part of my Dharma.

At our children's home we decided that all staff, as a prerequisite to employment, would participate in Insight I, which we would pay for. The amazing positive transformation in all of them was important to the success of our program.

Many of the children from the children's home participated in Teen Insight, either in El Paso Texas or Los Angeles. The results were astounding. The self worth and respect instilled in them through the Insight process was priceless and will serve them the rest of their lives.

A few years later, in Las Cruces New Mexico, I assisted at an Insight I. John-Roger was there to do a post Insight seminar. As assisting at Insight I requires long hours, I was exhausted. I was sitting against the wall, half asleep next to John Morton who is successor to John-Roger and now carries the keys to the Mystical Traveler Consciousness. In the middle of the seminar J-R was talking about the difficulty of raising children. "Wouldn't it be neat, if those of us past our twenties, if our Mothers and Fathers could be Insight graduates. And yet, right here in the state of New Mexico, you have that opportunity, not only with yourself, but Billy Whelan's working on Amigos de los Ninos. That's a hard road; to take kids in that aren't yours." I jolted wide-awake. "Often it's hard enough to put up with your own kids. But when they're not your own biologically but you're willing to put your body on the line, your emotions on the line and your mind on the line and your finances on the line and your house and reputation on the line to bring these youngsters in who didn't get the chance that a lot of you got and a lot of you didn't get. I don't know if you people know it or not but Billy's group works as a non-profit organization and if there's some place inside of you that could note the worthiness of what their doing, just to note the worthiness that's needed, then maybe you can also find it inside of you to be of service to that.

If you're saying, "I've got so much love and I don't

know what to do with it," go out tomorrow and dig a ditch for forty dollars and give the forty dollars to that organization. By the sweat of your brow, go ahead and do it. If you're tithing to your church then give an offering to them. And become a part of that organization, as valuable as the sun in the sky and the rain. You say, "Well, I don't have a hundred dollars, give them fifty cents, give them a penny, give them a nickel. Give. You know a lot of times you hear the old saying: "Give till it hurts." No, "give till it helps." Forget about the hurt. Because if you give and it hurts and it still doesn't help, it still didn't do it, you may say, "Well, yeah, it's easy J-R, for you to sit up there and say that but where are you on the issue?' I'll tell you where I am on the issue, I'm going to go back to Insight and MSIA and one of them, or maybe a combination of both of them, is going to come up with five thousand dollars within a week or so and it'll be made out to his organization.

You understand the difference in talking about it and living it and doing it? 'Cause a lot of people are gonna live their intentions, and never produce the method. And we're gonna produce the method! And you know whose money part of that will be? Part of yours, that you gave to take this training. I'm gonna see that part of your money goes to something else, because not only do we have to take responsibility for ourselves, but there are these youngsters that are coming up that are part of all us. And there are these youngsters that are going to be working with Billy and Susan and their part of us. And it's nice to say we love you and support you and walk away, that's nice and don't look down your nose at that. And it's nice to say, "You're in our prayers, too." And that's nice. Go ahead and pray too. And after you get through praying write a check and mail it. Is Insight affiliated with Amigos De Los Ninos? No, but are we? Yes! Do you understand that? No legal connection, but if you believe in anything in your own loving, in your own space of giving and sharing, then yeah you're affiliated with them. Some things in life are worthwhile to attach yourself to and say, 'Until it dies, I'm with it.' And children are worthwhile, for the simple reason that a child resides in each one of us and by giving to those children you give to the child in you that was never given to. I could probably go on all night about that.

And if I thought it would get him a couple hundred thousand dollars I'd lock the doors and go at it all night. Why? Because it's eminently worth it. The commitment to others is often the commitment to yourself."

Then he had everyone form a line around the room leading up to me and everyone gave me cash and checks. The pile became so large that it over-flowed onto the floor. And all I could do was sit there and cry. Our children's home was in serious financial difficulty. We raised over fourteen thousand dollars. He truly walks the walk.

Over these years, I decided if J-R was doing a seminar anywhere in New Mexico or Texas I would attend. Once he spoke in Dallas and I flew in for the seminar. Over the years I developed a technique where I got to hang out with him a lot. First I would arrive many hours early and scout out the hotel and I got pretty good at figuring out which corridor he would come down and I would casually be hanging out along the hall he would walk past. Of course we would have to hug and chat for a few minutes. Again, someone's gotta do it. Then I always arrived early to be first in line. When the doors opened I would immediately go to the front and in the second row place my coat on the end seat and sit in the second seat. (In the eighties, the front row was always for staff and if you sat in one of those seats you'd have to move, by that time the room was full and you'd end up in rear of the room) There was usually entertainment or announcements and eventually J-R would come down the isle and there wouldn't be anywhere for him to sit— except— next to me. Ha— and we'd have a few minutes to chat. I'm a dedicated groupie. I played this one for a couple of years and it always worked.

I never attempted it in L.A. as the first five or six rows

are allotted for anointed ones, which I never was. Once after a seminar in Dallas, I was asked to drop off a package at J-R's hotel. After delivering the package at the front desk, I was rapidly walking out when two very beautiful women walked in.

I turned to fill my eyes with candy continually walking fast and banged into someone almost knocking him down. Fortunately I was able to grab his arm preventing his fall. As I turned and saw it was J-R, I said, "Did you see that?" Enthusiastically he said, "YEAH!" I went out, he went in. Next day, waiting for my plane to El Paso, radar went down and our flight was cancelled. I couldn't believe what happened next. People were screaming at the desk attendants, like it was their fault. It was a sad mob scene. I walked across the room and stood next to another carrier where an attendant was working alone. I said to her "Can you believe that scene over there? What a bunch of animals. Like you guys caused the radar to go down."

She replied, "It goes with the job. Where are you going?" After I told her she said "Let me take a look. Maybe I can get you on one of our flights." Which she did and eventually received a refund from the first carrier. When I arrived at my terminal to await my flight, who is sitting there but J-R waiting for the same flight. So I had to spend an hour with J.R. prior to take off. Oh well, again, somebody's gotta do it. When I heard J-R was doing a seminar in El Paso, Texas, I called his office and asked if he would spend time with the kids from my children's home. They called back saying I had permission to bring two children, plus where and when. We arrived at his hotel room at the appointed time. Following us were a couple of my staff who were also involved with MSIA. After J-R spent time with the two boys, (one of whom called him an arse-hole,) he said to me, "Good luck with that one." We were walking down the hall when J-R called out to me in a heavy handed manner, "When you're told to bring only two children, don't bring the rest of your staff."

I replied: "You don't have my permission to be rude and disrespectful to me. I didn't bring them. They're here on their own," and started to walk away.

J-R said, "Billy, you're right. I apologize," and walked back into the room. My man. Also during this time, as I had done in the past, I requested dinner or lunch with J-R.

We had lunch in Las Cruces and during lunch J-R mentioned that I was the only one in the area that ever invited him. I replied that they were all afraid of him, but where I come from one is not afraid of their friends. And he was my best friend!

Later that year I was invited to a wedding in Santa Fe, New Mexico. Actually it was a re-wedding J-R was to perform and there were only a dozen guests. The couple went all out for the small reception. There were magnums of exquisite French Champagne. At one point I shared with J-R how much I used to love fine wine but didn't drink anymore as it made me sick. He replied, "Drink all you want and I'll take care of it." I didn't know what he meant but trusted him implicitly. A magnum contains approximately two large bottles of wine. I found a lovely fluted wine glass and over the next three hours polished off a full magnum. No drunk, no hangover, no sick, lots of pee. I so enjoyed that magnum. Thank you J-R He also told us we could take all the photos we wanted. I had borrowed a very expensive camera and took approximately 30 pictures. I was all over that place, snapping away. J-R suggested one of his staff members, Jsu take one of me and J-R. Jsu opened the camera and ruined all my shots. I was pissed! J-R was even more pissed and told him to go sit in the car for the rest of the day. I'm not mad at him anymore.

Years after my children's home closed, I was still living in Southern New Mexico and contracted a systemic arthritic like condition. The pain in all my joints was excruciating. This condition came on as I was including a bit of my own childhood abuse in my first book "Friends of the Children."

I had arranged darshan with Baba Hari Dass at Mount Madonna and the flight to Santa Cruz was painful. While waiting for Babaji in his library I randomly opened up one of his published books The passage read, "While recalling childhood abuse, be careful not to anchor it in your joints." BINGO!

Upon arriving home I called John-Roger and shared with him what was going on. His reply: "Forgive her!" That's all. I innately knew he was referring to my Mom. I was confused, as I truly loved her. Later that day, during my meditation, inside I heard:

I forgive myself for any karma, negativity, judgment or imbalance that I have created in any lifetime with my Mother. I forgive Mom!

This form of J-R's teaching, the inner communication, appealed to me. I was aware that I was the only one who could undo my own negative creations, that we are not victims, that we create it all, contrary to popular opinion. When I hear people say, "Poor dear, he suffered a heart attack." I immediately think, "No he didn't. He created it with his judgment, anger, negativity and, probably, diet. That evening, prior to sleep, I silently chanted this statement like a mantra for around thirty minutes. And continued every day for the next month. I really attempted to say this mantra from my heart with as much meaning as I could muster. Five weeks into the mantra, I came to tears as the catharsis washed over me. Next day the pain had lessened and at the end of the sixth week it was gone, never to return. I have used this amazing mantra with clients in my private practice and classes for years. While working as an outreach worker with the mentally ill/homeless, I was aware that I had karma with one of the Mental Health liaison therapists. She was occasionally nasty and angry with me including blowing up loudly at me at a staff meeting. I don't know why it took me so long to remember the mantra, but I finally started working it inside each evening. This one only took a week.

One evening, as I started the mantra, J-R said inside of me: "The karma is clear." Next morning she called me to thank me for some work I had done with a mutual client. I was incredulous as for the preceding six years she had been such a bitch. Even today, whenever I run into her, she always hugs me and is very pleasant.

The University of Wisconsin, Department of Educational Psychology, in their "A Process Model for Forgive", states:

Forgiveness research has been ongoing at the University of Wisconsin for over thirteen years. The head of the department states, 'The research on forgiveness by our colleagues may be as important to the treatment of emotional and mental disorders as the discovery of sulfa drugs and penicillin were to the treatment of infectious diseases.' Our experience and dedication to the teaching of forgiveness as a psychological health intervention have led to the development of a process model of interpersonal forgiving.

And early on, I realized that when I was having difficulty or just felt like heavy energy was around me all I had to do was go inside and ask J-R if he could lift anything. Over the years I'm used to two inner responses: (1) "I've got it," and immediately the discomfort is gone, or (2) "No," which I've come to understand means that whatever is going on I need to handle. This has been a truly effective tool that I still regularly use.

As I understand it, part of the work the *Mystical Traveler* does with students is to clear ninety percent of karma from the other side while we are responsible for the remaining ten percent here. This requires the student to live under certain rules:

- *Take care of yourself so you can take care of others.*
- *Don't hurt yourself and don't hurt others.*
- *Use everything for your upliftment.*
- *Regular S.E.'s*

Well, that's the J-R story. Like stated at the beginning of this chapter, he was my most important teacher! I believe all the other teachers prepared me for his work. It's been an extraordinary thirty some year ride and I look forward to many more.

Afterword

Truth is within ourselves; it takes no rise
From outward things; whate'er you may believe.
There is an inmost center in us all,
Where truth abides in fullness; and around,
Wall upon wall, the gross flesh hems it in.
This perfect, clear perception— which is truth.
A baffling and perverting carnal mesh
Binds it, and makes all error: and to KNOW,
Rather consists in opening out a way
Whence the imprisoned splendour may escape,
Than in effecting entry for a light
Supposed to be without
      From "Paracelsus", Robert Browning

Well, here I am at 73. I survived! I think. What an amazing forty-year ride. Part of that ride was the creation of a home for severally abused children in New Mexico. My book *Friends of the Children* about this home is available at our web site www.familypeacegroup.org. I also worked with the mentally ill/homeless in Hawaii on a federal grant for eight years.

What have I learned? Hmm, let's see.

I've learned:

- *I am the only one responsible for my Loving.*
- *Mankind is as addicted to illusion as to their next*

261

breath.

- *Duality— How sad the human condition goes against all the great spiritual teachings!*
- *The only way to take the Lord's name in vain is to use a negative after the words: "I am."*
- *That when you're right with spirit, it doesn't matter what anyone thinks of you.*
- *The positive power of forgiveness - It appears as though forgiveness is a cosmic delete button so we can literally erase or delete judgments, negative creations or karma.*
- *The negative power of judgments.*
- *We receive what we focus on. Focus on fear and we program our sub-conscious to create what we fear. Worry also programs the sub-conscious to create what we worry about.*
- *Focus on anger or hatred, we will receive anger or hatred.*
- *Focus on what you want tomorrow – today - because that's exactly what you'll get.*
- *Want love? Focus on love! Take charge. Give up your victim!*
- *Get in the habit of watching your thoughts and what comes out of your mouth.*
- *Practice – Practice – Practice!*
- *I've learned that all souls are equal, contrary to the New age statement: "He must be an old soul." The soul that's embodying for the first time and the soul that's finishing up many lifetimes are absolutely equal in spirit. One just has more experience.*
- *We are not victims; we create everything that happens to us. We absolutely create our future everyday. If you look closely at the poor dear that suffered a heart attack, you may find anger, judgments and/or crappy diet. Hardly a victim! We as a society have been programmed to believe that we are victims and have no responsibility for our outcomes. We create many of our problems through improper diet, judgments, gossip, anger, emotional instability or any of the myriad negative attributes*

> *we humans use to harm ourselves. The "What goes around, comes around," "What you put out comes back to you," "As ye sow, so shall you reap" or if you like, "Karma."*
> - *It appears if you heal an illness and you don't heal the things that produced it in the first place psychologically, it will either re-emerge later on down the road, or another lifetime or some other illness will emerge to take its place. There's definitely causality here. Unfortunately we don't teach our children to take responsibility for their loving and when we're separated from our loving; unloving things may happen to us. And n different forms they all said the same thing. It's all inside! It ain't in the world.*

The world will always let you down, it's designed that way. Go inside!

I've been into prevention for over twenty years. It's astonishing to me that Medicaid/Medicare will pay hundreds of thousands of dollars for heart surgery, but not 50 cents for prevention. I'm in my seventies and take no prescription medication and haven't seen a doctor in many years. I believe there are two reasons for my health - diet and attitude. I don't come from good genes, my Mom died of diabetes and Dad of a heart attack. I decided years ago to eliminate fast food and junk food from my diet and eat only organic fruits & veggies and lots of fish. I love beef, but haven't had any store bought in decades. Why? Because of all the hormones and chemicals in their feed. How many decades can the bodies filter system handle this volume of poison before breaking down? I also discovered decades ago that judgments, anger & negativity contribute to health or the lack of. We are not victims! I was asked why I've never been to the Senior Center. We-e-ll, no offence, but you people are depressing, with all your aches and pains and prescription drugs; problems that most of you created. YOU ARE NOT VICTIMS!

A study from "Diabetes Care" states that chemicals in the environment are making us more obese and more diabetic! Their claim is that our environment is loaded with toxins that we ingest, inhale, and take in through our skin every day.

However, the main source of "persistent organic pollutants" in humans is through dietary fats, primarily animal in origin. Once in our body, these fat-soluble chemicals, which are highly resistant to degradation, get stored in our own fat. As we carry more fat, more toxins get stored and become available to create metabolic disruptions. Metabolic disruptions then create all sorts of havoc, such as insulin resistance, which leads to diabetes. It's a vicious cycle of increasing fat, toxic overload, and metabolic maladies. Granted, our genes may be contributors to the problem but the role of toxins in promoting obesity is not good news for those struggling with their waist lines. I am living proof. I'm not concerned about how long I live. I'm concerned about being healthy while I'm here. If you want a healthy life, change your diet and your attitude.

The Miracle

AN EXTRAORDINARY EXAMPLE OF AURA BALANCING WAS an experience back in the early eighties, whereby I knew this form was part of my life's work. One of my acquaintances asked if I would do a balancing with her. I asked another person to hold the light. During the balancing it became clear she had been betrothed to Judas during the time of Jesus and I started to work with the negative Christian programming she had been exposed to. In the middle of the balancing, I became aware of a fourth person in the room. I was used to inner beings, angels, inner teachers, spiritual masters, etc. showing up in spirit during balancings, but this was different. This was a person in the physical body. I turned slightly to my right and standing in the corner, in a long gray robe, with the hood over his head, tied with a rope belt and sandals, silent, was the Lord Jesus. I turned to ask the light bearer if she was aware of anyone else in the room, but she had seen him before I did and was silently weeping. I was blown away, I mean JESUS H. CHRIST! Oh, excuse me, Lord. The balancee was unaware of his presence, so I had her sit up and look to her right. As soon as she saw him, she started weeping. She really lost it, wailing, snot faucet running.

When she was a bit under control he said to me inside, "Tell her to speak to me."

After more sobbing, she was able to gain a modicum of control and looking directly at him said, "I love you"! Then there was a poof sound and he de-materialized. Obviously the balancing was over. I'm really glad there were two other people in the room. Definitely, one of the loudest silent rings!

Epilogue

Seeking enlightenment is like looking for your car while sitting in it.

BILLY WHELAN

An awake person functions in the world just as others do, eating, sleeping, showing love and sadness— but inside there is non-attachment to the world. For that awake person, the world is nothing but God. For others, the world functions with no change; they feel the same attachment, love and hate throughout their lives. The awake person, after finding peace in the Supreme Reality, experiences bliss even while experiencing the mind and the senses.

When you are awake the dream is gone...

When you are Enlightened the "world of illusion" is gone.

BABA HARI DASS

I NEVER LIKED THE WORD ENLIGHTENMENT, AS MOST OF THE people who talk about it, have no idea what it is. "There's no understanding without experience!" (John-Roger) So I like to use the word awake or awakening, as we have all experienced this. The experience of knowing who we are. There is an awareness of the connection to being part of the Creator.

Awakening does not make one intelligent or wise. All too often, 'awake' people find themselves as a minority in a community of self-serving people. For this reason, humility and self-love are real virtues when awakening, as it assists one to survive. Before most people's awakening they are busy beavers, playing sports, arguing with their spouses, etc. But after awakening, there is a clear vision of how silly some of this activity is and how much effort is required to perform it.

It has been said that this level of awakening produces compassion and love and that many awake people forgo release into nirvana and reincarnate again and again until all souls are awake, the Bodhisattva vow and such. I always believed Bodhisattva vows were stupid. To vow to not get off the wheel of re-incarnation until everyone has made it. From what I've seen of this planet that's forever plus. None of this is true awakening. Becoming awake is not about morality or vows; it is simply existence in the now, that's all. It's also like: "When one looks in a mirror, one knows that what they see is a reflection of themselves, not themselves." (John-Roger) Awakening brings knowledge that this world is only a reflection of reality. It's important to understand that while nothing ultimately changes, in human terms much change takes place. This happens because once you understand what's going on; the main motivations of life begin to drop away. The level of dropping away is unique to the individual but is directly proportional to how much they desire to resolve into reality. This means it's possible to be awake and still retain a level of unconsciousness in order to interact in human affairs. As time passes this state is difficult to maintain. It's like going to the movies and pretending it's real. You cry and laugh and hope with the characters, etc. You do this for entertainment. This is the way real life is when one awakens. You know that it is just a display, a machine like emergence out of and as consciousness. Yet you believe it at some level or you will simply lose the ability to interact in the world. Occasionally awake ones isolate themselves or become hermits. I've personally struggled with this. How to know the truth and continue to interact with the world as if you believe it. You have to pretend to believe while always knowing the truth. Deliberate effort is an affront to reality where nothing is deliberate, everything is spontaneous, and nothing at all is going on. The natural outcome of becoming awake is less and less action, less and less thought. This is a natural development within the awake person.

Eventually all action will be spontaneous. Memory is also a tricky thing. The memories of your life are still there and can be jogged into awareness but as time progresses and you become more and more awake, your access to them becomes more difficult. Your awareness becomes centered in the events of the present, the now. This is natural since these are the only events that exist anyway. Everything outside of the now is illusion and doesn't exist. This is the point where rapport with the basic self is critical, as they are capable of giving you all you need to remember.

In reference to spiritual practice, most people just don't get it and most spiritual schools don't make it any easier for students to get it. There are all kinds of books on meditation and catalogs where you can buy all the cool silk clothes, cushions, gongs, incense and a bunch of other aids to spiritual practice. Most of this falls into the arena of "Spiritual Materialism". Once you have all that stuff and finally sit your butt down, close your eyes and start, what exactly are you doing? Why are you doing that? Why do you meditate? What are you trying to accomplish? Why do you watch your breath? Most people don't have a clue. The reason they don't is because they're asleep. If they were awake, then they might not even meditate anymore, or they might, it would make no difference. The truth that is missed by most meditators is that the act of sitting watching your breath is part of becoming awake. That's all. You're not doing something to gain something, just sitting there is awakening. In that still state with calmed mind, that is awakening, yet that annoying conversation over there interrupting your meditation, just that is awakening and that guy flipping you off in traffic is awakening. People meditate because it is popular or because they want to have a mystical experience or just relax. The latter reason may actually be the most legitimate for the average person. But no one I know says they meditate because they are deliberately engaging in an actless act, or attempting to resolve a false sense of being into a being - less existence.

Awakening carries with it the knowledge that there is no good/bad or right/wrong. And those who live in this belief are only into judgment. All that exists is "what is," now!

Check the Akashic records if you don't believe this. And what I've discovered is Spirit doesn't exist in illusion. Anything outside of now is illusion. Future doesn't exist, yet, and the past has already happened. So if you want to "partner with spirit," stay with "now". Every time you leave, "now", you're alone, every time you, like Ram Dass says, "Be Here Now," you link up with spirit. There are no blessings in illusion, only pain and confusion. Only intellectual convulsions, mental masturbation if you will, and you will!

My obsessive, many decade, spiritual quest has been about seeking experience of and gaining more awareness of the divine. And after all these years I've finally earned the sand box. I've found that what I'm seeking is found in the silence, as "silence speaks." I find the quest for enlightenment to be a joke. I believe we were created perfectly, lost our way and now need to wake up to our own divinity.

Many of the great religions state in myriad forms that we were created in God's likeness, perfectly. Look at the magnificence of the human body. When one awakens, there is a conscious awareness of the connection to being part of whatever you want to call that energy that spiritually rules.

Awakening does not make an individual intelligent or wise. Before awakening, societal and parental conditioning rule. Busy, busy, busy, making money, money and more money. Actively involved in any activity we can find to occupy our minds. To sate the tiny little person that lives between our ears and never shuts up. Well, I found a way to silence it. Spiritual Exercises. (See John-Roger chapter.)

In Martin Prechtel's "Long Life, Honey in the Heart" he states, 'Modern people seem to be proud of their despair, entirely imprisoned by their complacent respect for the overwhelming power of meaningless so popular today. The only thing that seems to have meaning is no meaning. Modern people are proud of it, and to them everything besides meaninglessness is meaningless."

And in Paul Twitchell's "The Tiger's Fang" It is stated: "It is a disgusting spectacle, the thousands of industrious and accomplished liars engaged in the mutual and systematic pursuit of their professions, salting their editorials, sermons and words with the sweetness and lightness of religious and philosophical platitudes."

Waking up is not about morality or vows. It is simply living in the now, and a return to self is all. Understand that while nothing ultimately changes, in human terms much change takes place. This happens because once you realize what's not going on, the main motivations of life begin to drop away. The level of dropping away is unique to the individual but is directly proportional to how much you desire to resolve into reality. It's possible to be awake and still try to retain a level of unconsciousness in order to interact in human affairs. This was my attempt for years, trying to fit in. As time passes, this state is harder to maintain. It is similar to suspending your belief when watching a movie. You pretend to believe the movie is real. You sob with the characters, laugh with them, hope with them, etc. You do this for the entertainment. This is the way real life is when you're awake. You know that it is just a display, a machine like emergence out of and as consciousness. Yet you must believe it at some level or you will simply lose the ability to interact in the world.

Many awake beings have isolated themselves or become hermits. For years this has been an issue I struggled with. How to know the truth and continue to interact with the world pretending you believe it. You have to pretend to believe while knowing the truth.

The great Chinese philosopher Lin Yu Tang eloquently stated, "If you can spend a perfectly useless afternoon, in a perfectly useless manner, you have learned how to live." I have learned how to live! A good gauge of your awakening is how well you understand his statement. And "Besides the noble art of getting things done, there is the noble art of leaving things undone. The wisdom of life consists in the elimination of non-essentials." Thank you, Mr. Tang! Definitely an awake being.

The natural outcome of awakening is less action, and less thought. This is a natural development. Eventually all action will be spontaneous.

Memory is also a tricky thing. The memories of your life are still there and can be jogged into awareness, but as time progresses and awakening begins to present itself, your access to them become more difficult. Your awareness becomes centered in the events of the present, the now. This is natural since these are the only events that actually exist. Everything outside of now is illusion and doesn't exist. Think about that statement. When you are sitting with a friend looking out at the ocean, that is the only thing happening in the world. Your now. You can't prove anything else, because in your "now" reality, that's all there is. The person and the ego are simply dissolving. They don't really exist in the first place but the illusion that they do becomes less a part of awareness. You don't remember and you don't care. We'd be closer to the truth if we would acknowledge that this world is a reflection of reality, like when you look into a mirror, you know that what you're seeing is only a reflection of yourself. (John-Roger)

Bibliography

BOOKS BY MEHER BABA

Beams from Meher Baba on the Spiritual Panorama.
The Everything and the Nothing.
God Speaks: The Theme of Creation and its Purpose
God Speaks, 2nd edition
God to Man and Man to God; the Discourses of Meher Baba.
Life at Its Best,
Listen, Humanity
Life At Its Best
The Advancing Stream of Life
Discourses

BOOKS BY BABA HARI DASS

Ashtanga Yoga Primer
Child's Garden of Yoga
Everyday Peace: Letters for Life
Fire Without Fuel
Hariakhan Baba
Mystic Monkey
The Path to Enlightenment Is Not a Highway
Silence Speaks: From the Chalkboard of Baba Hari Dass
Vinaya Chalisa: Forty Prayers
The Yellow Book: The Sayings of Baba Hari Dass

BOOKS BY JOHN-ROGER

Answers to Life's Questions
The Blessings Already Are
Divine Essence (Benjamin Franklin Award Winner)
Dream Voyages
Forgiveness: The Key to the Kingdom
God Is Your Partner
Health from the Inside Out
Inner Worlds of Meditation
Interviews with John Morton and John-Roger
Journey of a Soul
Living Love
Living Love, from the Spiritual Heart
Loving Each Day
Loving Each Day for Moms and Dads
Loving Each Day for Peacemakers
Momentum: Letting Love Lead
Manuel on Using the Light
The Path to Mastership
The Power Within You
Psychic Protection
Relationships: Love, Marriage and Spirit
The Rest of Your Life
Seeking the Light
Sex, Spirit and You
The Spiritual Family
Spiritual High
The Spiritual Promise
Spiritual Warrior (L.A. Times Bestseller)
Tao of Spirit
Timeless Wisdoms
The Way Out Book
Wealth & Higher Consciousness
What's It Like Being You?
When Are You Coming Home?
You Are the Blessings

CO-AUTHORED BOOKS WITH JOHN-ROGER

Do It! Lets Get Off Our Butts (New York Times Bestseller)
Life 101 (New York Times Bestseller)
The Rest of Your Life: Fulfilling Your Spiritual Promise
You Can't Afford the Luxury of a Negative Thought (UPI
   Bestseller)

BOOKLET BY ELLEVIVIAN POWER

The Auric Mirror

BOOKLET BY DR. HUNTER

Why a Karmic Life Reading

LaVergne, TN USA
10 August 2010
192818LV00006B/205/P

9 781616 670627